# SPACE WARFARE IN THE 21ST CENTURY

This book examines the growing threat of space warfare with a specific focus on the recent shift in US space policy.

The dual-use nature of the vast majority of space technology, meaning of value to both civilian and military communities, and being unable to differentiate offensive from defensive intent of military hardware makes space an area particularly ripe for a security dilemma. The evolving space capabilities of countries across the world has raised the threat perception within the US military and intelligence communities regarding the vulnerability of US space assets in an environment described as "congested, contested, and competitive." Consequently, the posture of the US military space program is becoming increasingly aggressive toward protection of those assets through a "deter, defend, and defeat" strategy. Though a broad-based view of that strategy has been traditionally encouraged, deterrence by punishment appears increasingly to dominate planning. This book analyzes whether these approaches will be effective or counterproductive, considers the potential consequences of pursuing the wrong course of action, and concludes by offering an alternative approach to addressing space challenges and achieving space goals.

This book will be of much interest to students of space policy, defence studies, foreign policy, security studies, and international relations.

**Joan Johnson-Freese** is a Professor and former Chair of National Security Affairs at the US Naval War College, Newport, Rhode Island, and author of several books.

# Cass Military Studies

A full list of titles in this series is available at:
www.routledge.com/Cass-Military-Studies/book-series/CMS

# SPACE WARFARE IN THE 21ST CENTURY

## Arming the heavens

*Joan Johnson-Freese*

Routledge
Taylor & Francis Group

LONDON AND NEW YORK

First published 2017
by Routledge
2 Park Square, Milton Park, Abingdon, Oxon OX14 4RN

and by Routledge
711 Third Avenue, New York, NY 10017

*Routledge is an imprint of the Taylor & Francis Group, an informa business*

© 2017 Joan Johnson-Freese

*British Library Cataloguing-in-Publication Data*
A catalogue record for this book is available from the British Library

*Library of Congress Cataloging in Publication Data*
Names: Johnson-Freese, Joan, author.
Title: Space warfare in the 21st century : arming the heavens / Joan
Johnson-Freese.
Description: New York, NY : Routledge, [2017] | Series: Cass military
studies | Includes bibliographical references and index.
Identifiers: LCCN 2016020667| ISBN 9781138693869 (hardback) | ISBN
9781138693883 (pbk.) | ISBN 9781315529172 (ebook)
Subjects: LCSH: Space warfare. | Astronautics, Military. | Outer space--
Government policy--United States. | Outer space--Strategic aspects. |
Space security.
Classification: LCC UG1520 .J65 2017 | DDC 358/.8--dc23
LC record available at https://lccn.loc.gov/2016020667

ISBN: 978-1-138-69386-9 (hbk)
ISBN: 978-1-138-69388-3 (pbk)
ISBN: 978-1-315-52917-2 (ebk)

Typeset in Bembo
by Saxon Graphics Ltd, Derby

# CONTENTS

# PREFACE

The sky is falling, again. Though the excitement that has been anticipated and awaited since the 1960s regarding space exploration and travel by a new generation of Buck Rogers- and Han Solo-type adventurers is finally beginning to take shape through NewSpace actors, a rising tide of global space nationalism and militarism is occurring in parallel. This militarism and nationalism is in response to mutual distrust and perceptions of nefarious intent in space, which may or may not be valid, and traditional geopolitics. Other countries refuse to be denied any of the benefits of space—military and otherwise—long afforded the United States and so are developing comparable capabilities. Consequently, that has significantly raised the threat perception within US military and intelligence communities regarding US space assets.

On April 26, 2015, Gen. John Hyten, chief of US Air Force Space Command, went on the popular television show *60 Minutes* and told the American public that the Global Positioning System (GPS) satellites they rely on every day for everything from getting cash from an automated teller machine (ATM) to watching television were at risk. The risks stemmed from naturally occurring, man-made, and geopolitical threats, including attack by anti-satellite weapons (ASATs), most specifically by ASATs being developed by the Chinese. Furthermore, the segment, titled "The Battle Above," explained the significant advantages the US military gains from space and that those too were at risk and, therefore, US national security threatened. But, said Gen. Hyten, if the United States is "threatened in space, we have the right of self-defense, and we'll make sure we can execute that right."[1] Asked if that meant using force, Gen. Hyten replied: "That's why we have a military. You know, I'm not NASA."

As both the segment title and the General himself implied, future warfighting in space is clearly anticipated. Further, there has been no hesitation in unequivocally stating both this anticipation and the US willingness and ability to respond. But given the size of the US military space program and, therefore, its reflective influence on other countries' military space programs, the apparently default, bipartisan US emphasis on fighting and winning battles in space without equal and pronounced effort toward deterring conflict in space is counterproductive and misaligned if protection of US space assets is the objective.

Gen. Hyten doesn't want to fight a war in space, but even more so, he doesn't want to lose a war in space.[2] As a military officer, that is the position that the warfighters he leads and the Americans they protect count on. As reassuring as Gen. Hyten's words sound, though, the problem is that, like so many other global issues the United States has faced of late, issues unquestionably putting vital US satellites at risk cannot be protected by military capabilities and actions alone. An environment where offensive options are cheaper and easier than defensive options, where the tyranny of both distance and physics prevail, and where ambiguity reigns makes reliance on military options to protect US space assets and the ability to use space inadequate. Military- and technology-based approaches are a necessary but insufficient part of a broader, more comprehensive strategy that is needed. Study after study has recommended a comprehensive, layered strategy toward achieving goals rather than one focused on a military approach,[3] and official US space policies and policy statements by US officials suggest recognition of the need for a layered strategy. Yet the United States continues to concentrate primarily on military shibboleths to complex space challenges, focused on fighting (and not losing) a space war without comparable efforts toward preventing a space war. Norms and diplomacy alone are not the answer to addressing the growing challenges of space either, but they are part of the answer.

Military options pursued alone can exacerbate challenges by creating security dilemmas where countries take actions against their own interests due to perceived risks that often involve attempting to match or counter technology advancements made by another country. While it might be expected that the potential for such security dilemmas would be anticipated and addressed as policy is developed, the policy process is not always conducive to such rational approaches.

The process behind development of such documents as the National Security Strategy (NSS), the National Space Policy (NSP), and the National Security Space Strategy (NSSS) affords opportunities for thoughtful policy considerations. But according to Georgetown University Professor David Edelstein and University of Minnesota Professor Ronald Krebs, they are also beehives of mischief, used as opportunities to create and exaggerate threats to serve developers' own bureaucratic budgetary purposes, which can fuel rather than avert a security dilemma.

> Strategizing is more than just unhelpful; it is also dangerous. The ritual of statecraft encourages participants to spin a narrative that magnifies the scope of the national interest and exaggerates global threats. The aggressive policies adopted in reaction to the perceived threats make them real: when states seek to defend themselves, they threaten others, prompting a response and

touching off a dangerous game of escalation—a classic security dilemma. Strategizing turns possible threats into all-too-real ones.[4]

Therefore, it is imperative that leadership periodically pauses to assess whether stated policy goals (ends) are correct and whether the strategies (means) being pursued to achieve those goals are appropriate. It is the purpose of this book to support such an assessment as it is my contention that the US is rapidly moving toward—if not already there—a posture where means and ends are misaligned.

In order to consider alignment, it is first necessary to review US space security goals. Hence, various US policy and strategy documents are reviewed in Chapter 1 along with the goals posited within them. Stability has long been recognized as the bedrock goal, foundational to others. Therefore, what numerous past studies have suggested as necessary to preserve stability in space is considered as well. Chapter 1 also introduces themes incorporated throughout the book: the need for a proactive focus on achievable goals; the need for a broad, balanced strategy that includes both carrots and sticks; and the counterproductive nature of bellicose rhetoric. And finally, the how, and why, of the incorporation of what has been called "the politics of fear" into space debates is considered as part of the context within which space policy is developed.

The space environment within which space goals must be achieved is regularly described by one of many three-word catchphrases favored by the US government: "congested, contested, and competitive." What each of those terms actually means, however, is rarely considered beyond a shallow extent. Therefore, each term is unpacked in Chapter 2 in order to assess if or how it is threatening the ability of the United States to fully use the space domain. Only with a full understanding of the issue can appropriate responses be identified. Because assessment of the environment, especially the "contested" aspect, is based largely on deciphering the "intentions" of other countries, the difficulties in making those assessments is also discussed. Finally, the growing movement toward integration of military space capabilities into defense plans as a consequence of the space environment being described as "congested, contested, and competitive" is noted as a prelude to consideration of whether space warfare is inevitable.

Because geostrategic conflict is inevitable, whether or not war between ruling and rising states is also inevitable has been the subject of considered academic debate, recently most often focused on the United States and China. Conflict can be resolved—more optimistically, "managed"—in many ways, warfare being just one. According to Prussian general and strategist Carl von Clauswitz, war is a "continuation of policy by other means."[5] As a continuation, there are implicitly other options as well. Regarding space, however, the inevitability of conflict turning into battle and hence the need to weaponize space was assumed in 2001 when the Commission to Assess National Space Security Management and Organization, chaired by Donald Rumseld, alerted the US to a potential "Space Pearl Harbor." "Inevitability" has since become one of four basic lenses through which individuals view the future of space security and have then developed space strategies. Each of these lenses, or schools, is considered in Chapter 3. Each is complicated by difficulties in even defining a space weapon due to the dual-use nature of space technology and the importance of deciphering intentions for use. Whereas the difficulties in assessing intentions are discussed previously, in this chapter, a focused look at perceived Chinese intentions is considered because, by default, capability has come to equal intent.

With the space environment considered "congested, contested, and competitive," the US has adopted a "deter, defend, defeat" approach to addressing those challenges. Ambiguity as to what each component of that responsive catchphrase specifically means, however, has served the US security community well. Vagueness leaves considerable room for maneuvering. Therefore, the component parts of "deter, defend, defeat" are examined in Chapter 4. Increasingly, only a narrow aspect of "deter" is being pursued—specifically, deterrence by punishment—with more emphasis on defend and defeat. However, without pursuing (as opposed to merely espousing) a more balanced, layered strategy for addressing space challenges, the space environment becomes subject to—to keep with the favored three-word government descriptors—mishaps, misperceptions, and miscalculations[6] that increase the risk of not just war in space, but escalation to or through terrestrial fighting as well. Deterrence requires both carrots and sticks, with the US conspicuously short on offering carrots and noticeably lacking in restraint when it comes to bellicose language. Effective deterrence also requires a consistency and clarity in signals and messaging that has been missing, most notably regarding, again, China. How the tyranny of distance plays into decision-making, long term and in crises, is also considered, especially regarding knowing what is going on in space.

The role of the military–industrial complex complicates space issues as well,[7] and so this is considered in Chapter 5. A vast array of parties involved in that complex have a vested interest in perpetuating the notion that with just one more contract, one or two more billion dollars, a technical problem can be solved, perhaps even the laws of physics defied. The revolving door of individuals moving between (or with simultaneous interests in multiple venues) defense firms, government positions, military billets, think tanks, Wall Street, lobbying firms, research labs, and even the media is astounding and growing. The number of general officers who retire from the military and take high-paying defense or aerospace jobs selling to their former employer, for example, has expanded significantly in the last 20 years. The bottom line is that there are individuals and organizations with a vested interest in seeing threats to which the US military must respond with weaponry because that is their product line—a product line with only one customer. The evolution and endurance of missile defense programs are examined as exemplary.

The turn to nationalism, militarization, and the weaponization of space that is increasingly evidenced not just in the US but in other major spacefaring countries as well is countered in Chapter 6 with a look at a blossoming of global space entrepreneurship and efforts at multilateral norm development. Companies financed by wealthy individuals or venture capitalists that are geared toward developing a space-related product not necessarily for government buyers have been dubbed NewSpace players. They work on different premises and with different business models than the traditional aerospace companies that are intertwined into the military–industrial complex. What they offer, what they need to succeed and what they mean to military aspirations for the "control" and "domination" of space will be important in future policy planning scenarios and implementation strategies.

Also important for the future will be the success or failure of initiatives to develop global norms for space activity. While Chinese and Russian calls for a treaty have been rejected by the US for what it considers legitimate reasons, efforts to develop guidelines through the United Nations have been stalled by the Russians as a move against the West generally and the US specifically on the larger geopolitical chessboard. Efforts through the United Nations to develop space norms toward greater stability had been developing ploddingly over the past five years, though with a light at the end of the tunnel visible through the end of 2015. But then the Russians interjected themselves in February 2016 as the "spoiler" with complex and barely intelligible substantive and procedural demands that temporarily stalled the process. Nevertheless, there has been a growing international consensus regarding the need for guidelines laying out acceptable norms and expectations toward maintaining stability in space, and gratefully, progress resumed in June 2016. Ultimately, a Wild West environment serves no one, least of all the Untied States given that it houses and relies upon more space assets than any other country.

Finally, a strategy forward is offered in Chapter 7, building on past lessons learned and drawing on the concept of cooperation spirals[8] rather than escalation spirals. In doing so, the intent is to encourage actually executing a comprehensive, layered US approach of strategic restraint to space security as opposed to a rhetorically bombastic and so counterproductive, technically infeasible primacist approach.

While the perspective presented here is clearly not the perspective currently prevalent in the United States, discussion and debate not only in the United States but internationally needs to continue. Further, it is not just the space policy and actions of the United States that must be considered toward stability in space, but that of the Russians, the Chinese, the Indians, the private sector, and others. If this book usefully contributes to understanding those issues and sparking discussion, then it will have served its purpose. With a new administration entering office in 2017, the time is ripe now for a change of direction—just as it was in 2009.

## Back to the Future

In the United States, there is a growing tendency to respond to challenges in space—and there are many—with military answers. This threatens the stability and hence the sustainability of the space environment. The United States has gone down this ill-conceived route before. Consequently, the parallels between space policy debates in 2009 as a new administration was entering office and in 2016 are striking. Space policy was at a crossroads in 2009 and is again now in 2016. The Obama Administration did make a policy change initially, moving away from the nationalistic, military-centric approach of the George W. Bush Administration and toward a more cooperative and commercial emphasis. Specifically, the administration returned the United States from the primacist policy of the Bush years to a traditional policy of strategic restraint in space and maintained that policy until 2013.

Under strategic restraint, the Obama Administration looked at stated US space policy goals and developed a menu of diverse, achievable means to address them. The rhetoric of "space control" and "domination" of the prior administration was toned down. Undeniably, some means were pursued with more vigor and were more successful than others. Consistently, however, technology development and hedging remained key strategy components. But just as the 1998 North Korean Taepo Dong launch triggered a sea change in US space policy that endured through 2009, so too did a May 2013 Chinese suborbital launch that nearly reached geosynchronous orbit.

Consequent to that 2013 Chinese launch, the Pentagon held a classified Strategic Space Portfolio Review, resulting in another sea change in policy away from strategic restraint, focusing instead on development of offensive counterspace capabilities and strategies for using these capabilities including, potentially, for preventive strikes. Primacy has returned. Back again is the chest-thumping rhetoric and a choir of declarations regarding the inevitability of war in space and the need to prepare for it. The costs of space warfare in terms of capabilities potentially lost would be enormous, and the risks of escalation would be high. And so now, with a new administration to take office in 2017, it is imperative that consideration be given to what means actually maximize the chances of achieving stated US goals in space while also minimizing the risks. But that won't be easy given the post-Cold War, post-9/11 American political culture that provides the context for space policy decision-making.

In many ways, America's unipolar decade of the 1990s did not serve America well. Political analyst Walter Russell Mead described it as a "bipartisan age of narcissism and hubris"[9] during which the United States saw itself as a benevolent hegemon, reveling in having ended the Cold War with a blessed whimper rather than a planet-destroying bang. With the triumph of liberal democracy over communism, books were written heralding the *End of History*.[10] Ideological battles seemed to have collapsed. Yet parts of the globe, particularly the Middle East, simmered in a stew of radical ideology, foreseen by some[11] but largely ignored by Americans in denial.[12] But the problem with being a hegemon—benevolent or otherwise—is that it is difficult to relinquish that position, even when circumstances change and make it impossible to sustain.

The relatively short history of the United States is replete with examples of exceptionalism. From its struggle for independence and the remarkable economic and geographic growth that followed (though not without a dark side) to its protection of personal liberties, its proclamation of offering sanctuary to immigrants on the Statue of Liberty, and its willingness and ability to accomplish remarkable feats—including sending the first men to the Moon and returning them safely to Earth—Americans have become accustomed to seeing themselves as "special." That feeling has become an expectation. When that psychological exceptionalism intersected with a moment of political unipolarism in the 1990s, it is perhaps not surprising that narcissism and hubris followed.

Those years were largely referred to as the post-Cold War era because nobody knew what else to call it. But as Thomas Friedman pointed out in his 1999 book *The Lexus and the Olive Tree*,[13] the world was nevertheless moving forward toward "the next big thing," and that thing was globalization with promises of widespread expanded wealth and individual empowerment. Some countries were winners in the globalization sweepstakes, while others were largely shut out. Goldman Sachs analyst Jim O'Neill dubbed Brazil, Russia, India, and China as "BRIC" in 2001, predicting them as destined to grow from then making up just 8 percent of the world economy to equaling those of the G6 by 2025.[14] While the global financial collapse of 2007–08 and the realities of trying to sustain high growth rates have intervened (Goldman Sachs closed its BRIC fund in 2015), the point is that the unipolar world of the 1990s was not frozen in time. Things changed. The United States has been reluctant to acknowledge that.

Even before the US unipolar moment on Earth, the United States and Russia dominated space. For many years, countries wanting to launch something into orbit were largely reliant on the goodwill of the United States to get it there. Then the United States handily won the race to the Moon against the Soviets, exacerbating an already-inflated sense of "controlling" the heavens. With the collapse of the Soviet Union, much of its space program became moribund, was mothballed, or was incorporated into US activities, specifically the International Space Station (ISS). The United States was on top geopolitically and certainly in terms of space capabilities. But the value of space assets to all aspects of life on Earth was becoming increasingly realized as part of globalization, and everybody wanted in on those benefits—benefits ranging from "informationalizing" militaries to being part of a burgeoning commercial space mining development effort worth potentially trillions of dollars. However, currently, rather than attempting to manage that inherent change in favor of its own best interests, the United States appears intent on trying to turn back time. As the biggest global space player by far, the space policies of the United States inherently affect those of other countries.

## An International Responsibility for Space

It would be both unfair and simply wrong to attribute the tenuous future of the space environment to the United States alone. All countries have a vested interest in sustaining the space environment so as to be able to reap the wide-ranging benefits it yields. That is the commonality all countries can and must build on. Hopefully, but not assuredly, all countries recognize the need for stability in order to facilitate the use of space assets.

China, with dreams of space travel dating back to the legendary Ming dynasty figure Wan Hu, has ambitious space plans linked to economic development, exploration, geostrategic leadership, and military modernization. But China irresponsibly conducted a high-altitude ASAT test in low Earth orbit in 2007, creating massive amounts of space debris. China's intrinsic opacity about its space activities creates tensions about intent as well. To that, China's generally aggressive geopolitical policies, particularly as related to the South China Sea, inherently create questions about its peaceful versus hostile and hegemonic terrestrial and celestial intentions.

Russia is now back with a vengeance after its post-Soviet-collapse domestic and global stall, including in space. While at times seemingly intent on playing an obstructionist role in diplomatic space efforts at the United Nations and making provocative maneuvers with its spacecraft in orbit,[15] it dismisses criticism of its behavior with a wave of the hand. Russian foreign policy is now the embodiment of President Vladimir Putin's soured view of the West. And yet, the ISS continues to be operated from mission control sites in both Russia and the United States, with the Russian taxi service to the ISS continuing on an uninterrupted basis, seemingly immune from geopolitics beyond rhetorical sniping.

Indian space plans have evolved from being largely focused on domestic development to including space exploration and military capabilities as well. The scope of its space program, civil and military, has broadened significantly in the past ten years, driven by geostrategic considerations. India's Mangalyaan spacecraft, which reached Mars in 2014, though certainly recognized for its scientific achievements, was primarily about getting India into the space record books previously dominated from among the Asian countries by China. Prestige, as it links to geopolitics, matters.

European countries are considering development of more autonomous military space capabilities. They do not want to be reliant on the United States—which is sometimes considered "stingy"—for such critical aspects of their security as satellite imagery. In fact, since consensus decision-making has often made follow-through more difficult than aspirations where joint European space activity is concerned, individual European countries are, in some instances, moving forward on their own. France, for example, boosted its military space budget for 2016, and this largely escaped budget cuts even after pressure to boost funding to fight terrorism after the Paris attacks.[16] Intelligence, surveillance, and reconnaissance are the top priorities for spending.

Japan has redefined its constitutional allowable space activity parameters, once limited to peaceful uses only, "peaceful" being defined narrowly as "nonmilitary." While for many years, Japan hid behind the ambiguity of dual-use technology to develop space technology that could be used for civil and, serendipitously, military purposes, in 2009 it reinterpreted "peaceful" to mean "non-aggressive." Since then, the Japanese Ministry of Defense has expressed interest in a range of space-based capabilities for national security purposes and has worked closely with the United States in that regard, specifically focusing on space situational awareness and space-based maritime domain awareness. Japanese cooperation with the United States on ballistic missile defense technology is especially controversial in the region given its perceived potential for use as an offensive anti-satellite weapon.[17]

There is not a country in the world that doesn't have a vested interest in space, even just as a "user" of information relayed through space assets. No country feels it can afford to forego the wide-ranging benefits space assets offer. Western countries are concerned about space activities in countries like North Korea and Iran, but they often put themselves in a position of making "do as we say, not as we do" pronouncements—especially the United States. In a globalized world with a globalized space industry, trying to deny countries—or companies or individuals—space technology is a futile effort at playing whack-a-mole.

The space environment is becoming more complex simply by virtue of more going on by more and more types of actors, governmental and nongovernmental. "Control" of the heavens has slipped away from the United States, if it ever really had it, simply by virtue of progress. Challenges regarding space debris, radio frequency access, real estate, new property rights questions and more abound. None of these challenges, however, requires or can be effectively dealt with through military answers. The complexity of the space environment means that all tools of national power must be used, with some degree of balance, toward addressing space challenges and achieving space goals. The United States must take the lead. A policy "tweak" likely will not suffice either; a paradigm shift is in order.

## Notes

1  Transcript of "The Battle Above," *60 Minutes*. David Martin (correspondent), Andy Court (producer). April 26, 2015. http://spacenews.com/transcript-of-60-minutes-air-force-space-command-segment/

2  Lee Billings, "War in space may be closer than ever," *Scientific American*, August 10, 2015. www.scientificamerican.com/article/war-in-space-may-be-closer-than-ever/; Gen. John Hyten, Speech at the 29th National Space Symposium, Colorado Springs, CO, 2015. www.afspc.af.mil/library/speeches/speech.asp?id=757

3  Forrest E. Morgan, *Deterrence and First-Strike Stability in Space*, RAND, Santa Monica, CA, 2010. www.rand.org/content/dam/rand/pubs/monographs/2010/RAND_MG916.pdf; Roger G. Harrison, Deron R. Jackson, and Collins G. Shackelford, "Space deterrence: the delicate balance of risk," *Space and Defense*, 3(1), Summer 2009, 1–51; Bruce W. MacDonald, *China, Space Weapons, and US Security*, Council on Foreign Relations Special Report No. 38, September 2008, Council on Foreign Relations, New York, pp. 10–11; Michael Krepon with Christopher Clary, *Space Assurance or Space Dominance: The Case Against Weaponizing Space*, The Henry L. Stimson Center, Washington, DC, 2003.

4  David M. Edelstein and Ronald R. Krebs, "Delusions of grand strategy," *Foreign Affairs*, November–December 2015, p. 114.

5  Carl von Clauswitz, *On War*, originally published by Dümmler in 1832, after his death.

6  Frank A. Rose, "Using diplomacy to advance the long-term sustainability and security of the outer space environment," Speech at the International Symposium on Ensuring

Stable Use of Outer Space, Tokyo, Japan, March 3, 2016. www.state.gov/t/avc/rls/253947.htm

7 Robert Jervis, "Cooperation under the security dilemma," *World Politics*, 30(2), January 1978, 167–214; see pp. 174–5.

8 Lyle Goldstein, *Meeting China Halfway*, Georgetown University Press, Washington, DC, 2015.

9 Walter Russell Mead, *Power, Terror, Peace and War*, Knopf, New York, 2004, p. 4.

10 Francis Fukuyama, *The End of History and the Last Man*, Free Press, New York, 1992.

11 Samuel Huntington, *The Clash of Civilizations and the Remaking of World Order*, Simon & Schuster, London, 1996.

12 Andrew J. Bacevich, *The Limits to Power: The End of American Exceptionalism*, Henry Holt and Company, New York, 2009.

13 Thomas Friedman, *The Lexus and the Olive Tree*, Farrar, Straus and Giroux, New York, 1999.

14 Jim O'Neill, *Building Better Global Economic BRICs*, Global Economics Paper No. 66, Goldman Sachs, November 30, 2001. www.goldmansachs.com/our-thinking/archive/archive-pdfs/build-better-brics.pdf

15 Mike Gruss, "Maneuvering Russian spacecraft has everyone's attention," *SpaceNews*, July 17, 2015. http://spacenews.com/maneuvering-russian-satellite-has-everyones-attention/

16 Peter B. de Selding, "Defense budget as new space programs ramp up," *SpaceNews*, November 19, 2015. http://spacenews.com/paris-attacks-pressure-french-defense-budget-as-new-space-programs-ramp-up/

17 Saadia M. Pekkanen, "U.S.-Japan military space alliance promises to grow in 'new ways,'" *Forbes*, October 27, 2015. www.forbes.com/sites/saadiampekkanen/2015/10/27/u-s-japan-military-space-alliance-promises-to-grow-in-new-ways/#3a39457241f9

# ACKNOWLEDGMENTS

Having now been observing, studying, writing about, and speaking on space issues for more than 30 years, I consider myself fortunate to have found and be part of such a collegial and sharing professional community. Perhaps because of the inherently international and interdisciplinary nature of the subject matter, from the technical geeks to the policy wonks, space professionals largely work together to improve the body of knowledge and literature. Well-intended individuals offer opinions and analyses that vary significantly on a wide range of issues, but everyone respects each other's views.

There are a number of individuals from the space community to whom I owe considerable thanks for their assistance and encouragement as I wrote this book. I asked Dr. David Finkleman, with his technical expertise and long and varied military and government service on space-related issues, to read multiple chapters to keep me honest on technical matters. Since he was dealing with a policy wonk, he did what he could in that regard and offered valuable general comments as well. Cynda Arsenault, President and co-founder of the Secure World Foundation (SWF), and Theresa Hitchens, Senior Research Scholar at the Center for International and Security Studies at the University of Maryland, read and commented on multiple chapters as well. I have had the pleasure of serving on the Advisory Committee of the SWF for two terms and greatly respect and appreciate Cynda's vision and the substantive work done by the SWF professionals. I had the pleasure of working with Theresa on another space strategy project in parallel to working on this book—a project where ideas were generated and which ultimately helped me focus my conclusions, for which I am very grateful. Commander Andrew Dittmer was a student in my class at the Naval War College in 2015–16. He learned the dangers of raising his hand the hard way after I asked for those with space experience to identify themselves. Andy ended up speaking at a conference for me after I had a scheduling conflict—and did a great job—as well as reading and commenting on almost every chapter. Jim Armor at Orbital ATK and Rich DalBello at Virgin Galactic kindly read and commented on material relating to commercial space and NewSpace and the differences between them. And David Kendall, with his long experience at the Canadian Space Agency and the UN Committee on the Peaceful Uses of Outer Space, provided great insight regarding multilateral space activities.

I am grateful as well to the Naval War College for its commitment to academic freedom. Allowing faculty members such as myself to engage in policy debates strengthens us as teachers and adds to the national and international dialogue on important policy issues. I have found the students at the Naval War College interested in and appreciative of faculty research and willing to be sounding boards for ideas, often adding nuance to arguments through the sharing of their operational experience.

Finally, I would like to thank my family and friends for their patience and tolerance while I was working on the book and tended, at times, to get a bit "focused," to the neglect of much else around me. I'm back now.

Clearly, I have had considerable support, encouragement, and assistance in this book project, and I am appreciative. Just as clearly, I am fully responsible for its contents, conclusions, and flaws. The views represented are mine alone and do not represent those of the Naval War College, the Department of Defense, or the US government.

# 1

# PROTECTING SPACE ASSETS

Unfortunately, aggressive leaders tend to be risk-acceptant optimists.

Forrest Morgan[1]

If you don't care where you're going, any road will take you there. Or so explained the Cheshire Cat to Alice in Lewis Carroll's *Alice's Adventures in Wonderland*.[2] However, notionally, policymakers and strategists do care where they are going and so work with goal achievement in mind; policymakers set the goals and strategists develop plans to achieve them. Regarding space, specifically US space security policy, protecting space assets has driven the work of policymakers and strategists for many years. Remarkably, there has been substantial consistency in studies focused on what needs to be done in order to achieve US space goals; basically, all elements of US power need to be employed.

The importance of protecting the space environment and US space assets in orbit has prompted strategic ends and means to be considered and reconsidered at many levels within multiple communities of the US government. The most recent US strategies related to or referencing space include the National Security Strategy (NSS) of 2010 and 2015, the National Space Policy (NSP) 2010, the Quadrennial Defense Review (QDR) 2010, and the National Security Space Strategy (NSSS) 2011.[3] Guidance in the 2015 NSS is simply stated thus:

> The world is connected by shared spaces—cyber, space, air, and oceans—that enable the free flow of people, goods, services, and ideas. They are the arteries of the global economy and civil society, and access is at risk due to increased competition and provocative behaviors. Therefore, we will continue to promote rules for responsible behavior while making sure we have the capabilities to assure access to these shared spaces.[4]

These general ideas—goals—are reiterated in the NSP as follows: "the United States considers the sustainability, stability, and free access to, and use of, space vital to its national interests."[5]

The same goals are reiterated in the NSSS, with others more directly related to security added. The NSSS also recognizes the importance of working with all spacefaring nations due to the nature of the space environment as "a domain that no nation owns but on which all rely," although, as per these government space documents, the space environment is benchmarked as increasingly "congested, contested, and competitive."[6] Specifically, because the United States does not own space, "partnering with responsible nations, international organizations, and commercial firms"[7] as well as seeking "common ground among all space-faring nations"[8] to maintain stability and address issues relevant to all becomes imperative. The assumed congested, contested, and competitive space environment presents both challenges and opportunities, if only through the self-interest of all spacefaring nations in sustaining that environment.

Within that now accepted description of the space environment, the security-specific NSSS goals are given as:

- Strengthen safety, stability, and security in space;
- Maintain and enhance the strategic national security advantages afforded to the United States by space; and
- Energize the space industrial base that supports U.S. national security.[9]

The NSSS means to achieving those goals are clearly stated, as follows:

> The National Security Space Strategy draws upon *all elements of national power* and requires active U.S. leadership in space. The United States *will pursue a set of interrelated strategic approaches* to meet our national security space objectives:
> - Promote responsible, peaceful, and safe use of space;
> - Provide improved U.S. space capabilities;
> - Partner with responsible nations, international organizations, and commercial firms;
> - Prevent and deter aggression against space infrastructure that supports U.S. national security; and
> - Prepare to defeat attacks and to operate in a degraded environment [emphasis added].[10]

The last two bullets include development of military capabilities to "deter, defend against, and defeat aggression"—language drawn from the 2010 Quadrennial Defense Review (QDR) and cited in the NSSS.[11] US goals in space have stayed relatively stable as might be assumed due to their enduring nature. The important question for analysts and strategists to address becomes, then, how best to implement the goals.

Bruce MacDonald, in a 2008 study for the Council on Foreign Relations, stated that "certain objectives are clearly in the interest of the United States. ... preventing space conflict should be a major US security objective, and ... all instruments of U.S. power, not just military measures, should be drawn upon to this end."[12] Similarly, Ambassador Roger Harrison, Deron Jackson, and Collins Shackelford of the Eisenhower Center for Space and Defense Studies at the US Air Force Academy conducted a study on space deterrence in 2009. The study was premised on the United States having "created a military structure that is heavily satellite-dependent without making corresponding improvements to the survivability of its space systems. The result is a classic opportunity for asymmetric, preemptive attack." Therefore, they asked "how to structure a strategy of deterrence to persuade potentially hostile actors that the costs of attack will nevertheless outweigh the benefits."[13] In other words, how can a war in space be prevented? In response, they recommended a four-tiered "layered approach"[14] to address the challenges of space deterrence: international norms, entanglement, retaliation, and denial. It is important to note that the first two layers focus on diplomatic and economic aspects of US national power rather than the military.

Forrest Morgan's 2010 RAND study presented a space deterrence strategy intended to protect US space assets by simultaneously addressing both sides of a potential adversary's cost–benefit decision calculus. While the strategy condemns the use of force in space, it also makes it clear that the United States would severely punish any attacks on its space systems and those of friendly states in ways, times, and places of its choosing—deterrence by punishment. But, specifically reiterating the fundamental interest in space stability, the strategy goes on to talk about appropriate approaches to achieve the policy goal, stating:

> such a policy would embrace diplomatic engagement, treaty negotiations, and other confidence-building measures, both for whatever stabilizing effects can be attained from such activities and because demonstrating leadership in these venues helps to characterize the United States as a responsible world actor with the moral authority to use its power to protect the interests of all spacefaring nations.[15]

The moral authority aspect of US space policy is not insignificant. If the United States expects other countries to follow its lead in space, it must itself be seen to be holding the moral high ground in terms of commitment to stability. In addition to deterrence by punishment, the strategy discusses the importance of deterrence by denial. In other words, space stability can only be achieved through layered activities, not a single focus.

And therein lies the problem. While a full complement of interrelated approaches utilizing all elements of US power is stressed throughout these documents and analyses as being necessary to effectively deal with space security issues, in practice focus is increasingly being put on military options—and even more specifically, deterrence by punishment—at best overshadowing and more realistically discounting or excluding others. Focusing on military options has too frequently become the US fallback position.

Though the United States is generally said to have diplomatic, informational, military, and economic tools of power available (referred to by the acronym DIME), since 9/11 especially, utilization can be characterized as primarily diMe. In his book *The New American Militarism*, Andrew Bacevich explains the rise of the "M" over other tools.

> In former times American policymakers treated (or at least pretended to treat) the use of force as evidence that diplomacy had failed. In our own time they have concluded (in the words of Vice President Dick Cheney) that force "makes your diplomacy more effective going forward … ." Policymakers have increasingly come to see coercion as a sort of all-purpose tool.[16]

Analysts including Sean Kay[17] and Steven Simon and Jonathan Stevenson[18] have argued that President Barack Obama tried to bring America back to a more traditional realist, noninterventionist position than that taken during the George W. Bush Administration. Additionally, in some policy areas, the Obama Administration worked decidedly, and against substantial criticism, to return to a more balanced use of policy tools, such being the case in normalizing relations with Cuba and negotiating a nuclear agreement with Iran. Space policy, however, was and is returning to being dominated by those who see every problem as a nail suited to a military hammer solution.

## Space Stability

"Space stability is a fundamental U.S. national security interest."[19] Stability sustains the space environment for continued use. The Secure World Foundation defines space sustainability as "the ability of all humanity to continue to use outer space for peaceful purposes and socioeconomic development over the long term."[20] A report published by the Union of Concerned Scientists states that "the United States has a vital interest in ensuring the sustainability of the space environment, keeping satellites safe and secure, and enhancing stability not only in space but also on the ground."[21] Sustainability, however, is a concept, or abstraction. As with most abstractions, as opposed to physical principles, there are many definitions and variations of definitions. While concepts are useful for general characterizations, they also allow for obfuscation and argumentation regarding why definitions are incorrect, needing refinement or further clarification. Space policy is rife with abstractions.

As an example of concept refinement, analysts have differentiated between first-strike stability and crisis stability. First-strike stability references the structural dynamics of nuclear deterrence. Charles Glaser has described crisis stability as "a measure of the countries' incentives not to preempt in a crisis, that is, not to attack first in order to beat the attack of the enemy."[22] RAND conducted a study on the effect of the Strategic Defense Initiative (SDI) on crisis stability in 1989.[23] The authors found instability was increased if an opponent perceived their offensive strategic forces to be threatened.

Regarding sustainability, the ability to use space can be seen as a consequence of stability; hence, stability is the end-state goal rather than sustainability being a goal in itself. In that view, sustainability is husbanding the resources that allow the ability. In any event, sustainability requires stability; maintaining space as an environment for hosting satellites upon which people in every country have become dependent is imperative and a fundamental US national security interest.

Global Positioning System (GPS) navigation satellites have become a global utility much like the Internet. GPS satellites do more than allow drivers to find their way from point A to point B. They transmit precise timing signals that facilitate communication transmissions necessary for drivers to use credit cards at the pump to purchase gas or for tourists from Iowa to use their bank ATM cards to withdraw money in Beijing. In fact, GPS satellites facilitate the global banking system. Further, trucking companies, taxi services, delivery companies, utility companies, and other trades heavily reliant on transportation as part of their business model use GPS to track their assets, offering demonstrated increased efficiencies in everything from fuel efficiency to overall productivity. With the advent of GPS, transoceanic airliners can fly closer together, increasing both efficiency and safety. A military program called Blue Force Tracker uses GPS to allow US forces to identify distant troops or vehicles as friend or foe. GPS is only one example of a space asset (GPS being a constellation of satellites) that provides terrestrial services.

Communication, weather, Earth observation, science, intelligence, and military satellites also orbit the Earth. These satellites provide the ability to track storms threatening populated areas, operate Unmanned Aerial Vehicles (UAVs), afford farmers information about maximizing crop rotations, and monitor activities in places otherwise inaccessible, like Syria, on a 24/7 basis as well as a plethora of other functions. Of the 1,381 satellites in orbit as of December 31, 2015, 568 belonged to the United States, followed by Russia's 133, China's 177, and the other 503 belonging to "others."[24] The United States clearly has the biggest stake in being able to use the space environment to facilitate the information technology that has become critical in everyday life as well as for national security. The Space Enterprise Council and the Marshall Institute launched a series of events in 2008 that effectively demonstrated the negative implications of "a day without space."[25] If there is only one consensus about space security, it is regarding the wide-ranging global value of space assets.

Therefore, if sustaining the space environment is imperative, then stability must be maintained. Stability, as Gen. Hyten pointed out, is threatened in several different ways, including those which are man-made. Some scientists, most notably Neil deGrasse Tyson, derided the movie *Gravity* for its technical inaccuracies.[26] But beyond its entertainment value, the movie did raise the level of awareness, or at least curiosity, about the very real problem of space debris—dangerous junk left in space over the course of 60 plus years of utilization, ranging from small flecks of paint to satellite bodies weighing tons—among the general public,[27] a public fairly oblivious to what and how information is regularly provided to them from space.

Nobody expects the average GPS user to understand the orbital dynamics that keep satellites in orbit or the engineering that facilitates the operation of navigation satellites any more than the average car driver is expected to understand combustion engines or airplane passengers, aerodynamics. But car drivers do understand the need for mechanics to perform maintenance, the need to add fuel, and the need for occasional tire and oil replacement—the fundamentals. That might not be the case regarding space assets. Even lawmakers have been known to lack a fundamental knowledge of space basics. A National Oceanic and Atmospheric Administration (NOAA) meteorologist testifying before Congress was told by a lawmaker that while he would like to fund a new weather satellite, he didn't see it as a priority since The Weather Channel was already available. Gen. Hyten has similarly expressed frustration regarding the lack of awareness even within the military regarding the importance of space, relaying a conversation he had with a flight rank officer: "We were talking about the threat that space was now coming under… and he pointed out to me it's really not that big a deal because if space goes away, we can just fly UAVs and we'll be fine."[28] Without basic knowledge regarding the nature and importance of space assets among lawmakers and the military, it is easy to understand how the public might easily accept incomplete conclusions about what is needed to protect the space environment and hence those assets— conclusions that omit consideration of the need for stability and how that is contradicted by current plans. But public support can be seen as valuable for continued funding of always-high-cost space activity.

In some ways, the notion of maintaining stability harkens back to the Cold War and nuclear deterrence. The international system during the Cold War was, however, a bipolar system, whereas today the international system is multipolar, whether or not American politicians want to or are willing to admit that to the populace. Doing so would be to admit that the United States' unipolar moment has passed and it can no longer dictate or control global, let alone celestial, actions. It is an increasingly multipolar world, the United States being clearly first among others but no longer able to unilaterally impose its will. But that inevitable fact can be politically twisted into a stump speech exhorting that someone dropped the "leadership" ball, resulting in American "decline," and only a political opponent to whoever dropped the ball can save America. Hence, it is safer for politicians not to address inconvenient realities with the voting public.

President Jimmy Carter's 1979 speech on energy policy came to be known as the "crisis of confidence" or "malaise" (though that word was never used) speech, the negative consequences of which became Lesson Number One for campaigning politicians. During the height of an oil crisis that required American drivers to get up before dawn to get in line for gasoline, sufficient a situation in itself to rile the citizenry, Carter had the audacity to tell Americans they needed to tighten their belts and live within their means. Consumption, he told them, "does not satisfy our longing for meaning. We've learned that piling up material goods cannot fill the emptiness of lives which have no confidence or purpose."[29] Not surprisingly, opposing candidate Ronald Reagan jumped on the opportunity presented him, assured the American people that they did not have to and they should not settle for less—they were, after all, hard-working Americans who deserved to reap the rewards of their hard work—and ran with that message all the way to the White House. The lesson learned for all future campaigning politicians was simple: Never tell the American public anything they don't want to hear because the American public had come to think of itself as special and America as "exceptional." Traditionally, exceptionalism referenced the character of the United States as based, somewhat uniquely, on constitutional freedoms and personal liberties, and perhaps a "special providence."[30] It also meant that the United States did things, like the Apollo Program, that other countries did not or could not. Exceptionalism, naturally, requires that the United States be not merely first among others, but superior to others (by as much as possible); hence, public aversion to the idea of multipolarity and the continuing emphasis by political candidates on exceptionalism, more recently defined by the public as entitlement.[31]

In some areas, however, intelligence agencies are less hesitant than politicians in being forthright. The two most recent reports of the US National Intelligence Council, *Global Trends 2025: A Transformed World* and *Global Trends 2030: Alternative Worlds*, accept a multipolar world as certainty. As part of the analysis in *Global Trends 2030*, seminars were conducted with international experts; relevant parts of the seminar findings are described thus:

> Emerging powers are likely to be particularly sensitive to future perceived slights by the US. Words like "humiliation" and "respect" cropped up repeatedly in the presentations and conversations, especially with experts from those regions. As emerging powers seek greater influence and recognition in the international order they are likely to clash diplomatically with the US. Elite and publics in emerging countries have increasingly objected to "hegemonic" behavior or extensive interventions abroad by the US. One of the attractions of a multipolar world for many of them is a lessened US dominance. Maintaining and protecting one's sovereignty would continue to be a preoccupation, particularly so long as they feel their place in the international order is not secured.[32]

While US hegemony is neither internationally desired nor appreciated, a continuing leadership role in a multipolar international system will be increasingly imperative to guide future stability, making it essential that the United States fully understands, accepts, and addresses the parameters of the international system within which it will operate and that it does so from a moral high ground. Specifically, a primacy approach to addressing issues is no longer an option, including and perhaps especially in space.

## Space Dominance: It's Déjà Vu All Over Again

*Joint Vision 2010*, produced by the Joint Chiefs of Staff, codified the military's answer to the question of "what is enough security?" There, it was said that, "[f]ull spectrum dominance will be the key characteristic we seek for our Armed Forces in the 21st century."[33] Full spectrum dominance basically means unambiguous dominance—differentiated from supremacy or preeminence—in all forms of warfare. Dominance rhetoric goes hand in hand with "control" rhetoric and primacy.

Space control is considered one of the military's four space missions, along with space force enhancement, space support, and force application. In 2002, the Joint Chiefs defined it as follows:

> Space control operations provide freedom of action in space for friendly forces while, when directed, denying it to an adversary, and include the broad aspect of protection of US and US allied space systems and negation of enemy adversary space systems. Space control operations encompass all elements of the space defense mission and include offensive and defensive operations by friendly forces to gain and maintain space superiority and situational awareness if events impact space operations.[34]

Basically, it allows the United States to do what it wants in space while denying others access to space.

In a 2013 article, Ambassador Roger Harrison explained both the pull and the empty promise of "space control."

> Space control is a politically potent doctrine. It appeals to American exceptionalism and our assumed vocation for international leadership, and it dominated space policy debate for a generation or more. Of course, this sort of power was always aspirational rather than real since (fantasy systems aside) we lacked both the means to enforce our will on recalcitrant actors in space, and the consent of those we thought of, and needed, as willing collaborators. We spoke loudly, but carried an imaginary stick. … But while dead for practical purposes, the notion of space control remains ideologically very much alive.[35]

While perhaps dead at the time of that writing in 2013, it soon thereafter rose again like a phoenix.

For many years, the United States and the Soviet Union, even at the height of the Cold War, viewed restraint as the best option for maintaining the vital interest of stability in space. A policy of strategic restraint, specifically restraint of military actions in space and favoring passive military systems to active systems, had prevailed through the "space race" years to avoid an expensive, unwinnable, and dangerous space arms race. These underlying premises of strategic thought made possible the 1967 Outer Space Treaty (OST), codifying aspects of the tacit US–Soviet restraint agreement that both countries thought would last forever and tamp down the military's tendency to inflate threats and hatch ill-conceived programs like Project A-119, a 1958 Air Force program to detonate a nuclear weapon on the dark side of the Moon as a show of US military might.[36] But strategies possible in a bipolar world proved more difficult, first in a unipolar world and then in today's multipolar world.

Even after the Anti-Ballistic Missile Treaty was signed in 1972, both countries pursued policies of contingent restraint regarding anti-satellite weapons (ASAT) technology, whereby restraint by one was contingent upon restraint of the other.[37] But restraint began to be challenged during the Clinton years and the Republican Contract with America. With the Cold War over and America enjoying its unipolar moment, primacy, with its emphasis on preserving America's hegemonic status for the good of America and assumedly the rest of the world, began to emerge, reaching its pinnacle during the George W. Bush years.

Space dominance rhetoric prevailed during the Bush Administration when "transformation" and "transformational" were the buzzwords used to describe every military program seeking Pentagon support for funding. Transformation, meaning use of technology to enable capability leaps, was Defense Secretary Donald Rumsfeld's preferred approach to war. Transformation went hand in hand with Rumsfeld's philosophy of "known knowns," "unknown knowns," and "unknown unknowns," drawn from an introduction written by Harvard economist Thomas Schelling for Roberta Wohlstetter's book *Pearl Harbor: Warning and Decision*. There, Schelling wrote: "There is a tendency in our planning to confuse the unfamiliar with the improbable. ... Furthermore, we made the terrible mistake ... of forgetting that a fine deterrent can make a superb target."[38] Therefore, it was imperative to expect the unexpected and to be able to respond with unmatched lethality and speed. Transformational capabilities demonstrated that lethality and speed with US "shock and awe" in Iraq. Transformation, it was professed, would allow the United States to remain a benevolent hegemon for its own good and that of others, whether they liked it or not.[39] The United States would not just be in charge, but would dominate. With space assets providing key force enhancement capabilities to US forces, clearly the United States must dominate space.

The genesis of primacy and control space rhetoric, and policy, can be traced through a series of documents primarily but not exclusively emanating from the Air Force. The *Joint Doctrine for Space Operations*, published by the Office of the Joint Chiefs of Staff in August 2002, stated that "[s]pace control supports freedom of action in space for friendly forces, and when necessary, defeats adversary efforts that interfere with or attack US or allied space systems and negates adversary space capabilities."[40] The Air Force's 2003 *Transformation Flight Plan*[41] followed soon thereafter. Reading the new political environment well, it included plans for orbiting weapons, including hypervelocity rod bundles, dubbed "Rods from God," that would send giant tungsten rods crashing to Earth from space with the force of a nuclear weapon but without any radioactivity.[42] The idea wasn't new or even original. Science fiction writer Jerry Pournelle conceived it while working at Boeing in the 1950s and called it "Thor." As he explained in a 2006 interview with the *New York Times*, "people periodically rediscover it."[43] The Air Force certainly had, but they dismissed their seriousness about development when it garnered attention in publications like *Popular Science*.[44] Citing the Air Force's 2004 *Transformation Flight Plan*, space analyst Theresa Hitchens and colleagues state that

> Air Force officials downplayed the 2003 Transformation Flight Plan as a "wish list," but the 2004 version describes the series as a "reporting document" that does "not represent new policy guidance or propose what the Air Force should do, but is instead intended to reflect decisions, information, and initiatives *already made and/or approved* [emphasis added] by the Air Force capability-based planning, programming and budget process."[45]

While Rods from God remains only a concept (as far as is known), the Air Force pushed forward with plans for weapons in space.

The *Tranformation Flight Plan* documents focused on hardware. The 2004 Air Force Doctrine Document 2-2.1 *Counterspace Operations* added another important component; that is, how and where to use them. The document states that the United States would seek

> [t]he degree of dominance in space of one force over another that permits the conduct of operations by the former and its related land, sea, air, space, and special operations forces at a given time and place without prohibitive interference by the opposing force.[46]

That definition is strikingly similar to the Department of Defense (DoD) definition of air superiority: "That degree of dominance in the air battle by one force that permits the conduct of its operations at a given time and place without prohibitive interference from air and missile threats."[47] The difficulty with transference is that an air battle takes place in a relatively small area, over a relatively short period of time, with a relatively high degree of ability for commanders to know what is going on and who is responsible for what actions, whereas in space, none of that may be true.

While the 2006 NSP abandoned restraint of any variety and adopted the primacist tone and policy direction of the military, the apparent hope was that few people would notice.

> Released on a Friday afternoon during a sleepy news cycle before the three-day Columbus Day weekend, the White House Office of Science and Technology Policy produced the long-awaited new policy, a sweeping document providing overarching guidance for America's multiple space programs. Initially there was little reaction, which was almost certainly the point of burying the story on a slow weekend. In fact, the document was signed by President Bush on August 31, but then apparently held for a few weeks and then released with as little fanfare as possible, thus continuing a

previously established administration approach regarding the direction of U.S. space policy of maintaining a low profile to avoid too much scrutiny and controversy.[48]

Eventually, however, it was noticed—and scrutinized—not just in the United States, but globally.

Bush supporters claimed the 2006 NSP was little different from the 1996 Clinton space policy. Like the 1996 policy, for example, it did not endorse space weapons. The changes were, in fact, subtle. Whereas the 1996 policy focused on civil programs first and military second, in the 2006 policy, the order was reversed. The Bush NSP de-emphasized arms control and barely mentioned international cooperation.[49] But those could be considered issues of prioritization expected to change from one administration to the next. The big difference was largely in tone. Whereas, for example, the 1996 NSP stated that the United States "rejects any limitations on the fundamental right *of sovereign nations* to acquire data from space," the 2006 NSP stated that it "rejects any limitations of the fundamental right *of the United States* to operate in and acquire data from space."[50] Rights extended to all nations in 1996 began to be reserved for the United States in 2006.

The same kind of language rollback shown in 2006 during the primacy years of the Bush Administration began to be seen again in 2014, this time regarding arms control. In statements as recent as 2014, Assistant Secretary of State for Arms Control, Verification and Compliance Frank Rose stated the United States was amenable to space arms control agreements if they are "equitable, effectively verifiable, and enhance the security of *all nations*."[51] Beyond those terms being complete abstractions, in his November 2015 remarks, Mr. Rose stated that the United States would consider arms control measures if they are "equitable, effectively verifiable, and enhance the national security of the United States *and its allies*."[52] It is unlikely that selection of the more recent wording was casual or a misstep as this phrase is one of the recurring talking points of US space policy. It also assumes it is up to the United States to determine what enhances another nation's security. Other countries, even allies, tend to balk at this.

The international perspective on the 2006 NSP was summed up best in an article in *The Times* of London entitled "America Wants it All – Life, the Universe, and Everything." The article stated that the 2006 policy no longer considered space the final frontier, but the "51st state of the United States," going on to say that "[t]he new National Space Policy that President Bush has signed is comically proprietary in tone about the U.S.'s right to control access to the rest of the solar system."[53] Bombastic, muscular, primacist language prevailed in space as in other post-9/11 areas of US policy and strategy.

The desire for dominance has, over the years, sometimes been overtly stated and sometimes couched in almost Orwellian, doublespeak terms like "offensive counterspace." Air Force doctrine began articulating the idea of offensive counterspace in 2004, detailing the planning and execution of operations against space systems and satellites for both offensive and defensive purposes.[54] Offensive counterspace includes space weapons. Further, it implies the potential inclusion of not just preemptive but also preventive operations.

Since a nineteenth-century formulation known as the Caroline test, preemptive self-defense has been upheld as within the bounds of customary international law if the necessity is "instant, overwhelming, and leaving no choice of means, and no moment for deliberation."[55] Prevention, however, involves actions taken in the short term to fend off a longer-term potential threat. It is strangling the baby in the cradle before it can grow up and become a threat. Given the ambiguous, dual-use nature of space technology and the tyranny of distance that comes into play with determining accountability for actions taking place hundreds, maybe thousands, of miles in space, the potential for error in determining, anticipating, and reacting to the activities of others is significant. So while offensive counterspace might profess preemptive, defensive actions, those actions might well be preventive[56] but with a subsequently high potential for mishap, misperception, and miscalculation.

When doublespeak is combined with dual-use technology, the result is, depending on one's perspective, either convenient or perplexing abstruseness. The United States has been conducting end-to-end system missile defense system tests since 2000[57] and considers this a defensive right. There is, however, a nearly symbiotic relationship between the capabilities required for missile defense and for an ASAT. Though the physics involved differ in terms of a much higher kinetic energy and closing rate being required for an ASAT than for missile defense, the fundamentals are the same. ASAT tests, however, are now—as opposed to the 1980s when both the United States and the Soviets were testing ASATs—internationally censured, whereas missile defense tests are politically acceptable. So countries have learned, primarily from the United States, that the way to test ASAT capabilities and avoid political condemnation is to refer to their tests as missile defense tests rather than ASAT tests and to conduct tests in such a way as to not create long-lived orbital debris.[58] Not only has China learned this lesson, but India too, as both appear determined to develop an ASAT capability.

India has been conducting missile defense-cum-ASAT intercept attempts since 2006.[59] India seems to be suffering a hangover from the Non-Proliferation Treaty, which excluded it from having nuclear status. It now seems determined to possess an ASAT capability before international arms control provisions potentially separate countries again into ASAT haves and have-nots. China began its "missile defense" testing in 2010—after its overt ASAT test in 2007 was internationally condemned—followed by further missile defense tests in 2013 and 2014.[60]

Space dominance rhetoric initially toned down during the Obama Administration years, replaced by a more restraintist approach to protecting space assets that continued research and development of a wide spectrum of technology but also sought to advance bilateral and multilateral diplomatic efforts. Policy, actions, and rhetoric were fairly aligned. Secretary of State Hillary Clinton announced support for an international code of conduct (ICOC) for space in 2012,[61] later endorsed by Air Force Space Command Chief William Shelton.[62]

Administration policy was that US space assets could best be protected through collectivizing key space functions, replacing the desire for national autonomy with globalized entanglement. Neglecting the potentially positive impact of globalization on space security has been argued before to be shortsighted,[63] but that argument was largely ignored during the Bush Administration. It makes sense, though, that the more satellites a country has at risk, the less likely they are to put them at risk. The Obama Administration seemed amenable, indeed committed, to a restraintist, balanced approach, at least for a while.

But the quest for dominance and control still simmered within parts of the military and policy community, with primacist rhetoric and eventually policy changes bubbling up again after a launch by China in May 2013, which they claimed was a science mission but the United States considered to be an ASAT test.[64] Concerns about the Chinese test were elevated all the way to President Obama, resulting in a concerted interagency effort, led by the National Security Council (NSC), to figure out what should be done to deal with the perceived heightened threat environment. Hitchens explained what happened next.

> The Pentagon in the summer of 2014 undertook a classified Space Portfolio Review that looked at threats, the survivability of satellites, and the capabilities to respond to the threats. Congress jumped into the fray in passing the fiscal year National Defense Authorization Act in late 2014, ordering the Defense Secretary and the Director of National Intelligence to report on the role of "offensive space operations" in deterring and defeating threats to U.S. spacecraft, as well as mandating new spending on the development of "offensive space control and active defense strategies and capabilities."[65]

Consequent to the Space Portfolio Review, the United States generally and the Air Force specifically have adopted an approach known informally as "space protection," defined only as being able to assure that the Pentagon and intelligence communities can make use of their satellites at any time.[66] The director of space policy at the White House National Security Council, Chirag Parikh, described the consequent change in thinking as "a paradigm shift."[67] Since then, defense officials from Deputy Defense Secretary Bob Work[68] to Strategic Command (STRATCOM) chief Admiral Cecil Haney[69] to Gen. Hyten on *60 Minutes* have publically advocated a dominant, muscular approach to protecting space assets.

Even Frank Rose, heretofore the Obama Administration "space diplomat," increasingly began focusing on the more muscular aspects of US space policy, as evidenced in his remarks at the 2015 Space Foundation symposium in Colorado Springs. Rose stated that "China's continued development of anti-satellite weapons remains a major challenge to the space environment." He quoted US space policy intent to "deter others from interference and attack, defend our space systems and contribute to the defense of allies space systems, and, if deterrence fails, defeat efforts to attack them." The last phrase references offensive counterspace. He also said in his speech that "we need to continue to call out the disruptive actions of countries like Russia and China both publicly and in cooperation with our allies and partners."[70]

The importance of strategic messaging and signaling cannot be overstated if deterrence is a serious part of US strategy. The 2010 RAND study explains why.

> While efforts to develop such [counterspace] plans and capabilities may be prudent, openly expressing U.S. intentions to dominate space does nothing to deter others from attacking U.S. space systems; rather, given the first-strike advantage so prevalent in the space strategic environment, it animates the efforts of potential adversaries to develop similar capabilities and, in a crisis, would provide motive and justification for their preemptive employment.
>
> A national space policy more conducive to deterring attacks on U.S. space systems would avoid provocative rhetoric about denying others the use of space and would, instead, explicitly condemn any use of force to, from, or in that domain, except in retribution for attacks on one's own space systems.[71]

While bravado about countering a threat may be seen as effective, perhaps even necessary, in persuading the American people and Congress of the need for budget increases, it is counterproductive in terms of successfully deterring a potential adversary from actions against US interests. Restraint does not mean that work on counterspace technologies stops; it means that diplomacy is a first choice effort while other options are pursued as well. That approach has been used before by both Republican and Democratic administrations.

Both President Jimmy Carter and President Ronald Reagan used a dual-track, or hedging, approach to tamp down security dilemmas associated with weapons systems. In the 1970s, President Jimmy Carter took a dual-track approach to the threat of ASAT weapons. He pursued negotiations with the Soviets on the issues, but in case that did not work—and to perhaps nudge them to the negotiating table—he also pursued advanced air-launched ASAT technologies.[72] NATO took a similar approach with deployment of intermediate nuclear forces in Europe in the 1980s under the Reagan Administration. NATO countered the introduction of Soviet SS-20s when deploying ground-launched cruise missiles and Pershing IIs in Europe while also seeking an arms control agreement. That dual-track approach led to the 1987 Intermediate-Range Nuclear Forces (INF) Treaty.

It might be argued that a similar dual-track or hedging approach is now being pursued regarding ASATs—developing offensive counterspace capabilities while pursuing diplomatic avenues through the United Nations (UN). However, brandishing US "space control" and "dominance" intentions while taking anything less than a leadership role in diplomatic efforts does not signal being serious about diplomatic goals. And once the iron dice are thrown, so to speak, it is often difficult to pull them back. Internal organizational behavior comes into play, furthering the case for war rather than diplomacy.

Andrew Bacevich points out the implications of space control and dominance expectations on the military.[73] Basically, dominance becomes a baseline from which to strive further. Supremacy comes to be seen as being merely adequate and any hesitancy in efforts to increase the margin of supremacy between the United States and all others, as evidence of falling behind. The consequences of that attitude are reflected in examples provided by Bacevich regarding both sea supremacy and space dominance.

> Thus, according to one typical study of the U.S. Navy's future, "sea supremacy at our shore lines and extending outward to distant theaters is a necessary condition for the defense of the U.S." Of course, the U.S. Navy already possesses unquestioned global preeminence: the real point of the study is to argue for the urgency of radical enhancements to that preeminence. The officer-authors of this study express confidence that given sufficient money the Navy can achieve ever greater supremacy, enabling the Navy of the future to enjoy "overwhelming precision firepower," "pervasive surveillance," and "dominant control of a maneuvering area, whether, sea, undersea, land, air, space or cyberspace." In this study and in virtually all others, political and strategic questions implicit in the proposition that supremacy in distant theaters forms a prerequisite of "defense" are left begging—indeed, are probably unrecognized. At times, this quest for military dominion takes on galactic proportions. Acknowledging that the United States enjoys "superiority in many aspects of space capability," a senior defense official nonetheless complains that "we don't have space dominance and we don't have space supremacy." Since outer space is "the ultimate high ground," which the United States must control, he urges immediate action to correct this deficiency. When it comes to military power, mere superiority will not suffice.[74]

Seeking dominance has become the military's quest for the Holy Grail.

Admiral Arthur Cebrowski, director of the Defense Department's Force Transformation Office from 2001 to 2005, explained the need for dominance differently, though with the same "quest" tenor. Cebrowski argued that the United States must not succumb to complacency even if it is far above all other countries in military space capabilities. In the following extract from *Twilight War: The Folly of Space Dominance*, Mike Moore cites Cebrowski in explaining what that means, adding his own noteworthy commentary.

> Cebrowski argued ... as the "sole superpower" it [the United States] must "*compete with itself to avoid stagnation.*" That last bit is worth pondering. Is it sound advice for a nation to "compete with itself" in building military capabilities? It might seem rational to some; to others, it suggests a straight-arrow highway to national bankruptcy.[75]

Moore is rightly suggesting that the feasibility of dominance needs to be questioned, especially in a resource-constrained environment.

The economic, technical and political feasibility of across-the-board unambiguous dominance is tenuous at best. An Improvised Explosive Devise (IED) on a road in Iraq or Afghanistan was effectively used to defy the best-equipped, best-trained fighting force in the world. In space, dominance is challenged by the tyranny of distance, the vastness of the area to be covered, and physics. And yet, again, the military–industrial complex and all its component parts is always willing to keep trying to discover unobtainium or impossibilium, even when inconsistent with the laws of physics, for the right price. And so, the quest for invincibility continues, often with the blessing of the public even though it is their money being thrown down a rabbit hole—a reaction to fear.

## The Politics of Fear

Former managing editor of *The National Interest* Robert Golan-Vilella tells of presidential candidate Barack Obama delivering a 2008 speech in Los Angeles where Obama said, "I don't want to just end the war, but I want to end the mindset that got us into this war in the first place." The mindset he was talking about, according to his advisors, was "the politics of fear." Golan-Vilella defines the politics of fear as "the absence of any sort of perspective or making sense of threats. It's the mentality that any potential threat to the United States is a 'critical' or 'extraordinary' one, and that almost any measures are therefore justified in confronting it."[76]

While Obama and his advisors largely conceived of the politics of fear as a reaction to 9/11 that was exploited by the George W. Bush Administration, utilizing the politics of fear was not a new tactic. The American Founding Fathers accused each other of all kinds of things, including conspiracies. Candidates of both parties have successfully used "fear" against their opponents. In the late 1940s and 1950s, Republicans accused the Truman Administration of losing China and being soft on communism. Joseph McCarthy went so far as claiming that communists were infiltrating key American institutions. The Kennedy Administration accused the Eisenhower Administration of allowing a missile gap to develop despite knowing that this wasn't true.[77] The internment of American citizens of Japanese descent during World War II and the categorizing of the Soviet Union as the "the Evil Empire" during the Cold War served fear-related purposes as well, though different purposes. Internment was responding to public fear, while dubbing the Soviet Union the Evil Empire created politically useful public fear.

Tufts Professor Michael Glennon suggests a rationale for politically useful public fear.[78] He concludes that within the United States, there are actually two parallel governments operating. The first includes the three branches of government everyone learns about (or used to) in civics class: the Executive, the Legislative and the Judicial branches. The second, the one that actually holds power, consists of a network of officials that makes up the nations security apparatus. These individuals "define security in military and intelligence terms rather than political and diplomatic ones."[79] Because there is no such thing as too much security and space dominance may be just one government contract away, creating fear serves to protect their own power bases, to insulate them from charges of not anticipating or responding to all perceived threats (and consequently facing something like a 9/11 Commission or Benghazi hearing[s]), and of course, to secure ever-increasing budgets.

The US military space budget has long exceeded those of all other countries in the world combined. In 2012, the DoD space budget authority was $26 billion, and had been above $20 billion since 2002. In 2013 when the DoD space budget was hit by sequestration,[80] Air Force Space Command officials said their budget dropped by $508 million that year and was slated to decrease by about $462 million in 2014. Gen. Shelton warned that with those budget cuts, "you will break every program."[81] According to analyst Loren Thompson at the Lexington Institute, however, even with the significantly reduced budget figures, military space was still left in "very good shape," especially considering budget cuts being made elsewhere in the federal budget.[82]

For fiscal year 2016, the Pentagon requested and got an increase of $5 billion for space security. When that increase was jeopardized in the spring of 2015 amidst fears of a continuing government budget resolution that would fund government activities only at prior-year levels, Gen. Hyten went before Congress and said that funding was absolutely necessary to ensure the military could continue using its satellites.[83] That dire declaration of the state of military space made the timing of the *60 Minutes* segment particularly fortuitous as a "the sky is falling" advocacy piece for the hefty increase in the space budget.

Defense Secretary Ash Carter, addressing San Francisco's Commonwealth Club in March 2016, put a price tag of $22 billion on Pentagon space spending for 2017, more than double what the Air Force had said it expected to spend on unclassified space efforts in that same time frame.[84] Discrepancies in figures are often due to which programs are included and which aren't, whether classified programs are included, and accounting methods. But the bottom line is that military space spending is healthy and hefty.

## The Imperative for Balance

A robust US military space program is an absolute imperative. But it needs to be a piece of a larger, well-thought-through, comprehensive, budget-responsible, non-fear-driven approach to achieving the ultimate goal of sustainability through stability. A provocative, primacist space strategy runs counter to deterrence goals and risks escalation. Bruce MacDonald's 2008 study for the Council on Foreign Relations addresses the potential for escalation of a space conflict between the United States and China, thus jeopardizing stability and sustainability. He says:

> As a result [of that potential escalation], both countries have interests in avoiding the actual use of counterspace weapons and shaping a more stable

and secure space environment for themselves and other spacefaring nations, which could easily be caught in the undertow of a more militarily competitive space domain.[85]

Space warfare runs two untenable risks: the creation of destructive debris and escalation to terrestrial, even nuclear, warfare. Kinetic warfare in space creates debris traveling at a speed of more than 17,000 miles per hour, which then in itself becomes a destructive weapon if it hits another object—even potentially triggering the so-called Kessler Syndrome,[86] exaggerated for dramatic effect in the movie *Gravity*. Ironically, both China and the United States learned the negative lessons of debris creation the hard way. In 1985, the United States tested a miniature homing vehicle (MHV) ASAT launched from an F-15 aircraft. The MHV intercepted and destroyed a defunct US satellite at an altitude of approximately 250 miles. It took almost 17 years for the debris resulting from that test to be fully eliminated by conflagration re-entering the Earth's atmosphere or being consumed by frictional forces, though no fragment had any adverse consequences to another satellite—in particular, no collisions. China irresponsibly tested a direct-ascent ASAT in 2007, destroying one if its defunct satellites. That test was at an altitude almost twice that of the 1985 US test. The debris created by the impact added 25 percent to the debris total in low Earth orbit[87] and will dissipate through the low Earth orbit, heavily populated with satellites, for decades, perhaps centuries, to come. Perhaps most ironically, because of superior US debris-tracking capabilities, the United States—even though not required to do so—has on more than one occasion warned China that it needed to maneuver one of its satellites to avoid a collision with debris China itself had likely created.[88] In 2013, a piece of Chinese space junk from the 2007 ASAT test collided with a Russian laser ranging nanosatellite called BLITS, creating still more debris.[89] The broader point is that all nations have a compelling common interest in avoiding the massive increase in space debris that would be created by a substantial ASAT conflict.

Gen. Hyten has said that not creating debris is "the one limiting factor" to space war. "Whatever you do," he warns, "don't create debris."[90] While that might appear an obvious "limiting factor," preparing to fight its way through a debris cloud had been a Pentagon consideration in the past. Now, however, sustaining the space environment has been incorporated into Pentagon space goals.

Beyond debris creation, MacDonald points out that as China becomes more militarily capable in space and there is more symmetry between the countries, other risks are created – specifically, escalation.

> That is, the United States could threaten to attack not just Chinese space assets, but also ground-based assets, including ASAT command-and-control centers and other military capabilities. But such actions, which would involve attacking Chinese soil and likely causing substantial direct casualties, would politically weigh much heavier than the U.S. loss of space hardware, and

thus might climb the escalatory ladder to a more damaging war that both sides would probably want to avoid.[91]

MacDonald isn't alone in concerns about escalation. Secure World Foundation analyst Victoria Samson has also voiced apprehension regarding US rhetoric that does not distinguish between actions against unclassified and classified US satellites, stating that "things can escalate pretty quickly should we come into a time of hostility."[92]

Theresa Hitchens explained the most frightening, but not implausible, risk of space war escalation in a 2012 *Time* magazine interview.

> Say you have a crisis between two nuclear-armed, space-faring countries, Nation A and Nation B, which have a long-standing border dispute. Nation A, with its satellite capability, sees that Nation B is mobilizing troops and opening up military depots in a region where things are very tense already, on the tipping point. Nation A thinks: "That's it, they're going to attack." So it might decide to pre-emptively strike the communications satellite used by Nation B to slow down its ability to move toward the border and give itself time to fortify. Say this happens and Nation B has no use of satellites for 12 hours, the time it takes it to get another satellite into position. What does Nation B do? It's blind, it's deaf, it's thinking all this time that it's about to be overwhelmed by an invasion or even nuked. This is possibly a real crisis escalation situation; something similar has been played out in U.S. Air Force war games, a scenario-planning exercise practiced by the U.S. military. The first game involving anti-satellite weapons stopped in five minutes because it went nuclear – bam. Nation B nuked Nation A. This is not a far-out, "The sky's falling in!" concern, it is something that has been played out over and over again in the gaming of these things, and I have real fears about it.[93]

While escalation to a nuclear exchange may seem unthinkable, in war games conducted by the military, nuclear weapons are treated as just another warfighting weapon.

Morgan also voiced concerns about escalation generally and nuclear escalation specifically in the 2010 RAND report, stating:

> The adversary would also likely be deterred from damaging U.S. satellite early-warning system (SEWS) assets to avoid risking inadvertent escalation to the nuclear threshold, but that firebreak would almost certainly collapse with the conclusion that such escalation is inevitable and that it is in the adversary's interest to launch a preemptive nuclear strike.[94]

Only recently, in contrast to past analyses, has the risk of escalation been downplayed—dismissed—in favor of moving forward with war plans. Analyst Elbridge Colby authored a 2016 study for the Center for a New American Security

(CNAS) in which he stated "no one really believes that a limited space attack would necessarily or even plausibly be a prelude to a total nuclear war."[95] As evidence, he says "senior responsible U.S. officials have telegraphed that the United States would indeed not necessarily respond massively to attacks against its space assets."[96] Whether that message was received or buried amidst other telegraphed messages of control, domination, and denying access is tenuous. That study, however, also argues for the need for the United States to prepare for a limited space war with tacit rules and (while not desirable) acceptable actions.

Colby offers an alternative goal to either stability or annihilation: non-annihilation. It is built on several premises and assumptions, including the assumption of "the consent of one's adversary."[97] Among the foundational premises of the framework are, for example, that "being the first to carry war into space is escalatory and irresponsible" and would be considered "presumptively illegitimate." But the framework goes on the reject a "no first use" pledge, stating that such a pledge "might unduly constrain the United States over the long-term if the space military balance develops unfavorably."[98] So apparently, the United States should reject the first use of space weapons unless it decides first use is in its best interest. Whether the United States would get the space war it wants, a limited space war, or something else is a significant risk.

Given the dangers of space warfare, MacDonald pointed out how space strategy was misaligned in 2008, applicable again in 2016. First, since 2002, US space policy documents have included language about the imperative of being able to deny the use of space assets by its adversaries—primacist language that has caused considerable angst among countries increasingly using space in many of the same ways as the United States. The United States has ranged from hinting to overtly stating its desire to "control" space. And yet, second, since the 2006 NSP, space has been considered a "vital interest" of the United States for all the reasons already explained. MacDonald then points out the incongruous nature of those two points.

> Identifying one's own space capabilities as a vital national interest while reserving the right to attack others in space (which would likely provoke retaliatory attacks against our "vital" space assets), appears internally inconsistent, even contradictory. … Attacking others' satellites would invite retaliation, putting at risk a "vital national interest" where the United States has much more to lose than the attacker.[99]

Rational decision-making is goal directed with internally consistent choices. Therefore, if the United States wants to maintain access to its vital interests, then avoiding an attack becomes equally as imperative as defending and defeating an attack. Yet to the detriment of US security, far less effort is being placed on deterrence by denial than deterrence by punishment.

A closer look at the "congested, contested, and competitive" space environment is important for understanding the backdrop within which threat assessments and strategies are being developed. While management of the environment is both useful and necessary, control of the environment is already out of reach of any one country. Pursuing control is not just a futile, costly quest but can be, and in some cases already has been, counterproductive.

## Notes

1 Forrest Morgan, *Deterrence and First-Strike Stability in Space: A Preliminary Assessment*, RAND, Santa Monica, CA, 2010, p. 28.
2 First published by Macmillan in 1865.
3 US Department of Defense and Office of the Director of National Intelligence, *National Security Space Strategy: Unclassified Summary*, January 2011. http://archive.defense.gov/home/features/2011/0111_nsss/docs/NationalSecuritySpaceStrategyUnclassifiedSummary_Jan2011.pdf
4 The White House, *National Security Strategy*, February, 2015, p. 12. https://www.whitehouse.gov/sites/default/files/docs/2015_national_security_strategy.pdf
5 The White House, *National Space Policy*, June 28, 2010, p. 3. https://www.whitehouse.gov/sites/default/files/national_space_policy_6-28-10.pdf
6 *National Security Space Strategy*, p. i.
7 Ibid., p. 8.
8 Ibid., p. 5.
9 Ibid., p. 4.
10 Ibid., p. 5 (italics added).
11 Ibid., p. 10.
12 Bruce W. MacDonald, *China, Space Weapons, and US Security*, CSR No. 38, Council on Foreign Relations, New York, September 2008, p. 10.
13 Roger G. Harrison, Deron R. Jackson, and Collins G. Shackelford, "Space deterrence: the delicate balance of risk," *Space and Defense*, 3(1), Summer 2009, 1–30: p. 1.
14 Ibid., p. 18.
15 Morgan, *Deterrence and First-Strike Stability*, p. xiv.
16 Andrew J. Bacevich, *The New American Militarism*, Oxford University Press, New York, 2013, p. 19.
17 Sean Kay, *America's Search for Security: The Triumph of Idealism and the Return to Realism*, Rowman and Littlefield, Lanham, MD, 2014.
18 Steven Simon and Jonathan Stevenson, "The end of Pax Americana," *Foreign Affairs*, 94(6), November–December 2015, 2–10.
19 Morgan, *Deterrence and First-Strike Stability*, p. ix.
20 "Space Sustainability." *Secure World Foundation*. http://swfound.org/our-focus/space-sustainability/
21 Laura Grego and David Wright, *Securing the Skies: Ten Steps the United States Should Take to Improve the Security and Sustainability of Space*, Union of Concerned Scientists, Cambridge, MA, November 2010, p. 1.
22 Charles Glaser, *Analyzing Strategic Nuclear Policy*, Princeton University Press, Princeton, NJ, 1990, p. 45 as cited in Morgan, *Deterrence and First-Strike Stability*, pp. 1–2.
23 Dean Wilkening, Kenneth Watman, Michel Kennedy, and Richard Darilek, *Strategic Defense and Crisis Stability*, RAND, Santa Monica, CA, 1989. https://www.rand.org/content/dam/rand/pubs/notes/2005/N2511.pdf

24 Union of Concerned Scientists, based on the USC Satellite Database. www.ucsusa.org/nuclear-weapons/space-weapons/satellite-database.html#.Vj0Bb4QbDq0

25 Jeff Kueter, "A day without space," Remarks to NSISC Space INFOSEC Symposium, George Marshall Institute, October 25, 2011. http://marshall.org/wp-content/uploads/2013/09/1022.pdf

26 Angela Watercutter, "Astrophysicist Neil deGrasse Tyson fact-checks Gravity on Twitter," *Wired*, October 7, 2013. www.wired.com/2013/10/neil-degrasse-tyson-gravity/

27 Joan Johnson-Freese, "Commentary, Gravity: it's all about the buzz," *SpaceNews*, October 14, 2013. http://spacenews.com/37693gravity-its-all-about-the-buzz/

28 Gen. John E. Hyten, Remarks at 2015 National Space Symposium, Colorado Springs, CO, 13–16 April, 2015. www.afspc.af.mil/About-Us/Leadership-Speeches/Speeches/Display/Article/731707/general-john-hyten-2015-space-symposium

29 Conveyed by Andrew J. Bacevich, *The Limits of Power: The End of American Exceptionalism*, Metropolitan Books, New York, 2008, p. 33.

30 Walter Russell Mead, *Special Providence: American Foreign Policy and How It Changed the World*, Routledge, New York, 2002.

31 Bacevich, *The Limits to Power*, Chapter 1, "The crisis of profligacy," pp. 15–66.

32 National Intelligence Council, *Global Trends 2030: Alternative Worlds*, NIC 2012-001, Office of the Director of National Intelligence, Washington, DC, December 2012, p. 102. www.dni.gov/nic/globaltrends

33 Chairman of the Joint Chiefs of Staff, *Joint Vision 2010*, Office of the Joint Chiefs of Staff, Washington, DC, p. 2. www.dtic.mil/jv2010/jv2010.pdf

34 Joint Chiefs of Staff, *Joint Doctrine for Space Operations*, Joint Publication 3-14, August 9, 2002, Office of the Joint Chiefs of Staff, Washington, DC, pp. ix–x. www.dtic.mil/doctrine/new_pubs/jp3_14.pdf

35 Roger G. Harrison, "Unpacking the three C's: congested, competitive, and contested space," *Astropolitics*, 11(3), 2013, 123–31: pp. 127–8.

36 Antony Barnett, "US planned one big nuclear blast for all mankind," *The Guardian*, May 14, 2000. https://www.theguardian.com/science/2000/may/14/spaceexploration.theobserver

37 Nancy Gallagher and John D. Steinbruner, *Reconsidering the Rules for Space Security*, American Academy of Arts & Sciences, Cambridge, MA, 2008, p. 11.

38 Cited in Robert D. Kaplan, "What Rumsfeld got right," *The Atlantic*, July/August 2008. www.theatlantic.com/magazine/archive/2008/07/what-rumsfeld-got-right/306870/

39 Mike Moore, *Twilight War: The Folly of US Space Dominance*, The Independent Institute, Oakland, CA, 2008, Chapter 2, "Full spectrum dominance," pp. 21–40.

40 Joint Chiefs of Staff, *Joint Doctrine for Space Operations*, p. xi.

41 U.S. Air Force, *Transformation Flight Plan*, November 2003, US Air Force, Washington, DC. www.au.af.mil/au/awc/awcgate/af/af_trans_flightplan_nov03.pdf

42 Ibid., Annex D.

43 Jonathan Shainin, "Rods from God," *The New York Times Magazine*, December 10, 2006. www.nytimes.com/2006/12/10/magazine/10section3a.t-9.html?_r=0

44 Eric Adams, "Rods from God," *Popular Science*, June 1, 2004. www.popsci.com/scitech/article/2004-06/rods-god

45 Theresa Hitchens, Michael Katz-Hyman, and Jeffrey Lewis, "U.S. space weapons: big intentions, little focus," *Non-Proliferation Review*, 13(1), March 2006, 35–56: pp. 37–8.

https://www.nonproliferation.org/wp-content/uploads/npr/131hitchens.pdf; citing The U.S. Air Force Transformation Flight Plan, Executive Summary, 2004, p. i.

46 Air Force Doctrine Document 2-21, *Counterspace Operations*, August 2, 2004, US Air Force, Washington, DC, p. 55. www.space-library.com/0408_afdd2-2.1.pdf

47 Department of Defense, *Dictionary of Military and Associated Terms*, Joint Publication 1-02, amended 15 February, 2016, p. 10. www.dtic.mil/doctrine/new_pubs/jp1_02. pdf

48 Joan Johnson-Freese, *Heavenly Ambitions: America's Quest to Dominate Space*, University of Pennsylvania Press, Philadelphia, PA, 2009, pp. 58–9.

49 See The Space Review's "Section-by-section comparison of 1996 and 2006 National Space Policy documents." www.thespacereview.com/archive/745a.pdf

50 Ibid. (italics added).

51 Frank A. Rose, "U.S. will continue to take the leadership in ensuring the long-term safety, and security of space," *Mission of the United States, Geneva*, June 10, 2014, (emphasisadded).https://geneva.usmission.gov/2014/06/10/u-s-will-continue-to-take-the-leadership-in-ensuring-the-long-term-safety-and-security-of-space/

52 Frank A. Rose, "Challenges to arms control in space and pragmatic way ahead," Remarks to 3rd ARF Workshop on Space Security, Beijing, China, November 30, 2015 (emphasis added). www.state.gov/t/avc/rls/2015/250231.htm

53 Bronwen Maddox, "America wants it all – life, the universe, and everything," *The Times*, October 19, 2006. www.timesonline.co.uk/tto/opinion/columnists/bronwen maddox/article20522770.ece

54 Theresa Hitchens, "US Air Force Counterspace Operation Doctrine: questions answered, questions raised," *Center for Defense Information*, October 3, 2004. www. space4peace.org/articles/counter_space_doctrine.htm

55 Anthony Clark Arends, "International law and the preemptive use of military force," *The Washington Quarterly*, 26(2), Spring 2003, 89–103: p. 91, citing Letter from Mr. Webster to Lord Ashburton, August 6, 1842. www.diplomaticlawguide.com/ Documents/03spring_arend-1.pdf

56 Joan Johnson-Freese, "Escalating US-Sino military space rhetoric," *China-US Focus*, July 21, 2015. www.chinausfocus.com/peace-security/escaling-u-s-sino-military-space-rhetoric/

57 "US Ballistic Missile Defense Timeline: 1945–2013," *Union of Concerned Scientists*. www.ucsusa.org/nuclear-weapons/us-missile-defense/missile-defense-timeline#bf-toc-2

58 Joan Johnson-Freese, "China's anti-satellite program: they're learning," *China-US Focus*, July 12, 2013. www.chinausfocus.com/peace-security/chinas-anti-satellite-program-theyre-learning/

59 Victoria Samson, "India's missile defense/anti-satellite nexus," *The Space Review*, May 10, 2010. www.thespacereview.com/article/1621/1

60 Ting Shi, "China says third missile defense test in four years successful," *Bloomberg News*, July24,2014.www.bloomberg.com/news/articles/2014-07-24/china-says-third-missile-defense-test-in-four-years-successful

61 "International Code of Conduct for Outer Space Activities," *US Department of State*, January 17, 2012. www.state.gov/secretary/20092013clinton/rm/2012/01/180969. htm

62 Sydney J. Freedberg, Jr., "Why the Pentagon wants an international 'code of conduct' for space," *Breaking Defense*, March 22, 2012. http://breakingdefense.com/2012/03/safe-passage-why-the-pentagon-wants-an-international-code-of-c/

63 Simon P. Worden and Joan Johnson-Freese, "Globalizing Space Security," *Joint Force Quarterly*, Winter 2002–2003, 65–71.

64 Brian Weeden, "Through a glass, darkly," *Secure World Foundation*, March 17, 2014. http://swfound.org/media/167224/through_a_glass_darkly_march2014.pdf; Zachery Keck, "China secretly tested an anti-satellite missile," *The Diplomat*, March 19, 2014. http://thediplomat.com/2014/03/china-secretly-tested-an-anti-satellite-missile/

65 Theresa Hitchens, "A pause button for militarizing space," *Aerospace America*, April 2016, 38–43: p. 42.

66 Mike Gruss, "Disaggregation giving way to broader space protection strategy," *SpaceNews*, April 26, 2015. http://spacenews.com/disaggregation-giving-way-to-broader-space-protection-strategy/

67 Mike Gruss, "Delays in U.S. military satellite studies could be limiting," *SpaceNews*, May 7, 2015. http://spacenews.com/delays-in-u-s-military-satellite-studies-could-be-limiting/

68 Colin Clark, "Deputy Secretary of Defense invokes 'space control': analysts fear space war escalation," *Breaking Defense*, April 15, 2015. http://breakingdefense.com/2015/04/depsecdef-work-invokes-space-control-analysts-fear-space-war-escalation/

69 Jim Garamone, "Stratcom Chief: US must maintain space dominance," *US Department of Defense*, February 6, 2015. www.defense.gov/News-Article-View/Article/604064

70 Frank A. Rose cited in Colin Clark, "US presses Russia, China on ASAT tests: space control spending triples," *Breaking Defense*, April 16, 2015. http://breakingdefense.com/2015/04/space-control-spending-triples/

71 Morgan, *Deterrence and First-Strike Stability*, p. 39.

72 Michael Krepon with Christopher Clary, *Space Assurance or Space Dominance? The Case Against Weaponizing Space*, The Henry L. Stimson Center, Washington, DC, 2003, p. 6.

73 Bacevich, *The New American Militarism*.

74 Ibid., p. 18.

75 Moore, *Twilight War*, p. 29.

76 Robert Golan-Vilella, "Why the politics of fear will never go away," *The National Interest*, October 29, 2014. http://nationalinterest.org/feature/the-politics-fear-will-never-go-away-11556

77 Judy Woodruff interviewing Beverly Gage and Stephen Walt on *PBS Newshour*, "What past elelctions can teach us about fear politics," *PBS*, January 26, 2016. www.pbs.org/newshour/bb/what-past-elections-can-teach-us-about-fear-politics/

78 Michael Glennon, "National security and double government," *Harvard National Security Journal*, 5(1), 114 pages. http://harvardnsj.org/wp-content/uploads/2014/01/Glennon-Final.pdf

79 Ibid., p. 26.

80 Aeronautics and Space Report of the President, Fiscal Year 2014 Activities. http://history.nasa.gov/presrep2014.pdf

81 Mike Gruss, "Shelton: sequestration could break military space program," *SpaceNews*, September 23, 2013. http://spacenews.com/37270shelton-sequestration-could-break-military-space-program/

82  Debra Werner, "US military space spending set at $8 billion for 2014," *SpaceNews*, April 17, 2013. www.space.com/20702-united-states-military-space-budget-2014.html

83  Reuters, "US officials urge funding to reduce vulnerabilities in space," March 25, 2015. www.reuters.com/article/2015/03/25/us-usa-military-space-threat-idUSKBN0ML2T M20150325#axZJdlumE3bMjKQo.97

84  Mike Gruss, "During Silicon Valley trip, Carter puts $22 billion price tag on Pentagon space spending," *SpaceNews*, March 2, 2016. http://spacenews.com/during-silicon-valley-trip-carter-puts-22-billion-price-tag-on-pentagon-space-spending/

85  MacDonald, *China, Space Weapons, and US Security*. p. 4.

86  David Finkleman, "New insights into the stability of the space debris environment," Paper presented at the 65th International Astronautical Congress, Toronto, Canada, September 29–October 3, 2014.

87  Point Paper on the Institute for Foreign Policy Analysis, Capitol Hill Roundtable, "Space-based sensors: missile defense and more," July 14, 2015. www.ifpa.org/pdf/ iwgRoundtablePointPaperSpaceBasedSensors.pdf. Figures on debris added to LEO sometimes vary accordingly to methodologies regarding what is counted. See also: T. S. Kelso, "Analysis of the 2007 Chinese ASAT test and the impact of its debris on the space environment," AMOS Conference, Maui, Hawaii, 2007. https://celestrak.com/ publications/AMOS/2007/AMOS-2007.pdf

88  "US warned China of debris threats 147 times last year," *SpaceNews*, June 20, 2011. http://spacenews.com/us-warned-china-debris-threats-147-times-last-year/

89  Karl Tate, "Russian satellite crash with Chinese ASAT debris explained," *Space.com*, March 8, 2013. www.space.com/20145-russian-satellite-chinese-debris-crash-infographic.html

90  Lee Billings, "War in space may be closer than ever," *Scientific American*, August 10, 2015. www.scientificamerican.com/article/war-in-space-may-be-closer-than-ever/

91  MacDonald, *China, Space Weapons, and US Security*, p. 4.

92  Cited in Colin Clark, "DepSecDef work invokes 'space control'; analysts fear space war escalation," *Breaking Defense*, April 15, 2015. http://breakingdefense.com/2015/04/ depsecdef-work-invokes-space-control-analysts-fear-space-war-escalation/

93  World Economic Forum, "What if space were the next frontier for war?" *Time*, October 3, 2012. http://world.time.com/2012/10/03/what-if-space-was-the-next-frontier-for-war/

94  Morgan, *Deterrence and First-Strike Stability*, p. xi.

95  Elbridge Colby, *From Sanctuary to Battlefield: A Framework for a U.S. Defense and Deterrence Strategy for Space*, Center for a New American Security, Washington, DC, January 2016, p. 17.

96  Ibid., p. 18.

97  Ibid., p. 20.

98  Ibid., p. 21.

99  MacDonald, *China, Space Weapons, and US Security*, p. 13.

# 2

# CONGESTED, CONTESTED, AND COMPETITIVE

Whatever happens will be for the worse. Therefore it is in our interests that as little happen as possible.

Nineteenth-century British Prime Minister Lord Salisbury[1]

Describing the space environment as congested, contested, and competitive presents an ominous picture, apparently to indicate an across-the-board threatening change from the past. The environment has certainly changed, and change bodes ill for those the status quo favors. Even in the 1960s though, "dominance" was likely an overstatement of the US position in the space environment. Then, it was the National Aeronautics and Space Administration (NASA), as the civilian face of the US space program, which established US preeminence(-cum-dominance) with the Apollo Program.[2] Apollo was part of a techno-nationalist "space race"[3] with the Soviet Union. While the United States handily won the race, its occurrence evidences that it was not the only country with considerable space capabilities. Even then, it was unlikely that the United States was able to "dominate" in the sense of being able to control Soviet access to and activity in space. The club of spacefaring nations, however, was clearly very exclusive.

The strategic environment of space has been described as congested, contested, and competitive—the terms used individually and in combination and often without definition—even before it was first officially used as a descriptor in the 2011 NSSS.[4] Analysts noted that it took longer for government officials to clarify exactly what was meant by congested, contested, and competitive than for the catchy phrase to be accepted as fact and as part of not only the US national security lexicon but internationally. Initially it was, as one analyst noted, part of a trend whereby "reducing complex strategic problems to acronyms, metaphors, or catch phrases is what passes these days for strategic thinking."[5] Another pointed out the danger of oversimplicity and that use of the "three Cs" continues "the 'lamentable tendency' in policy discussions to reduce complex ideas to slogans of three or fewer words … this consonantal alliteration is seriously misleading."[6] That the phrase was used for a considerable period before being defined suggests an intended use as a marketing tool for instituting the idea of "threats" to the public and Congress as much as it being meant as a serious descriptor.

Ambassador Gregory L. Schulte, as Deputy Assistant Secretary of Defense for Space Policy, provided definitions in 2012 in a presentation given in Singapore,[7] useful as a basis for further inquiry. Quite simply, space is considered congested by virtue of the quantity of "stuff" in orbit, including both active systems and trackable debris. In addition, space is considered increasingly competitive based on the growing number of actors in aerospace, including countries, consortiums and companies. But these two attributes of the space environment could be considered part of the natural evolution of space as both an industrial sector and space as an environment for exploration and development—both goals long supported by the United States. Each aspect presents both opportunities and challenges, and these are considered first. Then the "contested" aspect of space—defined as the number of countries developing counterspace capabilities and integrating them into their military doctrine and forces—is considered. It is the contested aspect of the space environment that appears to drive US national security space strategy and, consequently, signals of US intent that potentially influence other countries.

## Congested

Space was the exclusive, expensive domain of the United States and the Soviet Union for many years. Both countries used the space domain to their own advantage in order to ameliorate strategic weakness. For the United States, being able to position reconnaissance satellites to look behind the Iron Curtain provided important intelligence information that was otherwise unavailable. For the Soviet Union, intercontinental missiles provided the Soviets with the capabilities required for a nuclear standoff with the United States—mutually assured destruction (MAD). Satellites also provided the means for both countries to monitor the treaty activities (primarily nuclear) of the other; hence, in the Strategic Arms Limitation Treaty (SALT) signed in 1972, both parties agreed not to be first to interfere with these "national technical means of verification" (satellites). Additionally, the SALT negotiations led to the Anti-Ballistic Missile (ABM) Treaty, also signed in 1972, placing limitations on systems intended to shoot down missiles in order to avoid an arms race neither thought winnable.

In 1965, France became the third country to have space launch capability. It was followed by Japan and China in 1970. Between 1971 and 2012, the United Kingdom, the European Space Agency (ESA), India, Israel, Ukraine, Iran, and North Korea joined the list. While some countries have consolidated their efforts, especially the European countries through ESA, there are now more countries with space launch capability. Countries consider access to space to be important and their right, codified as a fundamental principle of the 1967 Outer Space Treaty. For the United States to expect other countries to accept anything less now would be to say that it expects other technologically and economically capable countries to forego capabilities that the United States not only admits but proudly proclaims provide it significant across-the-board advantages.

Further, it is not just the number of countries able to launch payloads into orbit that is growing. A number of private sector companies are now providing (relatively) low-cost access to space as well. They are part of the growing "NewSpace" companies that will shape the future and will take "control" even further away from government hands.[8] SpaceX, Blue Origin, Bigelow, Orbital ATF, Kistler, Starchaser, ARCA, and Virgin Galactic are among the firms developing new launch technology.

Beyond the increasing number of actors capable of providing launch capability, which inherently facilitates congestion, analysts and government reports have cited other indicators of "congestion," including debris, radio frequency access, and limited orbital real estate.[9] The increased number of small satellites (of various sizes) potentially to be launched in the future, and even space tourism, will further exacerbate the relatively congested nature of space, simply in terms of the number of objects in orbit. Debris is the most potentially threatening near-term issue of congestion.

Aerospace Corporation defines space debris as "any nonfunctioning human-made object orbiting Earth."[10] Everything from tools left by astronauts, rocket stages, and moribund satellites are among the tens of thousands of pieces of space debris larger than 10 centimeters that are detected, tracked, identified, and cataloged by the US Space Surveillance Network (SSN). The SSN encompasses the assets used to track space debris and follow-on operations. It is operated through the Joint Space Operations Center (JSPOC) located at Vandenberg Air Force Base in California. Some data is shared through the Space Track program. There is also an unknown number of smaller pieces, some too small and overall too many to keep track of, that are nevertheless dangerous. Because of the high velocity at which these small pieces travel, they can act like sandblasting or shrapnel when they come in contact with a satellite sensor or surface. More than once, the Space Shuttle had to have the windshield replaced after a mission due to damage from impact with even a small piece of debris. Nicholas Johnson, chief NASA scientist for space debris, has said the greatest debris risks come from non-trackable items.[11] Big pieces can be a threat too though. In 2011, the International Space Station (ISS) crew had to take emergency precautions when a substantial piece of space junk was determined to be on a potential collision course traveling at a speed of 29,000 miles per hour. While there is usually time to maneuver the station out of harm's way, that time there was only 15 hours' notice—not long enough to maneuver. The debris missed the station by only 1,100 feet.[12]

Before 2007, most space debris was junk from space missions. But China's 2007 kinetic anti-satellite test against one of their own moribund weather satellites added thousands of pieces of debris of various sizes.[13] Then in February 2009, a defunct

Russian satellite collided with and destroyed a functioning US Iridium commercial satellite. That collision added more than 2,000 additional pieces of trackable debris to the inventory of space junk.[14] These were not the first space collisions. In 1996, the French military reconnaissance satellite Cerise had a gravity gradient boom severed by impact with a fragment of debris, making it the first verified space collision.

But what are the odds of a catastrophic accident? According to NASA, very low.

> Operational spacecraft are struck by very small debris (and micrometeoroids) routinely with little or no effect. Debris shields can also protect spacecraft components from particles as large as 1 cm in diameter. The probability of two large objects (> 10 cm in diameter) accidentally colliding is very low. The worst such incident occurred on 10 February 2009 when an operational U.S. Iridium satellite and a derelict Russian Cosmos satellite collided.[15]

Beyond collisions, debris is created other ways as well.

In February 2014, a Defense Meteorological Satellite Program (DMSP) spacecraft exploded, caused by what engineers concluded was a battery rupturing in the spacecraft due to a design flaw; this created considerable debris in its polar orbit. Then in November 2015, a National Oceanic and Atmospheric Administration (NOAA) satellite broke up, again in a polar orbit, creating more debris. Fortunately, the JSPOC found the debris caused by the NOAA satellite posed no threat as of that time. A Japanese astronomy satellite malfunctioned in March 2016, also creating debris.[16] With the number of spacecraft in orbit on the rise, though, the number of collisions and accidents can be expected to increase.[17]

Therefore, perhaps the right question to ask is not by how much the data is increasing but whether the probability of a collision is increasing. Analyst Bob Butterworth provides an analogy: "For travel purposes, I don't care how many cars there are in northern Virginia; I care about how many are on the road at the same time and place as I."[18] Answering that question requires more exact knowledge about where objects are in space than the currently imperfect intelligence (which is partly due to not all space actors being willing to share information). In 2014, the JSPOC issued 671,727 conjunction (collision) warnings.[19] Not all of those result in avoidance maneuvers, and some are false positives—not mistakes, but non-threats identified as threats using good data and good processing.[20] Nevertheless, the need for increased space situational awareness (SSA) regarding the active and inactive material in orbit is clear, as reflected in its inclusion as a DoD policy directive[21] and it being the topic of multinational forum discussions. There have been efforts to address the debris issue nationally and internationally.

In February 2013, the Steering Committee of the Inter-Agency Debris Coordinating Committee (IADC)—a 12-member, intergovernmental agency that has worked since 1993 to follow and study the space debris issue—made a presentation to the UN Committee on the Peaceful Uses of Outer Space (COPUOS) on the stability of the future low Earth orbit (LEO) environment;

here, the IADC considered the risk of a catastrophic collision, concluding that it was increasing. Since 2005, some IADC members had independently studied the evolution of the far-term LEO satellite population under a variety of scenarios. The study aimed to answer the question: If serious mitigation efforts were undertaken, would the risks of space debris to space assets decrease? In 2009, the IADC decided to assess the stability of the LEO space object population and the need to use active debris removal (ADR) to stabilize the future LEO environment. In other words, did the world have to do more than watch carefully and act when needed? The IADC's Environment and Data Bases Working Group did the assessment, the principal participants in the study being from Italy, the ESA, India, Japan, the United States, and the United Kingdom. Subsequently, the IADC concluded that action is needed to protect the sustainability of space and that if only five large pieces of space junk were removed each year, the odds of a catastrophic event go down significantly.[22]

NASA issued the first guidelines for the mitigation of space debris in 1995. These were followed in 1997 by US Government Orbital Debris Mitigation Standard Practices.[23] Those US government guidelines were further developed by the IADC and issued as consensus guidelines in 2007, and these were then largely adopted by COPUOS with UN endorsement.[24] Basically, those guidelines require satellite owners to provide for a 25-year satellite lifetime with either post-lifetime atmospheric re-entry so that the satellite will burn up in orbit and not become space debris or placement of the satellite in a designated storage orbit. But the guidelines are executed nationally. In the United States, for example, a Federal Communications Commission (FCC) license is required for all US satellite radio transmissions. In 2004, the FCC amended its licensing rules to require a narrative description of the satellite operator's plan to mitigate orbital debris. In other words, at least theoretically, the creation of more satellite-related debris will be mitigated in the future. Whether all countries or operators abide by the prescribed guidelines, however, remains to be seen.

The technical challenges and cost of removing space junk, while formidable, are not the only showstoppers preventing taking action on the 2013 IADC recommendations. Removal would in all probability need be a joint international venture or, at the very least, require tacit international approval. Every piece of junk in orbit is the property of some country. While there have been proposals for space salvage laws to allow "abandoned" debris removal,[25] under the Outer Space Treaty, nations currently retain "jurisdiction and control" of their spacecraft even when inoperable or in pieces. Further, many of the proposed methods for removal, such as lasers and grappling hooks, have other potential applications as well, including as ASATs. Therefore, debris removal by even a single country would require "trust" among nations, a commodity sorely lacking and likely to get worse with global space militarism on the rise, and so would be impossible. Sadly, the most likely scenario that would bring about serious cooperation is a debris-caused space catastrophe that leads to deaths on Earth.[26] So while it is technically possible to do something about the debris congestion that the United States and other countries profess concern about, the politics of fear, inertia, and delay will likely prevail in the interim. In the meantime, more and more satellites are being launched into space.

Real estate in space, just as on Earth, is limited, at least in desirable orbits. Geostationary orbit is perhaps the Beverly Hills of space because the gravitational pull of the Earth, Moon, and other planets allows a satellite to remain in orbit over a single point of the Earth's surface. Geostationary orbit is located at an altitude of approximately 35,786 kilometers (22,236 miles) from the Earth's equator and has a radius of 42,164 kilometers (26,199 miles). While that is a substantial radius, it is not limitless. In addition, a satellite occupying a slot in space requires a specific radio frequency in the electromagnetic spectrum; hence, a link between radio frequency issues and real estate issues. These radio frequencies must be different, and satellites must maintain enough distance between them so there is not interference among transmissions. Moreover, only a limited number of slots exist appropriate for "bouncing" signals from Europe to North America and across the Pacific. There are currently 493 satellites in geostationary equatorial orbit (GEO),[27] which may be approaching capacity under current parameters.

The job of allocating orbital slots and radio frequencies falls to the International Telecommunications Union (ITU), an organization created in 1865 to govern transnational telegraph communications. It then moved on to governing radio links and, from there, orbital slots. During "the good ol' days" when it was largely just the United States and the Soviet Union that had the capability to place satellites in orbit, the job of the ITU was primarily to record satellite locations consequent to registration by the owners. With the advent of more place players complicating things, though, it has had to take on the thankless job of regulation.

There has already been competition for valuable orbital slots, the winner often declared by who gets there first. In 1993, Indonesia occupied an orbital slot claimed by Tonga.[28] In 2015, the Philippines complained that China had grabbed and occupied a slot that belonged to it.[29] These disputes often end up at the ITU for resolution.

Sometimes countries have tried to "squeeze" a satellite into a position despite the protests of other countries fearing signal interference with their own satellites. Such was the case of China's Apstar-2 satellite, which faced protests from the United States and Japan when Apstar-2 squeezed into a position next to Japan's Sakura 3a satellite in 1994, potentially interfering with Sakura 3a transmissions. A diplomatic spat between Tokyo and Beijing ensued with the stakes seen as potentially higher than just this one situation.

> Some analysts fear that if China flouts global rules, there could be a destructive and expensive breakdown of international order in satellite transmissions. China is aggressively seeking to promote its satellite-launch services as an inexpensive alternative to Western competitors.[30]

While international order did not collapse, this case made the value of GEO real estate and the need to address crowding issues clear.

With GEO slots heavily utilized, industry has had to step up its game and find ways to make the most of the valuable real estate. By 2008, advances in satellite technology made it possible to decrease the amount of required space between satellites from the original 3-degrees to 2-degree spacing[31] and, more recently, sometimes even less. Because real estate is so valuable, "paper satellites" have become a particular issue of late. These are satellites crafted only on paper and registered with the ITU in order to hold an orbital slot for a given country, with no actual intent to build or operate it. Consequently, the ITU has mandated that a satellite must be placed in orbit within seven years of registration rather than the previous nine years.

Certain radio frequency bands are also becoming in short supply, and there has been significant growth in radio frequency "congestion" as a result of increased band use. In 2011, Schulte explained the problem thus:

> As many as 9,000 satellite communications transponders are expected to be in orbit by 2015. As more transponders are placed in service, the greater the probability of radiofrequency interference. This congestion is complicating space operations for all that seek to benefit from space.[32]

The military has and continues to work with industry to find ways to mitigate interference issues, especially regarding electronic warfare.[33] Unquestionably, more satellites and the seemingly unquenchable demand for more bandwidth will mean more complex issues needing to be addressed internationally—and potentially more space debris.

Low Earth orbit (LEO) is also increasingly crowded because countries other than the United States want to reap the same benefits from space assets it has enjoyed for many years and because low(er)-cost launch services make LEO more accessible. Particularly relevant for the future is the expected proliferation of (variously named according to size) smallsats, nanosats, picosats, and cubesats,[34] many of them originally developed by universities for low-cost access to space. The British firm Surrey Satellite Technology was spun off from the University of Surrey, the brainchild of scientists who decided to build a satellite using commercial, off-the-shelf (COTS) components. It now proudly proclaims it has the world's most extensive track record in small satellite missions.

Cubesats were originally developed at California Polytechnic State University and Stanford University to allow universities worldwide to perform space science and exploration experimentation, and universities and others are doing just that. Cubesats can be do-it-yourself, shoebox-sized objects, made and launched for around $65,000 or even less. Tyvak Nano-Satellite Systems, a small company in California employing less than 25 engineers, sells their satellites starting at $45,000. Their client list ranges from well-funded high school science clubs to NASA.[35] But Cubesats cannot maneuver in orbit to avoid collisions, and some users have insufficient, or nonexistent, plans for deorbiting their assets. A team of researchers using a sophisticated computer model has predicted that "Cubesats will be responsible for millions of orbital near-misses, with a handful of these orbital encounters resulting in collisions, by 2043."[36] A Cubesat collision had already occurred in May 2013 with Ecuador consequently losing its first Cubesat, NEE-01 Pegaso. More LEO collisions can be anticipated.

Congestion, in short, means that there is more going on in space than there was in the past, and that increased activity creates issues. It also means that space is "developing" in a way that was always anticipated, indeed desired, unless mankind was supposed to remain terrestrial or *The Jetsons* were only to be Americans. Air space is congested as well; however, this is not considered a threat but, rather, a situation to be managed. The Federal Aviation Administration (FAA) began registering drones in 2015 as part of its management of US air space.[37] There are rules for managing global airspace that are in the interests of all stakeholders to obey. There are no such rules for space although both airplanes and spacecraft are dual-use technology. While each of the issues created by congestion is important and must be addressed for long-term sustainability, none of them can be "fixed" because the utilization of space will inherently continue to grow. But they can be, and must be, better managed. Otherwise, the first effects to be felt will be economic.

More space debris collisions will not mean that space orbits will not be used, but it will make utilization more expensive. Ambassador Roger Harrison succinctly stated the reality of the situation.

> Despite the alarms and excursions, the civil and commercial space sectors are proceeding as if all is well. One would think that people with actual money in the game would act like the proverbial "canary in the mineshaft." But long-term projects continue to go forward with no discount for the possibility that future satellites will be operating in a battle zone or a space junk yard. Underwriters and investors seem unconcerned. New commercial launcher companies proliferate. There is, after all, still a lot of space in space, and we are not a species that cares very much about the long term. Congested space may be a long-term reality, but the impact of that reality on what we actually do is, and will likely remain, negligible.[38]

Equally as important, none of the issues related to a congested space environment requires a military "counterspace" solution. They all require international cooperation.

## Competitive

If there are more actors in space challenging each other for orbital slots and bandwidth (and there are) and if all countries want the right to pursue their own aims in space (and they do), then by definition, space is more competitive than it was in the past. It also means that the relative dominance of the United States in space is less. Whether that then means that the security of the United States is inherently compromised by competitiveness is more tenuous. But exceptionalists, and the US military, are often uncomfortable with relativism and more comfortable with absolutism, despite this being increasingly unrealistic.

With the influx of new players, the United States is facing competition in space in a variety of ways—some positive, some negative, some appropriately addressed in military terms, and some made worse by sabre rattling. A positive aspect of competition has been lowered launch costs. Though the United States bemoaned high launch costs for decades, nothing was really done about it until upstart private companies like SpaceX came along, successfully launching its Falcon 9. Only then did the behemoth heritage companies begin to think about revising their business plans. Harvard historian Niall Ferguson, in his 2011 book *Civilization: The West and The Rest*, attributed competition among warring European countries as the spur to technical advances, allowing the West to eventually triumph over once-dominant China.[39] Competition can be a positive force, but staying ahead of competitors is both imperative and self-determinative, not achieved by trying to stifle others. History has shown repeatedly that attempts to quash others will be both ineffectual and potentially counterproductive.

The United States initially held a virtual monopoly on commercial launch services. But US restrictions on the launch of two Franco-German communication satellites called Symphonie-A and Symphonie-B in the 1970s, in order to protect Intelsat's monopoly on international satellite communications, at least partially facilitated the French goal of developing an independent European launcher. Hence, the Ariane launcher was approved as an ESA optional program in 1973.[40] In 1981, Ariane signed its first commercial payload contract, for an American GTE Spacenet telecommunications satellite. By 1985, Ariane was launching half of the ten commercial satellites sent into space in a 14-month period.[41] The American commercial launch monopoly was no more. Balancing cooperation with competition can only be expected to get more difficult in a connected, globalized world.

Beginning with the 1958 Space Act that created NASA, the United States has advocated international cooperation in space, but it has had to deal with the realities of economics and national security in doing so. That requires thinking through the second- and third-order effects of anticipated actions or non-actions—or dealing with unintended consequences later. Trying to stifle competition in telecommunications resulted in launch service competition in the 1980s. However, the United States maintained the largest market share in satellite sales for much longer—specifically, until after the 1999 report of the Select Committee on US National Security and Military/Commercial Concerns with the People's Republic of China, commonly known as the Cox Committee. In fact, the competitive satellite business environment that the United States now faces is, in many ways, one created as a self-inflicted wound consequent to that report.

The Cox Committee report presented findings of an imminent threat to US national security based on dubious claims of China stealing vital US nuclear secrets through Los Alamos scientist Dr. Wen Ho Lee[42] and being given assistance for its missile program by US aerospace companies through lax adherence to International Traffic in Arms Regulations (ITAR). The result was the imposition of draconian, Byzantine regulations on the US satellite industry, basically placing them under the same export restrictions as are applied to weapons systems. Consequently, US satellite companies began losing sales, and other countries were motivated to develop their own satellite industries beyond the reach of US controls.[43] Within two years of the Cox Committee report being issued and the new regulations being imposed, the US portion of global satellite sales plummeted from 75 percent to 45 percent.[44]

Advertising satellites as "ITAR free" became an advantageous marketing tool for European aerospace firms. In other words, the United States took careful aim and shot itself in the foot as countries took their satellite business elsewhere, and the United States ended up with less control of dual-use space technology than it had previously. It was not until the National Defense Authorization Act for Fiscal Year 2013 (NDAA 2013) that commercial satellites were removed from the ITAR list and clarification was given as to what was under ITAR control and what was not—ambiguity having been part of the problem since 1999.[45] These changes have allowed the US satellite industry to again become competitive in the export market though imports and exports from certain countries (from China, for example) remain prohibited. Nevertheless, while long discredited by the technical community,[46] die-hard Cox Committee supporters (still) tout the findings as justified and bipartisan. Many political and technical analysts then and now, however, have characterized it as a partisan ploy to jab at President Bill Clinton through his engagement policies with China; engagement with China has always been an easy target in Washington.[47] But the United States must move beyond the canard that it can stop the spread of space technology. The United States has always been perhaps the world's strongest proponent of a free market, so competition for commercial profits should be neither unexpected nor considered nefarious. Beyond profit, competition for prestige must be considered as well as it strongly links to leadership, which then links to exceptionalism and geopolitics.

European countries, for example, were motivated to initiate space programs in the 1960s due to fears of an unbreachable technology gap being created between spacefaring nations—then, the United States and Soviet Union—and all others. Further, space means technology, technology means industrialization, and industrialization means economic growth. Hence there are pragmatic reasons for space program development, then and now. Beyond pragmatism, however, there is more. Space represents the future in a way that stirs imaginations and indicates leadership.

Iran created a space agency in 2004, reconfigured with a substantial budget boost in 2010 and then unceremoniously disbanded in 2015. While most observers assumed it a cover for development of missiles—and there certainly are benefits accrued from development of rocket technology to development of missile technology—some analysts felt that international prestige and national pride was as much, or more, motivation for the Iranian satellite launch efforts.[48] As President, Mahmoud

Ahmadinejad was quoted as saying, "[w]hen we launch a satellite into space, there is a huge boost in the morale of the public."[49] Plans for numerous launches were announced in 2010 and left largely unfulfilled, though Iran did manage to launch some turtles and monkeys into orbit. The Iranian Space Agency seemed to fall victim to the realization that space travel is difficult and costly and that perhaps the price of prestige was more than anticipated or more than Iran was able to pay.

Even the names of spacecraft and space programs evoke powerful, prestige-generating imagery. Mercury, Gemini, and Apollo were critical programmatic steps in taking Americans to the Moon, while Thor, Atlas, and Titan, originally designed to carry warheads, were converted to carry satellites. Satellites named Voyager and Pioneer explored the solar system and beyond. The Russian Mir space station is alternately translated into English as "world," "peace," or "village."[50] The Chinese Shenzhou spacecraft that carries its astronauts aloft translates as "heavenly boat" or "divine craft." The Chinese robotic lunar program Chang'e is named after a mythical lunar princess. Iran's rockets include Kavoshgar (explorer) and Safir (ambassador). Sir Richard Branson cleverly named his space transportation company Virgin Galactic, only a slight variation from his transoceanic airline Virgin Atlantic, perhaps intending to indicate that eventually space travel will soon be as commonplace as terrestrial travel is today. Beyond stirring the imagination, space programs are indicators of technical prowess, prowess that can have leadership and, hence, geostrategic implications.

Two *Telstar* satellites developed by AT&T were the first able to transmit television signals across the Atlantic. Countries vied for which would be the first signal recipient—a signal showing a flag waving outside a receiving station in Maine—with France winning apparently only because the British had mistakenly set its antenna incorrectly.[51] Polls showed that in 1962, Telstar was better known in the United Kingdom than Sputnik had been in 1957. A British band called The Tornadoes immortalized the satellite in a 1962 song called "Telstar," which reached Number 1 on the US top 100 Billboard chart.[52] The fact that countries competed to be the first to receive the signal indicates that they thought doing so had some value. Similarly, countries have made significant investments in the development of launch technology[53] and satellites when there appeared no real business rationale (or even business plan). In 2015, Laos joined Nigeria, Venezuela, Pakistan, and Bolivia as countries with satellites in orbit, all financed, built, and launched by China. Belarus launched a satellite in orbit in 2016, making a point to state it was for commercial purposes and not just prestige.[54] Human spaceflight, however, is the ultimate brass ring for prestige.

As Roger Harrison has pointed out:

> The rational and economic arguments against human spaceflight are compelling, and the opportunity costs enormous. What might have been done in the advancement of science with the $120 billion so far invested in a space station whose crew members spend the overwhelming percentage of their time maintaining the station and staying alive?[55]

Critics of China's human spaceflight program have made similar economic arguments, especially early in the program.[56]

India's space program once specifically rejected human spaceflight. Dr. Vikram Sarabhai, considered the father of India's space program, clearly linked heavenly goals to terrestrial responsibilities. Until recently, the following quote from Sarabhai was on the homepage of the Indian Space Research Organization (ISRO) website:

> There are some who question the relevance of space activities in a developing nation. To us, there is no ambiguity of purpose. We do not have the fantasy of competing with the economically advanced nations in the exploration of the moon or the planets or manned spaceflight. But we are concerned that if we are to play a meaningful role nationally, and in the community of nations, we must be second to none in the application of advanced technologies to the real problems of man and society.

But India's outlook and plans for space have changed dramatically over the past decade.

India's space plans are outlined in *Space Vision 2025*, released in 2009. While still including such goals as satellite-based communications and navigation systems for rural connectivity as well as enhanced imaging capability for natural resource management and weather and climate change studies, it also now includes planetary exploration, development of a heavy lift launcher, reusable launch vehicles, and human spaceflight. The specifics initially included a man on the Moon by 2020 and robotic missions to Mars, to a nearby asteroid, and to an observable distance from the sun. In discussions with Indian analysts, this philosophical change is often explained as simply "evolutionary." In all likelihood, feeling pressured to not be seen as technically usurped by China has played into India's change of philosophy as well, most vividly demonstrated in India's successful quest to beat China to Mars in 2014.[57]

In September 2014, the Indian spacecraft Mangalyaan began orbiting Mars. With that, India became the first Asian country to reach Mars, the first country to orbit Mars on its first attempt, and the fourth country to orbit Mars. Only the United States, the Soviet Union, and Europe had reached Mars previously. With Mangalyaan, India made it into the space record books, and the importance of that should not be undervalued. Whereas China had been the primary Asian beneficiary of the prestige and corresponding regional and geostrategic influence that accompanies space achievements, now it was India's turn. The success of Mangalyaan also raised the credibility of sophisticated space technology produced by Anthrix—the commercial arm of India's Space Research Organization—credibility accompanied by potentially substantial economic returns.[58] And then, of course, there is the dual-use technology important to the aspiring Indian military space program. Space activity, in many ways, is the gift that just keeps giving.

India achieved its success reaching Mars in record-breaking time and on a comparatively shoestring budget. Feasibility studies for Mangalyaan, also called the

Mars Orbiter Mission (MOM), began in 2010. Spacecraft development commenced in 2012, the satellite was launched only 15 months later in November 2013, and Mangalyaan reached Mars only 9 months after that. ISRO states the mission cost as $76 million, far less than the American Maven mission costing $671 million (Maven, however, is significantly more complex) that entered Mars orbit the same week as Mangalyaan or even, as noted by Indian Prime Minister Narendra Modi, the $100 million Hollywood space blockbuster *Gravity*.[59] India's remarkable achievement wasn't, however, the result of India perfecting warp drive or having better science and engineering geeks than anyone else. It was the product of a confluence of domestic and geopolitical factors that worked out well for India.

Geopolitically, India had been left looking like one of several distant "also-ran" competitors in the Asian space race—along with Japan and, more recently, South Korea—compared to China's Shenzhou human spaceflight program and Chang'e robotic lunar program. Given that space exploration has traditionally carried with it significant technology leadership implications—witness the American Apollo program—India could not allow China's regional space leadership to go unchallenged.

India needed to do something that China had not done before; India needed to "beat" China. Going to the Moon wouldn't do it, but going to Mars would. China had attempted a Mars mission with Yinghuo-1, launched in 2011 by Russia. But the mission failed. That failure provided India with an open spot in the space record books and the geostrategic prestige that accompanies those coveted spots.

China's successes in space have occurred while the US human exploration program has been largely focused on ISS missions, giving the American public little to follow with the exception of astronaut Scott Kelly's one-year stay in space, which did generate considerable public interest. NASA's Journey to Mars is too distant and too amorphous to catch the public's attention. Consequently, the perception has been created that China is "beating" the United States in space. While China is not doing anything that the United States hasn't already done, years ago, perception becomes reality over time with the United States sometimes appearing an also-ran in a space race with China.[60] So when India sought NASA's help with deep space navigation and tracking support for Mangalyaan, NASA was happy to oblige. In return, American scientists were given the opportunity to have access to importance scientific data from the Indian spacecraft and US politicians got to watch China lose a spot in the space record book to a democratic country the United States has pledged to work with in space.[61]

The leadership connotations that accrue with spaceflight are considerable. The Space Studies Board (SSB) of the National Academies of Science regularly considers the leadership aspects of space in their studies, including *America's Future in Space* (2009); *NASA's Strategic Direction and the Need for a National Consensus* (2012); and *Pathways to Exploration* (2014).[62] Unfortunately for the United States, the general public often equates space leadership with human spaceflight; and with the US human spaceflight earthbound since the Space Shuttle was retired in 2011 except when it can hitch a ride from Russia to the ISS, this reliance on the Russians for transportation further adds to the perception that US space leadership is slipping away.[63] Juxtaposed against that perception, however, is the imagery and perception created by Gen. Hyten in "The Battle Above."

## Contested

The difference between space being considered both contested and competitive took a while to sort out, and there still are no definitions in the DoD dictionary[64] or space doctrine publication.[65] Roger Harrison suggested that "an interagency process in the United States … arrived at a definition of contested space, which is some combination of capability, motive and intent."[66] Harrison further submitted that it was Air Force Space General Robert Kehler (Space Command Chief from 2007 to 2011 and Strategic Command Chief from 2011 to 2013) who first utilized the term "contested" as an alternative to the illusory quest for "dominance," though without definitional specificity.

Philosophically, dominance and "space control" was part of the rhetoric of the unipolar post-Cold War world with the United States as the benevolent hegemon. The United States would, with an implied degree of *noblesse oblige*, keep space safe for "good actors" and deny it to "evildoers," as the United States determined them, for the benefit of all mankind. In contested space, the environment becomes a Hobbesian place where mankind has to look for itself and the devil take the hindmost. Though space control has a temptingly exceptionalist allure, in reality, space dominance and control are aspirational fallacies. So the threats to be addressed by space control had to be modified, made more achievable, in order to continue building technology to counter them—threats like a "contested" space environment. Together, capability, motive, and intent do constitute the constructs behind space being construed as contested. But since the overwhelming amount of space technology is dual-use, making motive and intent impossible to decipher, in actuality, it is capability that defines space as being contested. That characterization is also in line with traditional military thinking wherein capabilities equal threats. By definition, anything that is dual-use has a military capability and so can be, and has been, considered a threat. A consideration of Chinese space activities provides an example.

Deciphering Chinese intent regarding space is considerably more difficult than surveying known capabilities.[67] Analysis must be based on information from a variety of official and unofficial sources, interpretations falling along a spectrum. Underestimating capabilities and best-case intent evaluations risk being unprepared to deal with the threats posed; overestimating capabilities and worst-case intent evaluations can lead to actions which produce unintended consequences and potentially increase the threat to US capabilities. Therefore prudence, regarding both research and drawing conclusions, is imperative.

Open source material, particularly technical journals, are often used as sources of information regarding what space-related programs the Chinese are working on or even just thinking about. However, most technical journals are *very* technical, focusing on detailed discussions of optics, trajectories, sensors, etc. Those that do discuss intent have limited utility as well. As pointed out by longtime China watcher Larry Wortzel, part of the difficulty with "intent analysis" is that "most technical articles from the science digests in China, admittedly, only deal in the theoretical aspects of how to fight war in space and analyze U.S. strengths and vulnerabilities."[68]

Beyond technical journals, the volume of information and analysis produced within China and commercially available is increasing exponentially. Wider ranges of "tolerable" opinions are appearing within Chinese academia and the media. Media outlets are proliferating, driven by market competition. Whereas, however, (most) Americans understand the risks of relying on the *National Enquirer* or a lone blogger for "fact," the need for similar discrimination with open Chinese sources does not always seem similarly understood by US analysts. For example, while a statement on defense policy from a university professor or a War College student being encouraged to "think outside the box" is understood by Americans as not necessarily reflective of US government policy, the same appears not always true about the output of Chinese authors.

One of the most often cited Chinese quotes on "intent," dating back to 2000, is that of a junior military officer named Wang Hucheng: "For countries that can never win a war with the United States by using the methods of tanks and planes, attacking an American space system may be an irresistible and most tempting choice."[69] The quote is one of braggadocio—attempting to make the point that the United States, the sole superpower at the time, having demonstrated its military prowess and space capabilities during the 1990–91 Gulf War, could still be beat. Much of his "analysis" of US space vulnerabilities was simply copied from US government documents, including the 1997 and 2001 Quadrennial Defense Reviews and the 1998 Space Command Long-Term Plan.[70] It was propaganda intended to draw a reaction from the United States; and it did. The increase in information available from China from numerous sources also increases the potential for communication misfires. That being the case, careful source-checking by analysts is imperative. Unfortunately, both sensationalist interpretations and lax fact-checking was not uncommon during the "quest for domination" years and, according to some analyses, still continues.

For instance, Pentagon annual reports for fiscal years 2003 and 2004 on the military power of the People's Republic of China[71] contained references to Chinese "parasite" satellites for potential use as anti-satellite weapons. Union of Concerned Scientist researchers Gregory Kulacki and David Wright, however, found that a relatively easy Internet search in Chinese places the origin of the story about those satellites with a self-proclaimed "military enthusiast" named Hong Chaofei from a small town in Anhui.[72] After Hong's story first appeared on the Internet in October 2000, multiple iterations and citations followed, and it then found its way into Pentagon analyses. Hong's website also contained scores of stories on "secret" Chinese weapons to defeat America in a war over Taiwan. China is working on small satellites, but the parasite satellite appears more one man's fiction than fact.

There are other instances of misinterpretation as well. *Challenges to Space Superiority*, published by the National Air and Space Intelligence Center at

Wright-Patterson Air Force Base in March 2005, highlighted quotes by Liying Zhang of the Langfang Army Missile Academy suggesting that China will pose a threat to on-orbit assets.[73] Kulacki and Wright again tracked down the quotes and the source, finding several key errors, which are fully documented in a Union of Concerned Scientists research paper on Chinese military space capabilities.[74] Key words were omitted from the original Chinese quote, and there were misinterpretations of what was included. For example, "should" (indicating a recommendation about a decision not yet made) was misinterpreted as "will" (indicating what China intends to do or is doing). Further, the author was found to be a junior faculty member at a facility primarily responsible for live fire and simulated training of junior artillery officers where ASAT research is likely not going on and which has subsequently been shut down. It was not exactly an authoritative source for US government planning purposes.

Besides the annual Pentagon report, the US-China Economic and Security Review Commission (USCC) also issues an annual report on Chinese military capabilities, including those relating to space, where information has been questioned. In 2008, for example, testimony used in the report was found, through relatively easy Internet checking, to be factually incorrect.[75] The errors included referencing of a defunct Chinese organization as still in existence; reporting the successful launch of a Pioneer rocket that had not actually occurred; and suggesting China does not have a dedicated relay satellite when in fact one had already been launched with a considerable amount of Chinese press coverage. Problems continued, as pointed out by Kulacki in a 2014 blog post titled "The 2014 USCC Report: Still Sloppy After All These Years."[76] There, Kulacki cited problems with the USCC analysis of a Chinese nuclear submarine and suggested broader, ideological concerns about the Commission and the consistently ominous reports it releases regarding Chinese intentions, which are then used for policy and budget planning by organizations like Congress and the Pentagon.

Even without having ideological bents, organizations encounter not inconsequential difficulties in analyzing information regarding Chinese intentions in space. Three in particular stand out: language skills, poor source selection, and insufficient attention to assessing source material. Individuals with no, or limited, Chinese language skills are limited to assessment of only those sources translated into English by individuals themselves perhaps limited in their language abilities. Agencies, such as the Foreign Broadcasting Information Service (FBIS), who translate material for official organizations may not have familiarity with the technical language of aerospace and so limit their sources to, for instance, Chinese newspapers, magazines, and weblogs, some with questionable reliability and perhaps having ideological bias that is not noted. And finally, without a careful assessment of sources, opinion and advocacy pieces (such as often found in the United States as well) are equated with Chinese policy.[77] All of these issues complicate an issue already muddied by dual-use technology.

Deciphering the motivations and intentions behind the development of dual-use technology is speculation at best. It is important to remember too that most countries do not have the financial or industrial luxury of having a civil space program separate from a military space program and, thus, consider dual-use technology development as a good return on government investment. In order to maximize resources, many countries, including China, France, and Japan, deliberately develop technology or establish organizations and operations for dual-use purposes. They have far less separation between military and civilian space activities and organizations than in the United States, though the lines between US programs are often blurred as well. For example, prior to the Space Shuttle, US civilian launchers were born from missile programs, and the Space Shuttle cargo bay was specifically designed to be large enough to carry large US reconnaissance satellites. Overall, though, the United States is more the exception than the rule in its use of what can be a duplicative approach to space administration and technology development via its civilian and military space programs.

Because of the largely dual-use nature of space technology, virtually any space activity can be deemed as military. Therefore it is (relatively) easier to know *what* China, or any country, is doing in terms of space activities than *why* they are doing it. For example, a co-orbital rendezvous and proximity operation satellite in space can be observed. Whether the satellite is intended for such benign operations as assessing damage to another satellite or for nefarious purposes such as ramming into another satellite, or both, can rarely be determined based on hardware.

In 2008, "taikonaut" Zhai Zigang conducted China's first spacewalk as part of the Shenzhou 7 mission, an expected step in phase two of China's three-phase human spaceflight program. A small satellite, Banxing-1 (BX-1) dubbed Companionsat, was released from atop the spacecraft. It "relayed back images of Shenzhou 7 from close range, then backed to a distance of several kilometers, testing network technology with the Shenzhou and the orbital module after the deorbit of Shenzhou 7."[78] Subsequent speculation was rampant about BX-1's true purpose, real intent, and even whether it tried to approach (and thereby threaten) the ISS. For example, Richard Fisher, Senior Fellow at the International Assessment and Strategy Center in Washington DC, stated that

> [w]e do not know how close the BX-1 actually approached the ISS. But for me, at closure speeds of 3.1km/second, the Shenzhou-7 was already too close at 45 kilometers. I expect that in time leaks or questions from the Congress will lead to revelations of more data about the BX-1 pass-by of the ISS.[79]

While the actual danger posed by Companionsat to the ISS was highly questionable,[80] the allegations made for great hype.

Hardware does not disclose intent, only capabilities. China has launched a number of experimental satellites in recent years, specifically the Shiyuan, Chuangxin (Innovation) and Shijian (Practice) satellites. Their stated missions have included Earth observation, space weather experimentation, space debris observation, mechanical arm observations, and testing space maintenance technologies capabilities including close proximity operations. Chinese media refers to China's Yaogan (remote sensing) satellite series as intended for disaster relief, Earth observation, and scientific experimentation. However, the high-resolution optical or radar satellites are fully funded by the People's Liberation Army (PLA). Launches of these satellites have been accompanied by a considerable amount of speculation regarding their intended use. Speculation regarding these missions might be compared to the international curiosity concerning the intended use of the X-37B Orbital Test Vehicle by the United States—a classified project that has sparked speculation around the globe as to whether it is, or is intended to be, a space weapon.[81]

It isn't just China that is giving Washington headaches. In the post-Cold War years, the Clinton Administration saw cooperation with Russia in space as being in US interests, culminating in 1993 with an offer to Russia of full partnership in the ISS program. Not only could Russia bring considerable space experience to the program, and potentially some cost savings, there were also broader foreign policy considerations as well.[82] Specifically, it was not considered in Western interests to have unemployed Russian aerospace engineers roaming the world seeking employment after the collapse of the Soviet Union. But the political environment has changed. In 2014, the Obama Administration slapped sanctions on targeted Russian officials and in economic areas in the hope of persuading Russian President Vladimir Putin to change his aggressive and anti-American foreign policy. Subsequently, Russia's Deputy Prime Minister Dmitry Rogozin used his English-language Twitter account to send a message to the United States: "After analyzing the sanctions against our space industry, I suggest the U.S. delivers its astronauts to the ISS with a trampoline."[83]

While the United States has been reliant on Russia for astronaut transportation to and from the ISS since the Shuttle retired, it is unlikely Russia would give up the millions it gets to run that taxi service. The ISS is also controlled by centers in both Houston, Texas, and Korolev, Russia, outside of Moscow, which jointly handle operations. Further, the sustained cooperation on the ISS even during periods of intense political strife between Russia and the United States is worth noting as a "lesson learned" for the future. Ironically as well, the workhorse US Atlas rocket uses Russian-made RD-180 engines. There are considerable cross-dependencies between the United States and Russia in space. Right now, however, the United States seems more fixated on the resurgence of the Russian military space program. That resurgence, however, should not come as a big surprise.

Russia, in its Soviet Union days, led the world into space with Sputnik and Yuri Gagarin. While the United States won the gold medal in the space race through the Apollo Program, the Russians hold a considerable number of places in the space record book. Early Russian space accomplishments were, and remain, a source of considerable national pride, which had suffered in the post-Cold War years. Russia went from being a global superpower to being referred to as "Upper Volta with missiles,"[84] a reference Putin is acutely aware of. The United States assured Russia it would not expand NATO eastward to former Warsaw Pact countries in the 1990s in conjunction with Russia's acceptance of a unified

Germany[85] but, soon thereafter, did just that because it could and Russia was too weak to do anything about it. Republican candidate Mitt Romney was ridiculed when he said Russia was the number one foe of the United States in a 2012 presidential debate. Romney's prescience has been vindicated lately though. Rejuvenation of Russian space capabilities is just one way Putin intends to restore the loss of national pride, and respect, that Russia has suffered. The resurgent aspect of its military space program adds to that goal and also serves key national security interests.

Like China, Russia became determined not be left vulnerable by some unbreachable space technology gap after observing the advantages the US military has gained from space since Kosovo. Three space-enabled capabilities are highlighted in Russia's 2014 military doctrine as main external threats to the Russian Federation: "global strike," the "intention to station weapons in space," and "strategic non-nuclear precision weapons."[86] Clearly Russia feels compelled to be able to respond to each.

The Russians see the future of warfare as driven by information and have focused on development of information-strike operations. "An information-strike operation consists of coordinated 'information-strike battles, information-weapon engagements and information strikes, which are being conducted with the goal of disrupting the enemy troop command and control and weapon control systems and the destruction of his information resource.'"[87] Those goals require Russia to maintain access to space, which is why it, like China, refuses to be denied such. Like China, Russia sees its nuclear deterrence as the main guarantee of its national security; hence, Moscow's continued and bellicose objections to US missile defense on its perimeters— objections that can be more politically based than technically cogent.[88]

Whereas the United States has consistently argued that deployment of missile defense capabilities into Europe is not aimed at Russia (but, rather, Iran), Russia believes otherwise, or at least claims to. In 2013, to reassure Russia, Deputy Assistant Secretary of State Frank Rose restated a declaration of missile defense intents previously made at the Chicago NATO summit in 2012.

> "The NATO missile defense in Europe will not undermine strategic stability. NATO missile defense is not directed at Russia and will not undermine Russia's strategic deterrence capabilities." Through transparency and cooperation with the United States and NATO, Russia would see firsthand that this system is designed for ballistic missile threats from outside the Euro– Atlantic area, and that NATO missile defense systems can neither negate nor undermine Russia's strategic deterrent capabilities.[89]

Nevertheless, in Russia's 2014 military doctrine, missile defense was ranked fourth in its prioritization of threats, and Russia has threatened a range of countermeasures in response to missile defense deployment.[90] As with many other issues, Putin's defiant, aggressive, even provocative anti-Western (particularly anti-US) attitude serves him well with domestic audiences and distracts them from Russia's economic woes.

Russian needling doesn't seem to have terrestrial limits. In 2015, after some curious maneuvers, Russia parked one of its military satellites between two Intelsat satellites. The US military uses some Intelsat satellites for operations, including drone missions and communications, so the Russian satellite drew angst from the Pentagon. The Russians, however, shrugged off US concern, saying that "in no way can it [the Russian satellite] be an 'aggressor'"[91] and that the chances of a collision were small. This was not the only Russian activity in space that drew US attention though. Russian launches in 2013 and 2014 carried declared communications satellites and also small undeclared objects that conducted maneuvers around the declared payload, maneuvers watched and questioned by analysts regarding whether Russia was testing ASAT capabilities.[92]

Russia currently has advantages and disadvantages if it wants to reach, and potentially surpass, the United States in military space capabilities. Because many Russian military space systems were allowed to become moribund after the Soviet collapse, Russia is not as reliant on space systems as is the United States. Therefore, Russian satellites are not the attractive targets that US satellites might be; this is especially important to a country like Russia where favoring offense, even preemption, has been traditional military doctrine.[93] Whether by choice or necessity, Russia has historically opted for numerous less complex satellites which do not last long but which they are able to rapidly replace. They have a resilience capability that the US military must envy. But Russia also has a steep upward curve to climb in terms of matching space aspirations to capabilities, including both development of across-the-board capabilities and integration of those capabilities into operations. It is also, politically, offering use of what capabilities it has, such as its navigation and positioning system GLONASS, to other countries toward drawing users away from GPS and US influence. Russia is not alone in its use of deliberately provocative tactics to draw US and international ire.

On February 7, 2016, when North Korea successfully launched the country's second satellite—an Earth observation satellite called Kwangmyongsong-4— Pyongyang celebrated with fireworks and a government spokesman referenced international efforts to block the launch as nothing more than a "puppy barking at the moon."[94] Grandiosity, provocation, and defiance clearly remain the key elements of North Korean foreign policy. While claiming the satellite launch a peaceful use of outer space in accordance with international norms, the international community has viewed North Korean actions differently.

Whether a launch is actually intended to put a satellite into orbit can be discerned technically. Comparing the trajectory of a typical liquid-fueled intercontinental ballistic missile (ICBM) and the North Korean Unha launcher used for satellite launch attempts, David Wright from the Union of Concerned Scientists explains:

> The trajectory of a satellite launch and a ballistic missile are very different. ... They differ in shape and the length of time the rocket engines burn. ... ICBM engines burn for 300 seconds and the Unha-3 engines burn for nearly

twice that long. The ICBM gets up to high speed much faster and then goes much higher.[95]

Nevertheless, North Korea can learn a considerable amount about how to develop a successful ballistic missile from a successful satellite launch.

North Korea has become adept at taking advantage of the dual-use nature of space technology, mixed with sometimes nonsensical propaganda, in testing long-range ballistic missiles. While North Korea has a stable of missiles capable of reaching much of South Korea and Japan, it has, officially, yet to flight-test any missiles capable of reaching a distance of more than about 1,500 kilometers. But, North Korea has attempted to launch a satellite into orbit five times, and because the technology is basically the same, they can learn a great deal about long-range missiles from these attempted satellite launches.

The only successful North Korean satellite launch prior to February 2016 was in December 2012; even though the satellite reached orbit, it has appeared to be nonfunctioning. North Korea claimed the satellite transmitted the revolutionary "Song of General Kim Il Sung" and "Song of General Kim Jong Il" after achieving orbit, but that claim has never been substantiated by observers outside North Korea—and there are many who pay close attention to North Korean space activities. In 2009, North Korea had also proudly proclaimed a successful satellite launch and stated that the satellite was transmitting revolutionary songs back to Earth. North Korean officials were, then too, the only ones hearing such songs. That was not surprising because, as tracked by both the United States and South Korea, the satellite had failed to reach orbit and dropped into the sea.[96]

In 2016, however, US Strategic Command said it detected two items in association with the North Korean Kwangmyongsong-4 launch: a satellite and the final stage of the rocket booster. US officials reported soon after the launch that the satellite was tumbling in orbit and incapable of any useful functions.[97] If it had been able to communicate with the satellite, North Korea would have become more adept at satellite operations—a future concern of the increasing number of countries that have shown interest in counterspace operations. In the nearer term, the success of the launch puts North Korea one step closer to having an ICBM; though they have several issues, such as re-entry, still apparently out of their reach. But North Korean persistence in obtaining these capabilities, considered alongside their recent purported test of a hydrogen bomb, has the international community rightly alarmed given North Korea's often at best erratic behavior.

An emergency meeting of the UN Security Council was held in conjunction with the 2016 launch, resulting in condemnation of North Korea's violation of UN resolutions banning them from testing ballistic missile technology—under any guise—and a pledge of "significant measures" in response. What those measures will be, however, remains to be seen. Some UN officials have suggested that further economic sanctions on the already largely isolated country would be an appropriate response. China—North Korea's most important ally—has voiced objections to the "more sanctions" option. China is North Korea's primary trading partner and the country's main source of food, arms, and energy. China has helped to sustain Kim Jong-Un's regime and has been historically opposed to harsh international sanctions on North Korea as it fears an influx of refugees across their almost-900-mile, porous border if the regime were to collapse. The recent launch, however, puts pressure on China to get North Korea in line with the international community—a job China has become increasingly weary of given its own financial woes and North Korea's near constant antics.

The launch also complicates already prickly Asian geopolitical relations. Almost certainly, consequent to the February 2016 launch, the United States will expedite plans for a buildup of US missile defense systems in Asia. Specifically, US and South Korea officials have already said they will consider deployment of the Terminal High Altitude Area Defense system, or THAAD, to the Korean peninsula at the "earliest possible" date.[98] China, at odds with the United States over its construction of artificial islands in the South China Sea, objects to placement of a system that includes radar capable of penetrating Chinese territory. To complicate things further, China is also South Korea's biggest trading partner. As well, Japan and Australia are considering what responses each might take against North Korea as part of a UN response or unilaterally.

Meanwhile, North Korean officials continue to spout provocative declarations about intended further launches. This is a country that timed its satellite launch according to weather predictions and the Super Bowl, wanting to draw as much attention as possible from television viewing audiences. Nuclear and missile technology in the hands of such a narcissistic national actor tests the mettle both of the international community to address challenges to peace and of China to be a responsible part of that community and do its part. Hopefully both will step up forcefully as nobody wants North Korea to become another country creating doctrine and setting up structures to integrate military space capabilities into their defense plans. There are plenty of those already.

In June 2008, Indian Defense Minister Shri A. K. Antony announced the formation of an Integrated Space Cell under the aegis of the Integrated Defense Services Headquarters. The stated purpose was to counter the growing threat to Indian space assets. But further progression of India's ability to develop and integrate military space capabilities has been slow, largely due to inter-service bureaucracy issues. In 2012, V. K. Saraswat, then chief of the Defense Research and Development Agency (DRDO), emphasized a defensive strategy for India in the space domain, focused on the principle of no space weapons. Nevertheless, Saraswat went on to say that space security entails the creation of "a gamut of capabilities," including the protection of satellites and communications and navigation systems as well as denying the enemy the use of their own "space systems."[99] The cover of ambiguity courtesy of dual-use technology leaves lots of options for "protection," especially through missile defense development and testing.

In 2015, Russian Defense Minister Sergei Shoigu announced the creation of a new branch of the Russian armed forces: the Aerospace Force. That restructuring brings the Russian air forces, anti-air, anti-missile, and space forces under one unified command. Further, an article in the *Moscow Times* reported that the government is

> pouring 20 trillion rubles ($320 billion) into replacing 70 percent of the military's hardware with shiny new gear by the end of the decade, it's rejigging its military doctrines and organizational structures to reflect modern Russia's threat perceptions – which in recent years have largely centered on NATO expansion.[100]

Reportedly, 20 percent of that money was allocated to buy and develop systems such as the S-500, intended to have the ability to intercept targets, including ballistic missiles, at the edge of the atmosphere. Russia is expanding not just its military space capabilities but also its ability to use them, and they are not alone.

Reports began circulating in 2015 of a Chinese "space force" being stood up within the PLA. Subsequently, on December 31, 2015, the Second Artillery, which had been responsible for strategic missile forces, was renamed the Rocket Force. This was more than a name change; rather, it was part of what has been tectonic-level reorganization of the PLA to include widespread bureaucratic reforms initiated by Chinese President Xi Jinping. The Rocket Force will be responsible for all three legs of China's nuclear triad – as opposed to just the land-based nuclear missile under the control of the Second Artillery – as well as conventional missiles.

Similarly, the US Air Force stood up its first Space Mission Force in February 2016 as part of reorganization toward streamlining the chain of command. Earlier, Air Force Maj. Gen. Martin Wheeler, director of future operations, explained the rationale for the reorganization shortly after it was announced in 2015. Whelan said, "We've had a hard time integrating and synchronizing air, space and cyber" due to problems with the chain of command for space missions being sometimes dispersed.[101] Another part of the rationale was to make better use of skills learned by those in operational positions.

All of the reorganization and modernization efforts demonstrate both the utility of space assets and the challenges with integrating them into operational force use. Space provides capabilities that are needed everywhere, which inherently creates questions about who's in charge and, potentially, internal conflicts. Additionally, these efforts point out the necessity of both broad and narrow troop training to best fill crucial positions within the bureaucratic space structures.

In the context of a "congested, contested, and competitive" space environment, contested clearly takes on an aggressive, militaristic, zero-sum connotation – one that must be countered in a similar manner. Everyone wants assured access to space; having that access has been considered a universal right. But countries are becoming more proprietary and nationalistic, with the military as protector and guarantor of national rights. From that flows the long-standing assumption within the (many) militaries regarding the inevitability of space warfare. If space warfare is inevitable, then the United States would be remiss not to prepare to defend itself and, it has been suggested, perhaps strike first to get a tactical advantage; hence the need for expanded "offensive counterspace" programs. If, however, space warfare is *not* inevitable, then as much attention ought to be spent on prevention as on "defend and defeat" programs, which may serve as little more than totems of protection. And it is certainly not in the best interests of the United States to create self-fulfilling prophecies. Therefore, a closer look at the "inevitability" debate is in order.

## Notes

1   Quoted in Bernard Porter, *The Lion's Share: A History of British Imperialism 1850–2004*, 4th Edition, Pearson Education, Harlow, UK, 2004, p. 189.
2   It is noteworthy that with the exception of during the Apollo years and a brief blip in the mid to late 1990s, the military space budget has always equaled or exceeded the NASA space budget. Marcia S. Smith, *U.S. Space Programs: Civilian, Military and Commercial*, Congressional Research Service Status Report, updated May 24, 2005. www.spaceref.com/news/viewsr.html?pid=16917
3   For more on techno-nationalism and space, see Joan Johnson-Freese, "The geostrategic, techno-nationalist, push into space," *OASIS*, 20, July–December 2014, 9–22.
4   Gen. Kevin P. Chilton, "Assured access to space in a competitive world," *High Frontier*, 3(1), November 2006, p. 2. www.afspc.af.mil/Portals/3/documents/HF/AFD-061128-043.pdf; William J. Lynn III, Remarks on Space Policy at the US Strategic Command Space Conference, Omaha, NE, November 3, 2010. https://www.stratcom.mil/
speeches/2010/56/2010_Space_Symposium_-_Remarks_on_Space_Policy/
5   Roger G. Harrison, "Unpacking the three C's: congested, competitive, and contested space," *Astropolitics*, 11(3), 2013, 123–31: p. 123.
6   Bob Butterworth, "Obama Administration's 'three Cs' means a failing space policy," *Breaking Defense*, November 7, 2011. http://breakingdefense.com/2011/11/obama-administrations-three-cs-means-a-failing-space-policy/
7   Gregory L. Schulte, "Protecting global security in space," Presentation at the S. Rajaratnam School of International Studies, Nanyang Technological University, Singapore, May 9, 2012.
8   Bhavha Lal, "Reshaping Space Policies to Meet Global Trends, *Issues in Science and Technology*, Summer 2016. pp. 63–74.
9   Harrison, "Unpacking the three C's," pp. 123–6; Gregory L. Schulte, Testimony before the Senate Committee on Armed Services, Subcommittee on Strategic Forces, May 11, 2011.
10   Marlon E. Sorge and Mary Ellen Vojtek, "Space debris mitigation policy," *Aerospace, Crosslink Magazine*, Fall, December 10, 2015.
11   NASA, "Space Debris and Human Spaceflight," *NASA*, September 27, 2013. www.nasa.gov/mission_pages/station/news/orbital_debris.html
12   Kenneth Chang, "Debris gives space station crew a 29,000-m.p.h. close call," *The New York Times*, June 28, 2011. www.nytimes.com/2011/06/29/science/space/29junk.html?_r=0

13 Leonard David, "China's anti-satellite test: worrisome debris cloud circles Earth," *Space.com*, February 2, 2007. www.space.com/3415-china-anti-satellite-test-worrisome-debris-cloud-circles-earth.html

14 NASA, "Space Debris and Human Spaceflight."

15 NASA, "Orbital debris: frequently asked questions, No. 15," *NASA Orbital Debris Program Office*, updated March 2012. http://orbitaldebris.jsc.nasa.gov/faqs.html#15

16 Mike Gruss, "US Air Force: no evidence malfunctioning satellite was hit by debris," *SpaceNews*, March 29, 2016. http://spacenews.com/u-s-air-force-no-evidence-malfunctioning-japanese-satellite-was-hit-by-debris/

17 Jeff Foust, "NOAA weather satellite suffers in orbit breakup," *SpaceNews*, November 27, 2015. http://spacenews.com/noaa-weather-satellite-suffers-in-orbit-breakup/

18 Butterworth, "Obama Administration's 'three Cs.'"

19 U.S. Government Accountability Office, "Space situational awareness: status of efforts and planned budgets," GAO-16-6R, GAO, Washington, DC, October 8, 2015, p. 2. www.gao.gov/assets/680/672987.pdf

20 More detailed technical analysis of conjunction warnings point out the limitations of surveillance. David Finkleman, "State of the art in space surveillance and collision avoidance," International Astronautical Congress, Jerusalem, Israel, October 2015.

21 Department of Defense Directive 3100.10, *Space Policy*, October 18, 2012. www.dtic.mil/whs/directives/corres/pdf/310010p.pdf

22 Information is available at: www.iadc-online.org/index.cgi?item=docs_pub

23 U.S. Government Orbital Debris Mitigation Standard Practices, 1997. www.orbitaldebris.jsc.nasa.gov/library/USG_OD_Standard_Practices.pdf

24 United Nations Office for Outer Space Affairs, *Space Debris Mitigation Guidelines of the Committee on the Peaceful Uses of Outer Space*, United Nations, Vienna, 2010. http://orbitaldebris.jsc.nasa.gov/library/Space%20Debris%20Mitigation%20Guidelines_COPUOS.pdf

25 Wayne White, "The Space Pioneer Act," *The Space Review*, October 27, 2014. www.thespacereview.com/article/2627/1

26 Joan Johnson-Freese, "Taking out the space trash: a model for cooperation," *Breaking Defense*, May 2, 2014. http://breakingdefense.com/2014/05/taking-out-the-space-trash-a-model-for-space-cooperation/

27 As of December 31, 2015; Union of Concerned Scientists, based on the USC Satellite Database. www.ucsusa.org/nuclear-weapons/space-weapons/satellite-database.html#.VkSkSYS4nq0

28 "Space is running out in orbital parking lot," *Los Angeles Times*, September 20, 1993.

29 Kevin N, "Philippines satellite slot in outer space grabbed and occupied by China," *ManilaLivewire*, August 29, 2015. www.manilalivewire.com/2015/08/philippines-satellite-slot-in-outer-space-grabbed-and-occupied-by-china/

30 David Holley, "Tokyo says new Chinese satellite violates world pact," *Los Angeles Times*, July 25, 1994. http://articles.latimes.com/1994-07-25/business/fi-19621_1_apt-satellite

31 Mark Holmes, "Hot orbital slots: is there anything left?" *Via Satellite*, March 1, 2008. www.satellitetoday.com/publications/via-satellite-magazine/features/2008/03/01/hot-orbital-slots-is-there-anything-left/

32 Schulte, Testimony before the Senate Committee on Armed Services, p. 2.

33  John Keller, "Army approaches industry for ideas of RF interference mitigation in future electronic warfare," *Military Aerospace*, July 24, 2014. www.militaryaerospace. com/articles/2014/07/army-rim-rfi.html

34  Smallsats are those under 500 kilograms (1,100 pounds); microsats range from approximately 10 kilograms to 100 kilograms (22 to 220 pounds); nanosats have a wet mass of approximately 1 kilogram to 10 kilograms (2.2 to 22 pounds); cubesats are approximately 21 kilograms (2.2 pounds). There are other variations as well.

35  Dave Baiocchi and William Welser IV, "The democratization of space," *Foreign Affairs*, May–June 2015, p. 100.

36  K. Jayalakshmi, "Cubesats crowding low Earth orbit posing collision dangers for space users, warns experts," *International Business Times*, October 1, 2014. www.ibtimes. co.uk/cubesats-crowding-low-earth-orbit-posing-collision-dangers-space-users-warns-expert-1468017

37  Federal Aviation Administration, "Small Unmanned Aircraft Registration Begins Dec. 21," *FAA*. https://www.faa.gov/news/updates/?newsId=84384

38  Harrison, "Unpacking the three C's," pp. 125–6.

39  Niall Ferguson, *Civilization: The West and The Rest*, Penguin Books, New York, 2011, Chapter 1 "Competition," pp. 19–49.

40  For a more thorough consideration of Symphonie, see Richard Barnes, "Symphonie Launch Negotiations," reprinted in *News & Notes*, 23(1), February 2006, 1–5. http:// history.nasa.gov/nltr23-1.pdf

41  John H. Anderson, "Europe vs. America in space," *New York Times*, March 17, 1985. www.nytimes.com/1985/03/17/business/europe-vs-america-in-space. html?pagewanted=all

42  Dr. Lee was cleared of espionage charges and pleaded guilty to one charge of mishandling government documents as part of a settlement. Federal Judge James Parker apologized to Dr. Lee for government prosecutorial tactics; Bob Drogin, "Wen Ho Lee freed: judge scolds US over case tactics," *Los Angeles Times*, September 14, 2000. http://articles.latimes.com/2000/sep/14/news/mn-20908

43  Joan Johnson-Freese, "Alice in Licenseland: US satellite export controls since 1990," *Space Policy*, 16(3), 2000, 195–204; Joan Johnson-Freese, "Becoming Chinese: or, how export policy threatens national security," *Space Times*, January–February, 2001, 4–12.

44  Evelyn Iritani and Peter Pae, "Strict export controls bring US satellite sales crashing down," *Los Angeles Times*, December 12, 2000. www.sfgate.com/business/article/ Strict-Export-Controls-Bring-U-S-Satellite-Sales-2722146.php

45  US Department of State, Amendment to the International Traffic in Arms Regulations, Revision of US Munitions List Category XV, *Federal Register*, May 13, 2014. https:// www.federalregister.gov/articles/2014/05/13/2014-10806/ amendment-to-the-international-traffic-in-arms-regulations-revision-of-us-munitions-list-category-xv

46  See Alastair Iain Johnston, W. K. H. Panofsky, Marco Di Capua, and Lewis R. Franklin, *The Cox Committee: An Assessment*, Center for International Security and Cooperation, Stanford, CA, December 1999, http://fsi.stanford.edu/sites/default/ files/cox.pdf

47  Cox Committee commentary drawn from Joan Johnson-Freese and Theresa Hitchens, "Cox Committee Redux at NASA Ames," *SpaceNews*, February 18, 2013. http:// spacenews.com/33647cox-committee-redux-at-nasa-ames/

48 Abolghasem Bayyenat, "Pride in the future: the politics of Iran's space program," *ForeignPolicy*,July7,2011.www.foreignpolicyjournal.com/2011/07/07/pride-in-the-future-the-politics-of-irans-space-program/

49 Jassem Al Salami, "Iran just cancelled its space program," *War is Boring*, January 27, 2015. https://medium.com/war-is-boring/iran-just-cancelled-its-space-program-5b1d
5ce50bd6#.j5vi8ssb6

50 Frank Culbertson, "What's in a name?" Paper submitted to the Congress of the Association of Space Explorers, October 3, 1996. http://spaceflight.nasa.gov/history/shuttle-mir/references/r-documents-mirmeanings.htm

51 Mark Williamson, *Spacecraft: The Early Years*, IET History of Technology Series, Institution of Engineering and Technology, London, 2006, p. 176.

52 Elizabeth Howell, "Telstar: satellites beamed first T.V. signals across the Atlantic," *Space.com*, February 12, 2013. www.space.com/19756-telstar.html

53 Joan Johnson-Freese and Roger Handberg, *The Prestige Trap: A Comparative Study of the US, European and Japanese Space Programs*, Kendall-Hunt Publishing, Dubuque, 1994.

54 Peter B. de Selding, "First Belarusian satellite has a mission of profit, not prestige," *SpaceNews*,January18,2016.http://spacenews.com/belarus-puts-up-its-first-satellite-for-profit-not-prestige/

55 Harrison, "Unpacking the three C's," p. 127.

56 "Space mission generating national pride but also criticism," *AsiaNewsIT*, October 13, 2005. www.asianews.it/news-en/Space-mission-generating-national-pride-but-also-criticism-4350.html

57 Much of the Mangalyann account draws from Joan Johnson-Freese, "How the (political) planets aligned to get India to Mars," *The Diplomat*, June 24, 2015. http://thediplomat.com/2015/06/how-the-political-planets-aligned-to-get-india-to-mars/

58 Samantha Subramanian, "Why India went to Mars," *The New Yorker*, September 26, 2014. www.newyorker.com/business/currency/india-really-went-mars

59 "'Our Mars mission cheaper than the movie Gravity,' says PM Modi after PSLV C-23,"*NDTV*,June30,2014.www.ndtv.com/india-news/our-mars-mission-cheaper-than-the-movie-gravity-pm-modi-after-pslv-c-23-launch-582320

60 Eugene Chow, "The US is in an under-the-radar space race with China – and it's losing," *The Week*, February 11, 2014. http://theweek.com/articles/451227/undertheradar-space-race-china--losing; Adam Minter, "China has US in a space race," *Bloomberg View*, June 9, 2014. www.bloombergview.com/articles/2014-06-09/china-has-u-s-in-a-space-race

61 Office of the Spokesperson, "U.S.-India Joint Fact Sheet: Cooperation in Space," *U.S. Department of State*, June 24, 2013. www.state.gov/r/pa/prs/ps/2013/06/211029.htm

62 National Research Council of the National Academies, *America's Future in Space: Aligning the Civil Space Program with National Needs*, National Academies Press, Washington, DC, 2009; National Research Council of the National Academies, *NASA's Strategic Direction and the Need for a National Consensus*, National Academies Press, Washington, DC, 2012; National Research Council of the National Academies, *Pathways to Exploration: Rationales and Approaches for a US Program of Space Exploration*, National Academies Press, Washington, DC, 2014.

63  Joan Johnson-Freese, "Ceding American leadership in space," *The Fletcher Forum*, 39(1), Winter 2015, 91–8. www.fletcherforum.org/wp-content/uploads/2015/04/Johnson-Freese.pdf

64  DoD Dictionary of Military Terms. www.dtic.mil/doctrine/dod_dictionary/index.html

65  Joint Chiefs of Staff, *Joint Doctrine for Space Operations*, Joint Publication 3-14, August 9, 2002, Office of the Joint Chiefs of Staff, Washington, DC. www.dtic.mil/doctrine/new_pubs/jp3_14.pdf#search="space"

66  Harrison, "Unpacking the three C's," p. 127.

67  Some material in this section is drawn from Joan Johnson-Freese, Testimony before the US-China Economic and Security Review Commission, February 18, 2015. www.uscc.gov/sites/default/files/Johnson%20Freese_Testimony.pdf

68  Larry M. Wortzel, "China and the battlefield in space," *WebMemo 346 on Asia*, October 15, 2003. www.heritage.org/research/reports/2003/10/china-and-the-battlefield-in-space

69  Wang Hucheng, "The US military's soft ribs and strategic weaknesses," *Xinhua*, July 5, 2000.

70  Gregory Kulacki, *An Authoritative Source on China's Military Space Strategy*, Union of Concerned Scientists, Cambridge, MA, March 2014, p. 2. www.ucsusa.org/sites/default/files/legacy/assets/documents/nwgs/China-s-Military-Space-Strategy.pdf

71  Cited in Gregory Kulacki and David Wright, *A Military Intelligence Failure? The Case of the Parasite Satellite*, Union of Concerned Scientists, Cambridge, MA, August 16, 2004. www.ucsusa.org/sites/default/files/legacy/assets/documents/nwgs/parasite_satellite_8-17-04.pdf

72  Ibid.

73  Cited in Gregory Kulacki and David Wright, "New Questions About US Intelligence on China," September 15, 2005. www.ucsusa.org/sites/default/files/legacy/assets/documents/nwgs/nasic-analysis-final-9-15-05.pdf

74  Ibid.

75  Gregory Kulacki and Joan Johnson-Freese, Memo to US-China Economic Security and Review Commission. www.ucsusa.org/assets/documents/nwgs/memo-to-uscc.pdf

76  Gregory Kulacki, "The 2014 USCC report: still sloppy after all these years," *All Things Nuclear*, November 24, 2014. http://allthingsnuclear.org/gkulacki/the-2014-uscc-report-still-sloppy-after-all-these-years

77  Gregory Kulacki, *Anti-Satellite (ASAT) Technology in Chinese Open-Source Publications*, Union of Concerned Scientists, Cambridge, MA, July 1, 2009. www.ucsusa.org/sites/default/files/legacy/assets/documents/nwgs/Kulacki-Chinese-ASAT-Literature-6-10-09.pdf

78  "Shenzhou 7", *Encyclopedia Astronautica*. www.astronautix.com/flights/shezhou7.htm

79  Cited in Peter J. Brown, "China gets a jump on US in space," *Asia Times Online*, October 25, 2008. www.atimes.com/atimes/China/JJ25Ad02.html

80  David Wright and Gregory Kulacki, *Chinese Shenzhou 7 "Companionsat" (BX-1)*, Union of Concerned Scientists, Cambridge, MA, October 21, 2008. www.ucsusa.org/sites/default/files/legacy/testfolder/aa-migration-to-be-deleted/assets-delete-me/documents-delete-me/nuclear_weapons_global_sec-delete-me/UCS-Shenzhou7-CompanionSat-10-21-08.pdf

81   Sharon Weinberger, "X-37B: secrets of the military spaceplane," *BBC*, November 18, 2014. www.bbc.com/future/story/20121123-secrets-of-us-military-spaceplane

82   John Logsdon and James R. Miller, *US-Russian Cooperation in Human Spaceflight: Assessing the Impacts*, under contract from NASA, February 2001. www.nasa.gov/externalflash/iss-lessons-learned/docs/partners_us_russia.pdf

83   Cited in Adam Taylor, "Russia's Deputy PM tells US astronauts to go to space on a trampoline; the joke may be on him," *Washington Post*, April 30. 2014. https://www.washingtonpost.com/news/worldviews/wp/2014/04/30/russias-deputy-pm-tells-u-s-astronauts-to-go-to-space-on-a-trampoline-the-joke-may-be-on-him/

84   Alexander Golts, "Vladimir Putin wants to frighten the world into respecting Russia again," *Moscow Times*, July 11, 2014. www.huffingtonpost.com/alexander-golts/putin-russia-world-fear_b_6122028.html

85   Mary Alise Sarrotte, "A broken promise? What the West really told Moscow about NATO expansion," *Foreign Affairs*, September–October 2014. https://www.foreignaffairs.com/articles/russia-fsu/2014-08-11/broken-promise

86   James R. Clapper, *Worldwide Threat Assessment of the US Intelligence Community*, Senate Armed Services Committee, Office of the Director of National Intelligence, February 9, 2016, p. 9.

87   Jana Honkova, *The Russian Federation's Approach to Military Space and its Military Space Capabilities*, Policy Outlook, George C. Marshall Institute, Arlington, VA, November 2013, p. 3; citing Igor Morozov, Sergey Baushev, and Oleg Kaminskiy, "Space and the character of modern military activities," *Vozdushno-Kosmicheskaya I Obobona*, 4, 2009. http://marshall.org/wp-content/uploads/2013/11/Russian-Space-Nov-13.pdf

88   Joan Johnson-Freese and Ralph Savelsberg, "Why Russia keeps moving the football on European missile defense: politics," *Breaking Defense*, October 17, 2013. http://breakingdefense.com/2013/10/why-russia-keeps-moving-the-football-on-european-missile-defense-politics/

89   Frank A. Rose, Remarks on "Implementation of the European Phased Adaptive Approach," Polish National Defense University, Warsaw, Poland, April 18, 2013. www.state.gov/t/avc/rls/2013/207679.htm

90   Military Doctrine of the Russian Federation, December 25, 2014, https://www.offiziere.ch/wp-content/uploads-001/2015/08/Russia-s-2014-Military-Doctrine.pdf

91   Laurence Peter, "Russia shrugs off US anxiety over military satellite," *BBC News*, October 20, 2015. www.bbc.co.uk/news/world-europe-34581089

92   Laura Grego, "Russia's small maneuvering satellites: inspectors or ASATs?" *All Things Nuclear,*December1,2014.http://allthingsnuclear.org/lgrego/russias-small-maneuvering-satellites-inspectors-or-asats

93   Honkova, *The Russian Federation's Approach*, p. 4.

94   Analysis and information regarding the 2016 North Korean satellite launch was largely drawn from a CNN editorial on the event. See Joan Johnson-Freese, "Why North Korea's satellite launch is troubling," *CNN*, February 9, 2016. http://edition.cnn.com/2016/02/09/opinions/north-korea-satellite-launch-freese/

95   David Wright, "North Korea is launching a rocket soon: what do we know about it?" *Union of Concerned Scientists*, February 5, 2016. http://allthingsnuclear.org/dwright/north-korea-is-launching-a-rocket-soon-what-do-we-know-about-it

96   Tania Branigan, "North Korean rocket launch 'fails,'" *The Guardian*, April 5, 2009. www.theguardian.com/world/2009/apr/05/north-korea-rocket-launch

97  Nash Jenkins, "North Korea's satellite is tumbling in orbit," *Time*, February 9, 2016. http://time.com/4213428/north-korea-satellite-tumbling/

98  Anna Fifield, "South Korea, US to start talks on anti-missile system," *Washington Post*, February 7, 2016. https://www.washingtonpost.com/world/south-korea-united-states-to-start-talks-on-thaad-anti-missile-system/2016/02/07/1eaf2df8-9dc4-45e3-8ff1-d76a25673dbe_story.html

99  Amit Saksena, "India and space defense," *The Diplomat*, March 22, 2014. http://thediplomat.com/2014/03/india-and-space-defense/

100  Matthew Bodner, "Russian military merges air force and space command," *Moscow Times*, August 3, 2015. www.themoscowtimes.com/business/article/russian-military-merges-air-force-and-space-command/526672.html

101  Philip Swarts, "USAF revamping space command structure, general says," Air Force Times, October 6, 2015. www.airforcetimes.com/story/military/2015/10/06/usaf-revamping-space-command-structure-general-says/73218694/

# 3

# AVOIDING THUCYDIDES' TRAP

Peace is not the absence of conflict, but the ability to cope with conflict by peaceful means.

Ronald Reagan[1]

In a 2015 article for *The Atlantic* magazine, Harvard Professor Graham Allison stated that based on historical evidence, the odds of the United States and China going to war were "much more likely than recognized at the moment."[2] His assessment was based on an examination of 16 cases of a rising power confronting a ruling power over the past 500 years, a situation the fifth-century Greek historian Thucydides had considered in relation to the Peloponnesian War. Thucydides wrote, "It was the rise of Athens, and the fear that inspired in Sparta, that made war inevitable."[3] In the 16 cases considered by Allison and his team, war had occurred in 12 instances. Yet, Allison says, war with China is not inevitable. Chinese President Xi Jinping echoed that rejection of inevitability, saying: "There is no such thing as the so-called Thucydides Trap in the world. But should major countries time and again make the mistakes of strategic miscalculation, they might create such traps for themselves."[4] And therein lies the problem and the link between the Thucydides Trap generally and space specifically. Strategic miscalculation is often driven by structural inertia— the same kind of structural inertia created by the powerful and expansive military— industrial complex that is deeply embedded in and exacerbating the security dilemma gripping the United States and China regarding space.

Toward avoiding inevitability, Allison tells strategists looking for a (often politically necessary and budget-friendly) quick fix to step back.

What strategists need most at this moment is not a new strategy, but a long pause for reflection. If the tectonic shift caused by China's rise poses a challenge of genuinely Thucydidean proportions, declarations about "rebalancing," or revitalizing "engage and hedge," or presidential hopefuls' calls for more "muscular" or "robust" variants of the same, amount to little more than aspirin treating cancer. Future historians will compare such assertions to the reveries of British, German, and Russian leaders as they sleepwalked into 1914.

The rise of a 5,000-year-old civilization with 1.3 billion people is not a problem to be fixed. It is a condition—a chronic condition that will have to be managed over a generation.[5]

Whether US politicians have the patience, the wisdom, and the wherewithal to manage a fundamental, chronic challenge remains to be seen. Similarly, the leadership of China, Russia, North Korea, and other nations must rise to the challenge of seeing beyond the "soda straw" perspective of their own knee-jerk actions. Professor and diplomat John Stoessinger focused on the pivotal role of the personalities of leaders who take their nations, or their followers, across the threshold into war in his book *Why Nations Go To War*, originally published in 1971.[6] Leadership, and the character of leaders, matters.

The Thucydides Trap metaphor holds especially true for space because, as Allison points out in his example of Germany challenging Britain's naval power, all that mattered in Britain's assessments was capability, not intentions. Similarly, the US military characterization of space as "congested, contested, and competitive" is based on an assessment of potential competitor capabilities; regarding space, this refers largely to China, but, increasingly, Russia as well. Avoiding the Thucydides Trap therefore requires, as Allison says, more than trite strategy aimed at maintaining an unsustainable status quo; rather, it needs a serious reassessment of an inevitably changing situation.

## Is Space War Inevitable?

Four basic schools of thought have traditionally dominated space warfare debates in the United States, including one that says war in space is inevitable[7]. In his 1999 book *Space Power Theory*, James Oberg said, "At its core, the notion of weapons in space pits military pragmatists against idealistic futurists."[8] Since 1999, a more nuanced spectrum of views has emerged though those who viewed war in space as inevitable then, largely still do.

The first school argues that US reliance on space for both military and civilian capabilities makes space dominance essential as space represents the "ultimate high ground." The second states that weaponization is simply inevitable and therefore the United States would be remiss not to prepare. The third school asserts the military importance of space but seeks to maintain limits on the militarization of space, toward avoiding the weaponization of space, and advocates arms control agreements toward that end. Last, there is the space sanctuary school. In its purist form, the sanctuary school advocates for space to maintain a status much like

Antarctica. How to manage globally expanded space capabilities warrants a closer look at each school in the space warfare debate.

The view that space is the ultimate high ground is analogous to cavalry soldiers holding a hill as the best position to view the surrounding terrain and, if necessary, fight. Similarly, if air superiority is required to win wars, then space is the ultimate high altitude from which to gain military advantage on Earth. Space assets such as reconnaissance satellites can offer the military access to areas otherwise beyond its physical reach. It is important to note that none of the schools are pertinent only to US analyses. Kevin Pollpeter finds references to space as the high ground in Chinese space analyses as well. He states, "Chinese writers make the oft-repeated statement that 'whoever controls space will control the Earth' and that outer space is the new high ground of military operations."[9]

Space being perceived as "the high ground" comes, in large part, from the still-evolving nature of differentiating air and space domains. The US Air Force has described itself by various names:[10] an "air force," an "air and space force," an "aerospace force," and an "air, space and cyber" force. The Chinese appear to be having much the same dilemma in terms of defining and differentiating domains.[11]

But the "high ground" analogy between Earth and space goes only so far due to differences between the basic physical characteristics of space and the capabilities of ground and air forces. Ground troops can defend and conceal themselves atop a hill. Aircraft can perform rapid self-protective maneuvers in defense of air space. But space assets are bright objects against a dark sky that travel in a determined and predictable path, making them "sitting ducks."[12] Consequently, the advantages offered by space as the high ground come with risks as well. The "high ground" school simply extends a basic principle of military operations to another domain, though the validity of the transference assumptions is limited. The second school is based on a broader assumption.

The adage "Earth is two-thirds water and one-third space studies, most of them chaired by me" is often attributed to the former commander of Air Force Space Command, Gen. Tom Moorman, Jr. For better or worse, most of those studies were promptly relegated to a desk drawer or coffee table. That was not the case, though, when the chair of the study stepped immediately into the position of Secretary of Defense, as was the case with Donald Rumsfeld in 2001. The National Defense Authorization Act for Fiscal Year 2000 created a Commission to Assess National Security Space Management and Organization, to be chaired by Donald Rumsfeld. The report of the Commission, known as both the Rumsfeld Commission report[13] and the Space Commission report, was published in January 2001 just as Rumsfeld was about to become Secretary of Defense. Consequently, it was hardly forgotten but, instead, became the basis for US space policy. Key among the conclusions reached was that

> we know from history that every medium—air, land and sea—has seen conflict. Reality indicates that space will be no different. Given that virtual

certainty, the U.S. must develop the means to both deter and to defend against hostile acts in and from space.[14]

The inevitability of space weapons was assumed. The United States, the report warned, must act quickly and decisively if it was to avoid a "Space Pearl Harbor."[15] Consequently, the "ahooga" horn sounded throughout not just the Pentagon, but Washington generally.

Among the military officers agreeing with the inevitability of conflict in space was (then, in 2002) Air Force Colonel John Hyten. Writing in *Air & Space Power Journal*, Hyten charted a course forward from the assumption of inevitability, but also noted the need for space "rules."

> Conflict in space is inevitable. No frontier exploited or occupied by humans has ever been free from strife, but the United States has a chance to mold and shape the resolution of such conflict in the future. Opportunities exist through both formal and informal negotiations to define the commons of space and the rules of the road. At the same time, the United States cannot afford to be caught off guard in the future—and cannot afford to allow another country to deploy a space-based weapon first. To ensure that this doesn't happen, it must develop a robust program for an entire spectrum of space-control capabilities—deferring the decision to deploy operational, space-based weapons until a clear requirement exists.[16]

Admirably, Gen. Hyten still talks about rules of the road, but with qualifications.

In response to a question after the keynote speech he delivered at the Small Satellite 2015 conference, Gen. Hyten said,

> I hope the State Department has a role in it because I would like to make sure—I always believe that we should talk first, so I hope we do down that path and we develop—you know, we jointly develop what we believe are, you know, rules for responsible behavior in space across the international community.[17]

But the rapid speed required to keep up with adversaries, he said, means that "everybody is moving fast," and he sees the need to move even faster. Diplomacy, unfortunately, takes time. He again spoke of the need for rules of the road in space at the February 2016 Air Warfare Symposium in Orlando, Florida, saying there are defined rules in all other domains of military operation. He further stated that norms are important "because it's hard to develop rules of engagement without international norms."[18] History has shown, however, that the United States cannot dictate to other countries. Therefore, there must be some basis for other countries to be interested in rule development—a benefit to them as well as to the United States.

Just as the 2015 Allison study uses history as its basis for analysis, history is usually the basis for inevitability premises. It has happened in the past; therefore, it will happen in the future. History lessons are valuable, but as Allison points out, history does not dictate the future, especially if the lessons of history are learned and considered. Rather than beginning from assumptions regarding military operations or inevitability, the arms control school begins by asking what is in the long-term interest of the United States, since it is the United States that has the most assets in space and is most dependent on them, and then sets a course most likely to achieve those goals.

Arms control advocates argue that while space weapons might offer the United States a short-term advantage, in the long term they would actually weaken US security by instigating an arms race that cannot be won, by anyone. Further, space weapons could potentially provoke a first strike by an adversary, create a "use it or lose it" mentality among US forces, and risk rapid and dangerous—perhaps even nuclear—escalation.

The arms control approach was clearly rejected during the George W. Bush Administration. John Bolton, as Undersecretary of State for Arms Control and International Security, stated the US position clearly and succinctly as follows: "We are not prepared to negotiate on the so-called arms race in outer space. We just don't see that as a worthwhile enterprise."[19] The rationale was that the United States was ahead of everyone else and arms control would only serve to limit US efforts to maintain that position. Arms control is not specifically rejected now. Frank Rose stated in March 2016, "I would like to point out that the United States is not opposed to arms control in principle."[20] However, his qualifications in terms of "if they are equitable" and "effectively verifiable" nullifies many areas of effort.

A study on verification was conducted by the Eisenhower Center in 2010[21] with several interlocking key points emerging. First, the idea that maintaining the stability of the space environment could be done without reciprocal constraints on the behavior of all major actors was said to be an illusion. Second, no country will trust verification to another country. Rather, countries will insist upon independent verification and so agreement on constraints will be limited to those measures verifiable by the least capable country. Since the United States has the most capability, serious proposals (*vice* diplomatic feints) are unlikely to exceed its verification constraints. And third, verification depends both on technical capability and precision of language in describing specific measures. Key in this regard is that "[i]f specificity is sacrificed to consensus, the resulting regime of non-binding, qualified and/or vaguely-worded 'norms' may undermine rather than increase stability in space."[22] Arms control efforts are largely unknown to the public, neglected by the media and given far less focus by government officials than counterspace operations. Yet, they can garner the United States far more international traction toward space stabilization efforts than threats of punitive deterrence.

Each of the four schools clearly recognizes the immense value of military space assets. Satellite imagery, three-dimensional radar maps of targets and terrain, GPS-guided munitions, troop use of more than 100,000 lightweight GPS receivers, and a bevy of satellites for various uses were used in Operation Iraqi Freedom. This massive use of space assets "enabled military responses to occur in minutes rather than hours, resulting in a dramatic reduction in the 'kill-chain'"[23]—target identification, force dispatch to target, decision and order to attack the target, and target destruction. But if or when the speed of that kill chain becomes counterproductive, in terms of increasing the potential for mistakes or overreaction, must be considered as well.

The United States, Russia, China, India, Japan, Taiwan, and South Korea are all developing hypersonic missiles capable of traveling over Mach 5, which will reduce the kill chain time significantly. The US Conventional Prompt Global Strike (CPGS) effort aims to be able to deliver ordinance anywhere in the world within an hour. If, however, these weapons are suspected of carrying nuclear weapons, the potential for rapid escalation ensues.[24]

The fourth school is the sanctuary school, which in its purest form, seeks to maintain space as a sanctuary from military activity or at least to limit space to clearly passive rather than active programs. Dual-use technology, however, makes that differentiation difficult. Alternatively, space sanctuary has also been characterized as an alternative to the "inevitability" perspective,[25] more in line with the arms control approach. Clearly, space offers military advantages on the ground through force enhancement that all countries seek, making the maintenance of space as a pristine, military-free domain unlikely.

Perhaps ironically, Oberg points out, "the popular view of space as a sanctuary, is one carefully crafted by the United States."[26] In doing so even while having a military space program that dwarfed the rest of the world, the United States ensured that actions taken against it by other countries would be viewed in terms of those countries violating this sanctuary. The 2016 CNAS report *From Sanctuary to Battlefield* seems to bear out Oberg's view. There, it states that "US space assets enjoyed a degree of sanctuary for many years due to the significant technical challenges to being able to strike at or interfere with satellites."[27] Defense Secretary Ash Carter, in a March 2016 speech, reiterated the idea that the days of space sanctuary are gone, this being a rationale for why the Defense Department must now "prepare for, and seek to prevent, the possibility of a conflict that extends into space."[28] With other countries wanting the same rights to and advantages from space that the United States has enjoyed, they have worked assiduously to improve their technical capabilities.

An increasing number of countries are moving into or expanding their military space programs. In 2014, European Space Agency (ESA) Director Jean-Jacques Dordain commented on the likely future expansion of the military component of ESA activities.

> As concerns military space activities, this represents so far the largest deficit of Europe as compared to other space powers. Space in Europe has been started as a civilian activity and military space activities are limited in size and scope so far. However there is an increasing number of programmes that, even though civilian may have military or security-related users – such as Galileo or Copernicus. The ESA itself is not a civilian agency. It is an agency

for peaceful purposes and may have programmes with a security component. If and when Europe needs space as an enabling tool for its security and defence policy, ESA will be prepared to develop the required programmes.[29]

Besides working together, European countries also have their own national space efforts, and it is there that a considerable amount of work on military space occurs. For example, French spending on military space programs increased by over $500 million in 2016, focused on next-generation optical imaging spacecraft, signals intelligence, and satellite communications.[30] Even countries like Japan that once defined "the peaceful use of space" as meaning "nonmilitary" have now altered that definition to allow military use, simply as a reflection of reality. And perhaps most importantly, declaring space a sanctuary would, quite simply, not be in the best interests of the United States. But keeping space a sanctuary from violence has until recently been increasingly recognized as imperative.

Over time, there has also been more experience with the potentially deleterious and escalatory effects of space warfare through computer simulations and wargaming. Rarely, however, are these effects made known to the public in the same way that "The Battle Above" focused on revealing threats to the public. Since 2001, Air Force Space Command has been hosting the Schriever Wargames, named in honor of Air Force General Bernard Schriever. In 1961, Schriever was named the first commander of Air Force Systems Command, in charge of all missiles. The wargame began as a venue to examine the utility of advanced space technologies in various scenarios and evolved into an opportunity to consider policy and strategy issues as well as how diplomatic, economic, and information tools of power come into play. While originally focusing on issues related to space systems, cyber system challenges have been integrated into the game as well.[31] While the specifics of the scenarios that trigger conflict are classified, the first Schriever wargame was generally known "to pit a friendly 'Blue' force against a near space-peer adversary known as the 'Red' force. 'Red' has been threatening a smaller, neighboring 'Brown' nation, and 'Blue' intervenes on 'Brown's' behalf."[32] It would not be difficult for anyone, or any country, to imagine that Blue represented the United States, Red represented China, and Brown represented Taiwan.[33] China certainly had no such difficulty.

Over the years, a plethora of issues and lessons learned have been identified. Perhaps key among them are the dangers of rapid escalation and the far-reaching consequences of space warfare. Military space assets are not the only assets that would become jeopardized in space warfare. Commercial space assets and military assets widely used by the civilian sector, such as GPS, are all put at risk. Writing after the Schriever V wargame, Congressional Representative Terry Everett, who played the US President in the game, wrote about the reach of space conflict in the midst of a still-deepening crisis.

I wondered how to explain to the American people that we had worked tirelessly with our coalition partners to defuse a crisis which had already resulted in the loss of global transport and communications services—services which deprived the people of the world the information they needed every day for national security, commerce, to transport goods, and maintain their way of life.[34]

The conditions on Earth which provide conflict "firebreaks"—borders, coastlines, mountain ranges, which cause troops and operations to pause—do not exist in space, making it an inherently unstable environment susceptible to rapid escalation. Further, there are no history books to pull from that provide "war-ending" lessons learned.[35]

Only recently, in the 2016 CNAS report, have the escalatory risks of space warfare, regularly noted in past analyses, been largely dismissed and assumptions made of "reasonable" responses to attacks—though few have been evidenced prior in wargames—or an anticipated "fog of war."

> Would the United States respond with a major strategic strike if China or Russia, in the context of a regional conflict with the United States, struck discriminately at implicated U.S. space assets in the attempt to defang U.S. power projection, all while leaving the broader U.S. space architecture alone? Not only does such a massive response seem unlikely – it would be positively foolish and irresponsible. Furthermore, would other nations regard attacks on assets the United States was actively employing for a local war as off limits to attack? Indeed, any reasonable observer would have to judge that such discriminate attacks on U.S. space assets would not necessarily be illegitimate, as, by the United States' own admission, it relies greatly on its space architecture for conventional power projection.[36]

Assuming that an adversary, or even the United States, would be prudent and reasonable if one or more of its space assets were under attack is a dangerous gamble for both doctrinal and structural reasons.

Challenges regarding command and control of space assets and the need for integration and prior coordination with allies have also emerged from the Schriever games, with no easy answers. The ability for the military to protect valuable space assets, including by preemptive and even preventive strikes, may well rest on its ability to act quickly and decisively. Yet ceding authority to take rapid action to the military comes with risks as well. Ambassador Lincoln Bloomfield addressed that conundrum after Schriever V.

> The question for the National Command Authority is, what if the worst-case characterization of the threat is incorrect? What if the first destructive action was an accident? Or a one-off demonstration intended as a political warning to the US relating to broader issues between the two adversaries? What if the attribution to a particular adversary was incorrect—perhaps even manipulated through offensive cyber operations by a third party *provocateur*? The point here is two-fold. As with any escalating crisis, the protagonists in

a conflict are political actors, and the issues being contested are geopolitical; and thus the US management of the crisis must of necessity include the civilian as well as military leadership. Second, a hair-trigger kinetic response in space by the US confers more risk than advantage, and should be avoided as a matter of operational tradecraft, to allow a discrete period for better characterization of the intent of the adversary before irrevocably harmful escalation is undertaken.[37]

The risk of escalation has not abated but, instead, potentially increased with the advent of technology that increasingly cuts into decision-making time and kill chains as well as the increased potential for mistakes and miscalculation due to congestion and more actors. The potentially complicating considerations of more actors as stakeholders in space have come to light as well.

The need for international coordination was recognized and addressed in the first international version of the Schriever Wargame in 2012 (SW12I), conducted at Nellis Air Force Base in Nevada. The intent was to emulate a notional NATO operation with reliance on space-based capabilities provided by member countries. Nine NATO nations, Australia, six NATO groups, nine US organizations, and representatives of the commercial space industry participated. One of the takeaways from the game was a recognition of the need for all countries and organizations to develop coordination and cooperation mechanisms that set standards and guidelines in the area of Space Situational Awareness (SSA), which often means others adopting US Air Force standards. The post-game report noted that "[t]he challenges of developing the right channels of cooperation during an on-going operation is time sensitive and risky."[38] The competing needs of acting quickly in a high-risk environment while dealing with the multiple challenges of a fast-moving situation have become a recurring theme in even the unclassified space wargaming reports.

For the 2015 wargame, some 175 military and civilian experts from various US government agencies as well as representatives from Australia, Canada, and the United Kingdom participated. Though the results are classified, the annual press releases do provide insight.

> As the wargame unfolded, a regional crisis quickly escalated, partly because of the interconnectedness of a multi-domain fight involving a capable adversary. The wargame participants emphasized the challenges in containing horizontal escalation once space control capabilities are employed to achieve limited national objectives.[39]

In other words, events spiraled rapidly.

Prudence requires that based on past analyses, simulations, and even statements by warfighters, it must be assumed events could and would likely escalate rapidly and dreadfully in space warfare. Alternatively, if it is to be assumed that limited space war is possible and adversaries would understand and agree to US expectations for non-escalatory responses, then taking steps to assure that other countries clearly understand and agree to those US assumptions is a necessary component of that approach. That requires dialogue and actions not currently being pursued with the same vigor as war plans. Yet the complications of space dialogue and space arms control are no less challenging than the complications of the inevitability school.

## Weapons in Space

A corollary question to whether space warfare is inevitable is that of whether weapons in space are inevitable. Space has been militarized at least since Wernher Von Braun and Walter Dornberger launched the first V-2 rocket at Pennemünde in Northern Germany. But the Rubicon of space weapons has yet to be "officially" crossed, at least under arms. The problem with differentiating *de jure* and *de facto* weaponization, however, is in defining space weapons.

Sometimes making the differentiation is easy. The "Rods From God" concept that *Popular Science* covered in 2004 would clearly be a space weapon—an orbiting platform capable of dropping tungsten rods to earth at hypersonic velocities to vaporize targets on terrestrial targets.[40] But in most instances, because most space technology is dual-use, intent is the only questionable issue.

In 2013 and 2014, for example, four Russian space launches drew the interest of the Pentagon, as Secure World Foundation technical analyst Brian Weeden explained.

> Three of the launches placed small Russian military satellites into LEO [low Earth orbit]; two of those satellites have conducted RPO [rendezvous and proximity operations] activities with Russian rocket states, and one appears to have "bumped" into the rocket stage near which it was maneuvering. The fourth launch was a Russian military satellite to geostationary Earth orbit (GSO). In the one year since its launch, the satellite has moved several times to different positions in the GSO belt of activities.[41]

While RPO activities can be benign, they also provide a destructive ASAT capability. Missile defense technology can also be ambiguous as to intent.

In November 2015, Russia reportedly tested an anti–satellite missile called Nudol[42] under the guise of a missile defense test. No debris was reported from an impact, so Moscow was officially able to maintain its missile defense pretense by virtue of ambiguity. Using ballistic missile technology to shoot down a failing satellite makes questions of capability less ambiguous and likely heightens questions regarding intent. That happened in 2008 when the United States executed Operation Burnt Frost only months after the 2007 Chinese ASAT test.

Whether through serendipitous coincidence or conscious design, the United States had the opportunity in February 2008 to use a modified version of the Navy's Aegis missile defense system for a "one-time mission"[43] to destroy a malfunctioning US satellite (USA 193) as it fell back to Earth carrying half a ton of toxic hydrazine fuel.[44] The timing of the shoot-down added to speculation that a public health risk from the hydrazine (the official US justification) may not have been the only reason, or even the real reason, the United States decided the satellite had to be destroyed. There was speculation that this was a chest-thumping display for China or action to assure that no pieces of the falling satellite large enough to be technologically valuable ended up in Chinese hands.[45] The latter suggestion was fueled by scientific risk calculations. MIT professor Geoffrey Forden and his colleagues calculated that, based on the amount of pressure on the tank during re-entry being 50 times the gravitational force on Earth, the chances of the toxic gas making it to Earth were near zero.[46] MIT astrophysicist Jonathan McDowell extended those calculations, commenting on what might happen if the satellite overcame the odds against making it through the atmosphere: "The chances the hydrazine will land within 100 yards of someone if the tank makes it through Earth's atmosphere are … about 2 in 100," and "if people just walk away from it, they won't be harmed."[47] Nevertheless, the shoot-down occurred, and it was successful.

The *Washington Post* heralded the carefully controlled operation, which successfully minimized the amount of space debris created, as demonstrating that "the Pentagon has a new weapon in its arsenal—an anti-satellite missile adapted from the nation's missile defense program."[48] The *Los Angeles Times* credited the hit with bolstering "the credibility of America's long-troubled missile defense system,"[49] while abroad, fears and doubts about America's intentions for missile defense heightened. An article in the UK *Independent*, for example, stated that, "almost nobody believes the public health rationale offered for the missile strike."[50] The ESA's Jules Verne Automatic Transfer Vehicle (ATV) re-entered the atmosphere in September 2008[51] carrying even more hydrazine than USA 193, but with little fanfare or health concerns, further implying that hydrazine was not the real justification for Burnt Frost. Whatever the intent,[52] Operation Burnt Frost clearly demonstrated the prowess and multifaceted capabilities of US missile defense technology, for both offense and defensive purposes, to the rest of the world. The ambiguity created by the overwhelmingly dual-use nature of space technology worked in favor of the United States in this instance.

Arms control talks have been challenged at best—more often, simply stifled—by the difficulty in defining dual-use space technology as weapons. Supporters of the "high ground" and "inevitability" schools contend that until space weapons can be defined, talks regarding limiting, prohibiting, or otherwise regulating space weapons are pointless. In November 2015, Deputy Assistant Secretary of State Frank Rose reiterated the difficulty in defining space weapons, thus presenting a presumably insurmountable challenge to space arms control efforts.[53] Nevertheless, many analysts have tried to define space weapons only to be countered with—annoyingly but correctly—confounding "what if" questions, mostly focused on capability versus purpose. The Chinese SY-7 satellite, the Russian Object 2014-28E, and the US XSS-11 are all maneuverable, giving them the capability to be weapons if used to ram into another space asset, though perhaps that is not their official purpose.

Defining space weapons has almost become a cottage industry over the years. A chronological look at a sampling of attempts reveals the difficulties yet to be unraveled. In 1999, Air Force Major David Ziegler defined a space weapon simply as "any system that directly works to defeat space assets from terrestrial- or space-based locations or terrestrial-based targets from space."[54] But what does "directly works" mean? That phrase leaves room for debate regarding what is and is not included. In 2003, Bruce DeBlois defined a space weapon as "that which is built with destructive intent to be used in a terrestrial-to-space, space-to-space or space-to-terrestrial capacity."[55] That definition requires a determination of intent, which is difficult or impossible because of the dual-use nature of most space technology. In 2005, Michael Krepon and Michael Katz-Hyman wrote:

> We define space weapons and offensive space warfare initiatives as terrestrially-based devices specifically designed and flight-tested to physically attack, impair or destroy objects in space, or space-based devices designed and flight-tested to attack, impair or destroy objects in space or on earth.[56]

Here as well, the phrase "specifically designed and flight-tested" toward use as a weapon leaves room for varying interpretations.

Russia and China attempted to define space weapons in their 2008 draft treaty proposal on Prevention of the Placement of Weapons in Outer Space (PPWT).

> The term "weapon in outer space" means any device placed in outer space, based on any physical principle, which has been specially produced or converted to destroy, damage or disrupt the normal functioning of objects in outer space, on the Earth or in the Earth's atmosphere, or to eliminate a population or components of the biosphere which are important to human existence or inflict damage on them.[57]

That definition omits all terrestrially based systems, such as China tested in 2007.

Canadian space analyst and diplomat Phil Baines later proposed the following: "A device based on any physical principle, specifically designed or modified, to injure or kill a person, irreparably damage or destroy an object, or render any place unusable."[58] If a system wasn't "specifically designed or modified" as a weapon, but is nevertheless used as one, does it fit within this definition?

Erik Seedhouse offered perhaps the simplest definition in his 2010 book: "Any system whose use destroys or damages objects in or from space."[59] However, since the word "object" is used, the definition does not specify whether damage must be permanent or whether it must be physical damage as opposed to, for example, damage to software. The loopholes in space weapon definitions seem endless, especially when including non-kinetic damage or destruction such as jamming.

Beyond definitions, issues with jamming are also difficult to deal with due to often self-inflicted wounds and technical abnormalities. In 2015, there were over 260 cases of US signals being jammed between the satellite and the ground station. According to Gen. Hyten, it is improbable that any of those were adversarial and, more likely, were caused by US radio or radar transmissions unintentionally causing interference.[60] In 2010, Intelsat officials announced that a Galaxy 15, C–Band telecommunications satellite had gone out of control in a geostationary orbit.[61] It was quickly dubbed a zombie satellite because controllers couldn't switch it off and it refused to die on its own. Although the incident raised concerns about unintentional electromagnetic interference,[62] this was prevented through the quick collaboration of five international COMSAT operators, demonstrating the need for trust and cooperation. Both cases highlight the potential for mishap, misperception, and miscalculation regarding incidents in space, which can trigger an action from one country to another.

Definitional difficulties are not likely to be overcome with a lucky stroke of a pen, nor are all technical issues likely to be overcome. What has been shown by inherent technical issues and the unsuccessful quest for a definition of a space weapon over decades is that perhaps a different approach to space arms control is needed.

## Chinese Intentions

The "ahooga moment" for China regarding the advantages of military space capabilities, and the technology gap developing between the United States and other countries, was the 1990–91 Gulf War. Then Air Force Chief of Staff Merrill McPeak referred to that war as "the first space war." There, for the first time, space systems were integrated with terrestrial systems as highly effective force multipliers with significant positive impact on mission effectiveness. The use of GPS was particularly important in Desert Storm because of the terrain with few distinguishable landmarks where forces would operate.

> GPS provided real-time, passive navigation updates to virtually every weapon system in theater. Planes, helicopters, tanks, ships, cruise missiles—even trucks used to deliver food to the front—relied on GPS receivers to precisely establish their position, speed and altitude (for aircraft).[63]

The demand for GPS receivers was such that, initially, demand outstripped availability, supply being held up by normal production times and government acquisition red tape. This resulted, in some cases, in commercial receivers being mailed to troops by their families and soldiers writing contractors directly for receivers.

Without GPS, Gen. Norman Schwarzkopf could never have pulled off the flanking assault on Iraqi forces that proved decisive. Schwarzkopf wanted to avoid a direct frontal assault on heavily dug-in Iraqi defenders, fearing thousands of allied casualties. But Schwarzkopf's tactical commanders questioned whether more than 150,000 troops, with all their equipment and 60 days of supplies, could be moved undetected over a desert with only rough roads. Schwarzkopf hoped that if his commanders doubted the veracity of the plan, the Iraqis would as well, and he knew that the Iraqis lacked the space reconnaissance to know it was actually underway. Using GPS, the allied forces pulled off what came to be known as Schwarzkopf's "Hail Mary" maneuver.

The Chinese watched attentively as coalition forces led by Americans roundly defeated the Iraqi army after a five-week aerial campaign and 100 hours of ground combat. Consequently, the People's Liberation Army (PLA) became determined to modernize from having troop size as its primary strength to being prepared to engage in "informationized" warfare in which troop size mattered much less. Over the next two decades, the Chinese military adopted information warfare concepts as appropriate to its own structure and doctrine, combining its own traditional tactics, Soviet military concepts, and doctrine learned from the United States to bring the Chinese military up the learning curve.[64]

There are differing American views on the intentions and successes of Chinese military modernization efforts and, subsequently, about the status and intentions of Chinese military space efforts.[65] While some are on a range, many are polarized along lines sometimes obliquely referred to as "dragon slayers" and "panda huggers," specifically applied to space as "space hawks" and "space doves." The characterization (perhaps intentionally) creates the impression that dragon slayers are strong and bravely fighting against evil forces, while panda huggers are naïve and weak. That aligns with conservative Washington characterizations of normalization of relations with Cuba as appeasement[66] and diplomacy and negotiation with Iran as weak.[67] More accurately, one group focuses on primarily military, primacist approaches to dealing with China, while the other favors a wider range of options.

The warning in the 2001 Rumsfeld report[68] of a potential "Space Pearl Harbor" and the inevitability of space warfare changed thinking not only in the United States but in China as well. It is likely not coincidental that it was in 2001 that the Chinese authors of their annual *The Science of Military Strategy* changed their view of space considerably from that presented in past editions; they "began to characterize space warfare as inevitable, and spent considerably more time assessing its role in future wars."[69] The Chinese made assumptions based on US rhetoric, and the United States made assumptions as well. Specifically, the assumption has prevailed in the United States that China intended to exploit US military reliance on space systems through asymmetric means, attacking US space systems.

American analysts have referred to American military reliance on its space systems as its "Achilles' Heel."[70] Carnegie Associate Ashley Tellis authored a 2007 analysis with the title *Punching the US Military's "Soft Ribs": China's Anti-Satellite Weapon Test in Strategic Perspective*, based on space being referenced as America's "soft ribs" in a Chinese propagandistic publication.[71] US national security space policy has been built around the assumption that China was building capabilities toward an asymmetric approach to countering otherwise overwhelming US forces.[72]

An alternative view of Chinese intentions was presented in 2014 in an assessment[73] of a 2003 Chinese PLA Second Artillery (now called the Rocket Force) text;[74] the assessment questioned whether asymmetric attack was indeed Chinese intent. The text being analysed was not intended for foreign or even domestic audiences; indeed, it was internally classified, so unlike many other non-authoritative sources referenced toward deciphering Chinese intent, it was not written with potential propagandistic value in mind. According to Gregory Kulacki, the author,

> The discussion of outer space in the Second Artillery text demonstrates that the PLA, like the U.S. military, places a high priority on maintaining normal functioning of these core military space capabilities in a time of conflict.
>
> [...]
>
> China was not pursuing an asymmetric strategy in space.[75]

The analysis further states that there was no mention of ASAT operations in the text. Rather, the text indicated that China was attempting to mirror US use in order to achieve the force enhancement advantages gained by them in space, demonstrated by the United States in the 1990–91 Gulf War. Similarly, in a March 2016 Congressional Research Service report on the Chinese military, it was stated that the PLA sees space assets "as a major force multiplier for modern military operations."[76]

If force enhancement advantages are the intent of Chinese military space efforts, then Chinese investments in space technology and its military applications are intended to narrow the technology gap between China and the United States rather than seeking to exploit asymmetry in space, just as fear of a technology gap drove Europe into space earlier. Space development has consistently been stated in Chinese white papers as part of overall national economic development plans.[77]

According to Kulacki's analysis, China seeks to use military space primarily for force enhancement protection of its missiles, which China considers to be strategic assets and essential to the eventual outcome of a conflict.[78] Kulacki suggested that the often-cited Chinese word *shashoujian*, or "assassin's mace," is confused with the similarly sounding word *sashoujian*, meaning "trump card," and states that the latter should be considered in conjunction with Chinese reliance on missiles. In that context, it would reference the ability to deliver

> a decisive thrust at just the right moment in just the right place that a technologically or materially outmatched opponent can use to prevail over a stronger adversary. It connotes an ability to prevail in a difficult situation by using skill or strategy over superior armaments or technology. It is an attribute, not a particular weapon.[79]

Thus, it is a strategy for ending a conflict, not starting one.

US satellites that can find these Chinese missiles are considered a threat. Rather than attacking other countries' satellites, Chinese strategy focuses on hiding their own missiles through camouflage, concealment, and deception. Under this interpretation of Chinese intent, US satellites are vulnerable to being fooled, not to physical attack.[80] Equally important, Kulacki's analysis suggests that China values its satellites and that "the Second Artillery's reliance on military space systems will necessarily increase, not decrease."[81] If that is the case, Chinese intent to use an

ASAT to exploit an asymmetric advantage, thereby putting its own satellites at risk, may be significantly lower than currently characterized by the United States. It also puts into question why China is clearly working to develop ASAT weapons.

The 2007 Chinese ASAT test was the culmination of a program that began in the 1980s when the United States and Russia were still testing their own ASAT technology. That it kept a slow pace for decades could be considered as evidence that China was attempting to avoid a technology gap, which is very different than initiation of a crash program toward development of an asset to be urgently incorporated into tactics. The General Armaments Division (GAD) of the PLA developed the technology tested in 2007. The GAD is responsible for technology and weapons development; it is composed largely of engineers. When engineers (in any country) build something, they want to test it. So not surprisingly, the GAD developers were anxious to test their technology and demonstrate success, and they likely downplayed or mischaracterized to their superiors the debris that would be created by a high-altitude LEO kinetic test. Assuming the developers would also want to maximize their chances of success, hitting a moribund satellite traveling in a predictable orbit would be cheaper and easier than attempting to hit a missile in flight.

Nevertheless, the Chinese are nothing if not cautious in their approach to technology development and testing. The 2007 impact was not their first test. They had previously launched two interceptors without an interception, whether by intent or failure, and they knew that the United States had the ability to observe those launches. The United States said nothing in response to those tests—perhaps because it did not want to reveal its observation capabilities, perhaps because it wanted to observe Chinese impact capabilities (which were more advanced than expected), or perhaps for some other, political, reason. But the degree of international condemnation that followed the impact was clearly unanticipated, leaving the Chinese politically unprepared to respond for 12 days. The tyranny of distance, the ambiguity of dual-use technology, and a plethora of other obstacles make a conclusive analysis of Chinese intentions in space impossible. It is more clearly known *what* China has done to build its space capabilities than *why*.

In 2015, China published a national military strategy that included the following reference to space:

> Outer space has become a commanding height in international strategic competition. Countries concerned are developing their space forces and instruments, and the first signs of weaponization of outer space have appeared. China has all along advocated the peaceful use of outer space, opposed the weaponization of and arms race in outer space, and taken an active part in international space cooperation. China will keep abreast of the dynamics of outer space, deal with security threats and challenges in that domain, and secure its assets to serve its national economic and social development, and maintain outer space security.[82]

China considers space as having both a security component and a development component.

Additionally, and importantly, space capabilities provide the Chinese leadership with credibility and self-confidence. The self-confidence point is addressed in a 2012 Brookings Institution report titled *Addressing US-China Strategic Distrust*, co-authored by prominent American China specialist Kenneth Lieberthal and prominent Chinese scholar/official Wang Jisi.[83] Wang Jisi's narrative includes reference to the Chinese space program. "China's outer space projects and advanced weaponry have also contributed to Beijing's self-confidence. Chinese leaders do not credit these successes to the United States or to the US-led world order."[84] From this statement, it can be inferred that China has suffered from a lack of self-confidence. China's near pathological opacity has been evidenced in its reluctance to let anyone get too close a look at its spacecraft or facilities, which relative to the United States, are still quite spartan. While a lack of self-confidence within any person or country leadership can result in overly aggressive, compensating actions, too much self-confidence can cross the line to hubris and lead to bravado. China must be encouraged into being a responsible member of the international community, likely through areas of self-interest.

China has made major advancements in its space capabilities over the past 20 years. Most notably, it has an expansive, ambitious human spaceflight program that has garnered international attention. China's most publicized space activities are those related to the Shenzhou human spaceflight and the robotic Chang'e lunar programs.[85]

Originally known simply as Project 921, the Shenzhou program was approved as a three-step plan for human spaceflight in 1992. Contrary to its normal proclivity, China has been relatively open about the programmatic goals and accomplishments because it has recognized that in order to get the publicity and recognition(-cum-prestige and geopolitical influence) it seeks, it must be open. China has stuck to the three-step plan announced in 1992: send humans into orbit, demonstrate advanced capabilities through a small laboratory (Tiangong), and finally, build a large space station. The Tiangong spacecrafts are not space stations intended for long-term use or to be permanently manned, but to form the basis for a small laboratory to test technologies similar to those tested by the United States during the Gemini program, including rendezvous, docking, and life support. Tiangong will host manned missions later in its evolution. At 8.5 tons, Tiangong is smaller than both Skylab (about 80 tons) and the 30-ton space station China has always planned as the culmination of Project 921.

The prototype Tiangong-1 (Heavenly Palace) was used to conduct experiments in conjunction with the Shenzhou 8-10 spacecraft. Tiangong-2 was to be a marginally improved version of Tiangong-1, and it was originally scheduled to be launched in 2014. That date was delayed when it became clear that more than marginal changes needed to be made in order to achieve the intended mission goals, including docking with a cargo vehicle. Consequently, it appears that expanded capabilities planned, originally, for a Tiangong-3 spacecraft are to be incorporated into a new version of Tiangong-2, scheduled for launch in September 2016; though there still seems to be some ambiguity regarding final Chinese plans. What has been announced by Chinese officials is that a crew of two persons will live on Tiangong-2 for 30 days.[86]

China is executing the robust Shenzhou human spaceflight program at a pace simultaneously incremental and accelerated: incremental in following almost the same timeline milestones as the United States did during Mercury, Gemini, and Apollo; and accelerated in that it accomplished these milestones with fewer flights.[87] For example, between Yang Liwei's first-ever manned flight in 2003 and Zhai Zhigang's spacewalk in 2008, there was only one other Shenzhou program flight. Compare that to the number of flights that occurred during the Mercury (six crewed flights) and Gemini (ten crewed flights) programs and clearly the United States executed more launches, though with smaller steps taken by each. Shenzhou 9, launched in June 2012, included China's first female taikonaut, Liu Yang.

Although sometimes presented by the media as fact, China does not yet have an approved human lunar spaceflight program. Such a program is under discussion. China currently does have an approved human spaceflight program and an approved robotic lunar program. Together, these two programs are developing and testing the component parts for a human lunar spaceflight program. It is unlikely that China will take the step of announcing such a program until it completes its large space station, leaving a lunar focus until the 2025/2030 time frame.

Chang'e is the mythical Chinese Moon goddess for whom the robotic Chinese Lunar Exploration Program vehicle is named. Chang'e 1 was launched in 2007 and operated until 2009; it demonstrated China's capability both to put satellites into lunar orbit and to return imagery. Chang'e 2 was launched in 2010. After flying in a closer-to-the-surface lunar orbit and providing imagery with a high-resolution camera—pictures essential for an anticipated soft landing for Chang'e 3 mission in 2013—Chang'e 2 left lunar orbit for the Earth-Sun L2 Lagrangian Point in order to test Chinese tracking and control capabilities; these capabilities are also valuable to the military. Using a nonmilitary program to test technology of potential value to the military is not exclusive to China. The US Clementine spacecraft in the 1990s was a joint program between the Ballistic Missile Defense Organization (BMDO) and the National Aeronautic and Space Administration (NASA) to test BMDO technology by mapping the Moon. Prior to China, only the United States and the ESA had visited L2. Chang'e 2 then set out for an extended mission to asteroid 4179 Toutatis.

Chang'e 3 was launched in December 2013 and became the first lunar soft lander since the Soviet Luna 24 spacecraft in 1974. Chang'e 3 carried with it the lunar rover Yutu, or Jade Rabbit. In February 2014, the Chinese and international press followed the success, demise, and revival of the anthropomorphized rover with great interest. Chang'e 5-T1 (formerly Chang'e 4, as a backup to Chang'e 3) was launched and returned to Earth in October 2014, conducting atmospheric re-entry tests as a precursor to a planned Chang'e 5 sample return mission, scheduled for 2017.

Beyond its human spaceflight and exploration plans, China is also expanding its military space capabilities in all areas of command, control, communications, computers, intelligence, surveillance, and reconnaissance (C4ISR) that have proved critical in enhancing terrestrial force effectiveness and in space weapons. While there are still significant gaps in China's capabilities in areas such as surveillance, Beijing has supplemented its needs through purchases from such providers as Spot Image (Europe), Infoterra (Europe), MDA (Canada), Antrix (India), GeoEye (United States), and Digital Globe (United States).[88] It is not just a globalized world, but a globalized space industry. Commercial access to space technology and space-based information is widely available to China while it develops its own capabilities. Conversely, China is also vulnerable to the other side of space being globalized and privatized. The commercial satellite imagery company ImageSat International first disclosed China's placement of surface-to-air missiles in the South China Sea.[89] China has a regional (and expanding) satellite navigation system, ocean-monitoring satellites, a data relay satellite, synthetic aperture radar (SAR) satellites, and improved communication and remote sensing satellites.

But as analyst Kevin Pollpeter has pointed out, China seems to not yet have an official space doctrine and most of what Chinese authors write about in terms of "space control" is aspirational, or assumed to be aspirational. Pollpeter states that integration of space into the PLA is part of China's development of an "informationalized force,"[90] which could either align with the idea of using space for force enhancement—rather than taking an asymmetric approach to dealing with US space advantages—or mirror US aspirations for dominance. Chinese development of its military space capabilities aligns with its military modernization plans in general but these capabilities are also in line with the parameters for a classic security dilemma[91] with the United States, which would create subsequent problems regarding cooperation between the countries.

With regard to aspirations for space control, which Pollpeter stated as the nearly unanimous aim in the multiple sources he consulted, Chinese military goals in space appear remarkably reflective of US goals; that is, the ability to freely use space and to deny its use to adversaries. Both countries clearly consider access to space as essential to their security. But the challenges of the increasingly internationalized and privatized nature of space, the tyranny of physics, offense being cheaper and technically easier than defense, and the limited budgets that together made "dominance" and "control" beyond the reach of the United States during the George W. Bush years hold true today for all countries, including China.

Pollpeter's analysis states that Chinese writers see the need to "develop ASAT weapons to paralyze an adversary by debilitating its C4ISR network."[92] Whether or not the Chinese could actually achieve debilitation of the American C4ISR network is questionable. While an attack on one or more US satellites would unquestionably degrade US force capabilities, by how much is another matter.

The inevitability of conflict in space has been widely assumed and accepted by the military. That assumption, however, increasingly seems to be creating a self-fulfilling prophecy. While "deter, defend, defeat" rolls off the tongue easily, so does mishap, misinterpretation, and miscalculation—all are relevant to potential space events that could act as that trigger. Therefore, consideration of what the United States is doing with regard to each element of "deter, defend, defeat," is warranted to move toward slowing or abating the security dilemma.

## Notes

1 Ronald Reagan, Commencement Address, Eureka College, May 9, 1982: www. reaganfoundation.org/reagan-quotes-detail.aspx?tx=2096

2 Graham Allison, "The Thucydides Trap: are the US and China headed for war?" *The Atlantic*, September 24, 2015: www.theatlantic.com/international/archive/2015/09/united-states-china-war-thucydides-trap/406756/

3 Thucydides, *The History of the Peloponnesian War*, written 431 BCE, trans. Richard Crawley. http://classics.mit.edu/Thucydides/pelopwar.1.first.html

4 Cited in Allison, "The Thucydides Trap."

5 Allison, "The Thucydides Trap."

6 John Stoessinger, *Why Nations Go To War*, St. Martin's Press, New York, 1971.

7 See, for example, Bruce M. DeBlois, "Space sanctuary, a viable national strategy," *Airpower Journal*, 12(4), Winter 1998, 42–57; James Oberg, *Space Power Theory*, US Air Force Academy, Colorado Springs, CO, 1999.

8 Oberg, *Space Power Theory*, p. 146.

9 Kevin Pollpeter, "Space, the new domain: space operations and Chinese military reforms," Presented at Reshaping the People's Liberation Army since the 18th Party Congress, conference organized by the China Program and Military Transformations Program, Institute of Defense and Strategic Studies, S. Rajaratnam School of International Studies, Nanyang Technological University, October 1–2, 2015, p. 3.

10 Joan Johnson-Freese, *Transitioning to a Space and Air Force: Moving Beyond Rhetoric*, INSS-sponsored paper, 1998. www.dtic.mil/dtic/tr/fulltext/u2/a367211.pdf

11 Kevin Pollpeter and Jonathan Ray, "The conceptual evolution of space operations as seen in the science of military strategy," in *China's Evolving Space Strategy*, ed. Joe McReynolds, The Jamestown Foundation, Washington, DC, forthcoming.

12 Captain David C. Hardesty (US Navy), "Space-based weapons: long-term strategic implications and alternatives," *Naval War College Review*, 58(2), Spring 2005, 45–68: see pp. 46–8. https://www.usnwc.edu/getattachment/5caf64d6-6ffc-4c00-b934-6cc9c02b77af/Space-Based-Weapons--Long-Term-Strategic-Implicati.aspx

13 Donald Rumsfeld chaired two important committees related to space prior to assuming the position of Secretary of Defense, both sometimes referred to as the Rumsfeld Report: the Space Report which came out in 2001, and the report of the Commission to Assess the Ballistic Missile Threat, issued in 1998.

14 Commission to Assess United States National Security Space Management and Organization, *Report of the Commission to Assess United States National Security Space Management and Organization, Executive Summary*, Pursuant to Public Law 106-65, January 11, 2001. p. 10. www.dod.gov/pubs/spaceintro.pdf

15 Commission to Assess United States National Security Space Management and Organization, p. 8.

16 Colonel John E. Hyten, "A sea of peace or a theater of war: dealing with the inevitable conflict in space," *Air & Space Power Journal*, 16(3), Fall 2002, 78–92. www.airpower. maxwell.af.mil/airchronicles/apj/apj02/fal02/hyten.html

17 Gen. John E. Hyten, Keynote speech, Small Satellite Conference 2015, Utah State University, August 10, 2015. www.afspc.af.mil/About-Us/Leadership-Speeches/ Speeches/Display/Article/731705/small-satellite-2015-keynote-speech

18 Cited in Jennifer Hlad, "Space rules of engagement," *Air Force Magazine*, March 1, 2016. www.airforcemag.com/drarchive/pages/2016/march%202016/march%2001%2 02016/space-rules-of-engagement.aspx

19 Cited in "State's Bolton says US favors treaty to ban fissile materials," *IIP Digital* September 13, 2004. http://iipdigital.usembassy.gov/st/english/texttrans/2004/09/200 40913160101sjhtrop0.2767298.html#axzz3sEGFYpxa

20 Frank A. Rose, "Using diplomacy to advance long-term sustainability and security of the outer space environment," Remarks at the International Symposium on Ensuring Stable Use of Outer Space: Enhancing Space Security and Resiliency, Tokyo, Japan, March 3, 2016. www.state.gov/t/avc/rls/253947.htm

21 Ambassador Roger G. Harrison, *Space and Verification, Volume 1: Policy Implications*, Eisenhower Center for Space and Defense Studies. http://swfound.org/media/37101/ space%20and%20verification%20vol%201%20-%20policy%20implications.pdf

22 Ambassador Roger G. Harrison, *Space and Verification*, under "Key points."

23 Erik Seedhouse, *The New Space Race: China vs. USA*, Praxis, Chichester, UK, 2010, p. 80.

24 Eleni Ekmecktsioglou, "How hypersonic missiles push America and China toward war," *The National Interest*, June 28, 2015. http://nationalinterest.org/feature/ how-hypersonic-missiles-push-america-china-towards-war-13205

25 DeBlois, "Space sanctuary."

26 Oberg, *Space Power Theory*, p. 148.

27 Elbridge Colby, *From Sanctuary to Battlefield: A Framework for a U.S. Defense and Deterrence Strategy for Space*, January 2016, Center for a New American Security, Washington, DC, p. 7.

28 Cited in Mike Gruss, "During Silicon Valley trip, Carter puts $22 billion price tag on Pentagon space spending," *SpaceNews*, March 2, 2016. http://spacenews.com/ during-silicon-valley-trip-carter-puts-22-billion-price-tag-on-pentagon-space-spending/

29 "The European Space Agency Director – in interview," *ESA*, February 10, 2014. www.esa.int/About_Us/Jean-Jacques_Dordain/ The_European_Space_Agency_director_general_in_interview

30 Amy Svitak, "French military space program spending," *Aviation Week & Space Technology*, December 16, 2015. http://aviationweek.com/space/french-spending-military-space-programs-rising-2016

31 "Schriever Wargame concludes," *Air Force Space Command*, February 18, 2015. www. schriever.af.mil/news/story.asp?id=123439473

32 "Air Force gains insight from first wargame," *Space Daily*, January 29, 2001. www. spacedaily.com/news/milspace-01d.html

33 Seedhouse, *The New Space Race*, p. 223.

34 US Representative Terry Everett, "Building the political consensus to deter attacks on our nation's space systems," *High Frontier*, 5(4), August 2009, 3–8: p. 3. www.afspc. af.mil/shared/media/document/AFD-101020-017.pdf

35 Everett, "Building the political consensus to deter attacks," p. 4.

36 Colby, *From Sanctuary to Battlefield*, pp. 17–18.

37 Ambassador Lincoln P. Broomfield, "A space doctrine for soldier, scientist, and citizen: what it will take to secure the space domain," *High Frontier*, 5(4), August 2009, 17–22: pp. 20–21. www.afspc.af.mil/shared/media/document/AFD-101020-017.pdf

38 *Schriever Wargame 2012 International: HQ SACT Report*, p. iv. www.act.nato.int/images/ stories/events/2012/sw12i/sw12i_report.pdf

39 "Schriever Wargame concludes," *Air Force Print News Today*, February 18, 2015. www. schriever.af.mil/News/Article-Display/Article/735507/schriever-wargame-concludes

40 Eric Adams, "Is this what war will come to?" *Popular Science*, May 12, 2004. www. popsci.com/military-aviation-space/article/2004-05/what-war-will-come

41 Brian Weeden, "Dancing in the dark redux: recent Russian proximity and rendezvous operations in space," *The Space Review*, October 5, 2015. www.thespacereview.com/ article/2839/1

42 Patrick Tucker, "USAF stands up Space Mission Force to counter Russia, China," *Defense One*, February 1, 2016. www.defenseone.com/technology/2016/02/usaf-stands-space-mission-force-counter-russia-china/125568/

43 "One-time mission: Operation Burnt Frost," *Missile Defense Agency*. www.mda.mil/ system/aegis_one_time_mission.html

44 Marc Kaufman and Josh White, "Spy satellite downing shows a new US weapon capability," *Washington Post*, February 22, 2008, A03.

45 Associated Press, "Pentagon: smashed satellite debris poses no danger," *Fox News*, February 28, 2008. www.foxnews.com/story/2008/02/21/pentagon-smashed-satellite-debris-poses-no-danger.html

46 Cited in Associated Press, "Pentagon missile hits dying satellite," February 21, 2008. www.sptimes.com/2008/02/21/Worldandnation/Pentagon_missile_hits.shtml

47 Cited in ibid.

48 Kaufman and White, "Spy satellite downing shows a new US weapon capability."

49 Greg Miller, "Missile's Bull's Eye on Satellite Echoes Far, Experts Say," *Los Angeles Times*, Feb. 22, 2008.

50 Andrew Gumbel, "Mystery of the toxic satellite," *The Independent*, February 17, 2008.

51 Tariq Malik, "What happens when satellites fall," *Space.com*, January 23, 2009. www. space.com/6349-satellites-fall.html

52 James Oberg refuted claims that the shoot-down was for any purpose other than public safety in "Down in flames," *The New Atlantis*, Spring 2009. www.thenewatlantis.com/ publications/down-in-flames. That refutation was countered as well by Yousaf Butt, "On the technical study of USA 193's fuel tank reentry," *The Space Review*, September 2, 2008. www.thespacereview.com/article/1200/1

53 Frank A. Rose, Remarks at the Third ARF Workshop on Space Security, ASEAN Regional Forum, Beijing, China, November 30, 2015. www.state.gov/t/avc/ rls/2015/250231.htm

54 David W. Ziegler, "Safe heavens: military strategy and space sanctuary," in *Beyond the Paths of Heaven*, ed. Bruce M. DeBlois, Air University Press, Maxwell Airforce Base,

Alabama, 1999, 185–245: p. 191. www.au.af.mil/au/awc/space/books/deblois/ch04.pdf

55 Bruce M. DeBlois, "The advent of space weapons," *Astropolitics*, 1(1), Spring 2003, 29–53: p. 30.

56 Michael Krepon and Michael Katz-Hyman, "Space weapons and proliferation," *Nonproliferation Review*, 12(2), July 2005, 323–41.

57 Russian Federation and People's Republic of China, Draft Treaty on the Prevention of the Placement of Weapons in Outer Space, the Threat or Use of Force against Outer Space Objects, Article 1(c). https://documents-dds-ny.un.org/doc/UNDOC/GEN/G08/604/02/PDF/G0860402.pdf?OpenElement

58 Cited by Michael Krepon, "What is a space weapon?" *ArmsControlWonk*, March 18, 2010. www.armscontrolwonk.com/archive/402665/what-is-a-space-weapon/

59 Seedhouse, *The New Space Race*, p. 81.

60 Cited in Sydney J. Freeberg, Jr., "US jammed own satellites 261 times. What if enemy did?" *Breaking Defense*, December 2, 2015. http://breakingdefense.com/2015/12/us-jammed-own-satellites-261-times-in-2015-what-if-an-enemy-tried/?utm_content=buffer0ba87&utm_medium=social&utm_source=facebook.com&utm_campaign=buffer

61 Peter B. de Selding, "Runaway zombie satellite Galaxy 15 continues to pose interference threat," *Space.com*, October 15, 2010. www.space.com/9340-runaway-zombie-satellite-galaxy-15-continues-pose-interference-threat.html

62 In an unexpected twist, the satellite sprung back to life after several months adrift. Denise Chow, "'Zombie' satellite comes back to life," *Space.com*, December 29, 2010. www.space.com/9677-galaxy15-zombie-satellite-life.html

63 Thomas S. Moorman, "Space: a new strategic frontier," in *The Future of Airpower in the Aftermath of the Gulf War,* ed. Richard Schultz, Jr. and Robert Pfaltzgraff, Jr., Air University Press, Maxwell Air Force Base, Alabama, 1992, 235–49: p. 241.

64 Larry M. Wortzel, *The People's Liberation Army and Information Warfare*, Strategic Studies Institute and US Army War College Press, Carlisle, PA, March 2014. p. 1. www.strategicstudiesinstitute.army.mil/pdffiles/pub1191.pdf

65 James Clay Moltz, *Asia's Space Race*, Columbia University Press, New York, 2011. Andrew S. Erickson, "Eyes in the sky," *Proceedings*, 136(4), April 2010, 36–41; Gregory Kulacki and Jeffrey Lewis, *A Place for One's Mat: China's Space Program, 1956–2003*, American Academy of Arts & Sciences, Cambridge, MA, 2009; Kevin Pollpeter, *Building the Future: China's Progress in Space Technology During the Tenth 5-Year Plan and the US Response,* Strategic Studies Institute, Carlisle, PA, 2008; Dean Cheng, "Prospects for China's military space efforts," in *Beyond the Straight*, ed. Roy Kamphausen, David Lai, and Andrew Scobell, Strategic Studies Institute, Carlisle, PA, 2008, 211–52; Wortzel, *The Chinese People's Liberation Army in Space Warfare*; Roger Handberg and Zhen Li, *Chinese Space Policy: A Study in Domestic and International Politics*, Routledge, Abingdon, 2007; Gregory P. Meltzer, "China in space: implications for US military," *Joint Force Quarterly*, 47, 2007; Kevin Pollpeter, "The Chinese view of space military operations," in *China's Revolution in Doctrinal Affairs*, ed. James Mulvenon and David Finkleman, CNA, Alexandria, VA, 2005, 329–69.

66 Katie Glueck and Seung Min Kim, "Republicans livid over Cuba talks," *Politico*, December 17, 2014. www.politico.com/story/2014/12/marco-rubio-says-cuba-talks-are-absurd-113639; Herbert London, "Obama's overture to Cuba adds to his record of

appeasement," *Washington Times*, December 30, 2014. www.washingtontimes.com/news/2014/dec/30/herbert-london-obama-appeasement-of-enemies-in-ira/

67  Thomas Joscelyn, "Obama's weak diplomacy with Iran," *The Weekly Standard*, November 7, 2014. www.weeklystandard.com/blogs/obama-s-weak-diplomacy-iran_818410.html

68  *Report of the Commission to Assess United States National Security Space Management and Organization.*

69  Pollpeter and Ray, "The conceptual evolution of space," p. 1.

70  James P. Finch, "Bringing space crisis stability down to earth," *Joint Force Quarterly*, January 2015, p. 16. http://ndupress.ndu.edu/JFQ/JointForceQuarterly76/BringingSpaceCrisisStabilityDowntoEarth.aspx

71  Ashley J. Tellis, *Punching the US Military's "Soft Ribs": China's Anti-Satellite Weapon Test in Strategic Perspective*, Carnegie Endowment for International Peace, Policy Brief 51, June 2007. http://carnegieendowment.org/files/pb_51_tellis_final.pdf

72  Forrest Morgan, *Deterrence and First-Strike Stability in Space: A Preliminary Assessment*, RAND, Santa Monica, CA, 2010, p. 1.

73  Gregory Kulacki, *An Authoritative Source on China's Military Space Strategy*, Union of Concerned Scientists, Cambridge, MA, March 2014. www.ucsusa.org/sites/default/files/legacy/assets/documents/nwgs/China-s-Military-Space-Strategy.pdf

74  The analyzed text is a military textbook published in 2003 by the General Command of the PLA titled *The Science of Second Artillery Operations.*

75  Kulacki, *An Authoritative Source on China's Military Space Strategy*, pp. 1–2.

76  Ian E. Reinhart, *The Chinese Military: Overview and Issues for Congress*, Congressional Research Service, Washington, DC, March 24, 2016, p. 17. https://www.fas.org/sgp/crs/row/R44196.pdf

77  Marc Boucher, "China releases white paper – China's space activities in 2011," *SpaceRef*, December 29, 2011. www.spaceref.com/news/viewnews.html?id=1598

78  Kulacki, *An Authoritative Source on China's Military Space Strategy*, p. 7.

79  Ibid., p. 7.

80  Ibid., p. 5.

81  Ibid., p. 4.

82  China's Military Strategy, The State Council Information Office of the People's Republic of China, Beijing, May 2015, p. 10.

83  Kenneth Lieberthal and Wang Jisi, *Addressing US-China Strategic Distrust*, John L. Thornton China Center Monograph Series, Number 4, Brookings Institution, Washington, DC., March 2012.

84  Ibid, p. 9.

85  Much of the information on the Chinese Shenzhou and Chang'e programs was drawn from Joan Johnson-Freese, Testimony before the US-China Economic and Security Review Commission, February 18, 2015. www.uscc.gov/sites/default/files/Johnson%20Freese_Testimony.pdf

86  Morris Jones, "Moving in to Tiangong 2," *Space Daily*, March 2, 2016. www.spacedaily.com/reports/Moving_in_to_Tiangong_2_999.html

87  Brian Weeden, *Timeline of Human Spaceflight Programs*, Secure World Foundation Fact Sheet, updated September 7, 2012. http://swfound.org/media/90819/swf_human_space_programs_fact_sheet.pdf

88 Office of the Secretary of Defense, *Annual Report to Congress, Military and Security Developments Involving the People's Republic of China* 2010, Department of Defense, Washington, DC. www.defense.gov/Portals/1/Documents/pubs/2010_CMPR_Final. pdf

89 CBS/AP, "China: focus on light houses, not anti-aircraft missiles," *CBS News*, February 17, 2016. www.cbsnews.com/news/china-anti-aircraft-missiles-woody-island-parcels-south-china-sea/

90 Kevin Pollpeter, "PLA Space Doctrine," in *Chinese Aerospace Power*, ed. Andrew S. Erikson and Lyle J. Goldstein, China Maritime Studies Institute and Naval Institute Press, Carlisle, PA, 2011, 50–65.

91 Robert Jervis, "Cooperation under the security dilemma," *World Politics*, 30(2), January 1978, 167–214.

92 Pollpeter, "PLA Space Doctrine," p. 51.

# 4

# DETER, DEFEND, DEFEAT

Preventive war is like committing suicide out of fear of death.

Otto von Bismarck[1]

US government documents and official statements clearly state US intentions to "deter, defend against, and defeat aggression" in space. Space assets are critical to the civilian and military sectors and so a key national interest. However, while the phrase "deter, defend, defeat" has an easily remembered, jingoistic ring to it, whether all three words were carefully thought through before inclusion or whether they were selected largely for alliteration value is arguable. Whereas US efforts in the areas of defend and defeat are increasingly robust and muscular, US attention and commitment to deterrence by anything other than punishment appears increasingly thin.

## Deter

American economist, professor of national security, and game theorist Thomas Schelling presented concepts critical to space security in his seminal 1966 book *Arms and Influence*,[2] specifically deterrence and compellence—concepts often used subsequently with loose fidelity. Deterrence refers to preventing a change in the status quo, whereas compellence refers to causing a change;[3] so deterrence refers to stopping an action before it has occurred and compellence seeks to change behavior that has already started. Compellence is often more difficult; hence, trying to persuade countries against acquiring nuclear weapons before rather than after the fact.

In game theory, a player must have a clear goal in order to create a winning strategy to achieve the goal. With the goal in mind, player A can determine how best to persuade, including by coercion, player B to act in a manner suitable to player A. Circumstances make a significant difference, however—whether these involve total war (where annihilation of the opponent is the central aim) or, more likely, peacetime or limited war—as Thomas Christensen explains:

> In the world of coercive diplomacy, threats and assurances must be balanced through a process of clear and credible signaling, and enforceable bargains must be struck short of total defeat or victory for either side. Without credible threats, coercion is obviously ineffective. But what is less well understood is that coercion is also unlikely to be effective without simultaneously transmitted credible assurances that the threat is fully conditional upon the target's behavior and that the target's key security interests will not be harmed if it complies with the demands of those leveling the threats. Without receiving both threats and assurances in concert, the target of a coercive threat has little incentive to comply with the demands being made.[4]

Deterrence requires both threats and assurances. Threats of punishment alone are not just insufficient, but also potentially counterproductive. Therefore Christensen's points regarding goals, signaling, bargains, and assurances as related to deterrence in space deserve further scrutiny.

In the case of space security, the dual-use nature of space technology makes it difficult if not impossible to deter the development of, or compel the abandonment of, space technology that could be used as a weapon. That reality then raises several questions. What specific actions does the United States seek to deter? What bargains and assurances are being offered toward achieving US goals short of annihilation? What are the signals being sent as related to goals and assurances? It is unrealistic to expect countries to forego the use of space for both civilian and military purposes. So what does a responsible space player look like? If the United States provides the model, it appears that a responsible space player can have a missile defense program and a large military space program with a broad spectrum of capabilities, including ASAT capabilities. But that does not appear to be the case. Whatever the US expects of other countries, the tone of US space policy since 2013 is very different than that which was being officially conveyed by the Obama Administration previously.

In 2011, US Deputy Secretary of Defense William J. Lynn III described the US approach to the space environment in *The Washington Quarterly*; while the environment was described as congested, contested, and competitive, Lynn said the Pentagon was "taking a hard look at how its own policies can help foster a more cooperative space environment."[5] He went on to say: "we can no longer rely solely on the threat of retaliation to protect space systems from attack. We must expand our traditional concepts of deterrence. Accordingly, the National Security Space Strategy outlines the multilayered approach we will take to deter aggression."[6] First among the initiatives listed as important to the multilayered approach was an international space code of conduct to promote international norms of responsible behavior. Those norms would have clearly stated what signatory countries were looking for other countries to do and how it would conduct itself. It is reasonable to assume these norms would link to the US space goals discussed in Chapter 1: security, sustainability, free access, and stability.

Based on statements by Gen. Hyten and others, avoiding the creation of space debris is considered a more specific yet integral part of those goals. Beyond that, however, the goals become murkier. If space control seeks to provide freedom of action in space for friendly forces while, when directed, denying it to an adversary, then the "free access" guarantees of the Outer Space Treaty appear subject to erosion. Without a clear statement, or code, it is unclear what it is exactly that the United States does not want China (or Russia, or other countries) to do, or not do. To date, nothing China has done in space has been beyond the permissible boundaries of international law. In order for deterrence to be effective, goals must be clearly signaled along with the benefits to be accrued by following them.

Increasingly, the United States is signaling that it is preparing for "The Battle Above"; the only bargain being offered is one of an unrealistic playbook of what the battle will look like, while, not unexpectedly, the military, particularly the Air Force, has been overt and muscular in its words and tone. But the State Department has been subtly changing its rhetoric as well in alignment with the Pentagon. The State Department, as the voice of US diplomacy, has been and ought to be the organization offering both bargains and assurances in efforts to deter space warfare and protect the space environment.

In 2012, for example, Secretary of State Hillary Clinton[7] and then Air Force Space Command chief Gen. William Shelton endorsed the concept of a voluntary space code of conduct similar to that which governs activities on international waters, with a European draft as the starting place for international negotiations. Analogies between maritime matters and space are limited though. Codes of conduct say, for example, that collisions should be avoided. Maritime practices go beyond that kind of general statement and include measures such as always passing to port to avoid collisions. These practices are more akin to "rules of the road." But international agreement, even on a more general code of conduct, has been elusive. Even within the United States, there have been objections, including that a code would restrict the United States more than other countries, that other countries would not abide by a code, and that a code would make voluntary things that are already required by law in the Outer Space Treaty.

Though US support for an international code of conduct was never enthusiastic, it had been pragmatically agreeable. Gen. Shelton stated that increased transparency regarding keeping track of more objects in space (reflected as space situational awareness [SSA] now being a stated US goal in space), more governance of issues related to radio frequency interference, and other issues connected to "safe passage" in space all made a code to the benefit of the United States.[8] Given that the United States has consistently rejected efforts through the United Nations toward a treaty banning weapons in space, a voluntary code of conduct was thought the best potential option to maintain stability, thereby sustaining the space environment.

Unfortunately, the European Union lacked the persuasive powers and especially the diplomatic finesse to incentivize other countries to partake.[9] Initially, Russia, China, India, and other countries hesitated for a variety of reasons—including the usual "we weren't consulted" complaint, though having little to offer in terms of alternative proposals—and the United States showed little staying power, or leadership, to take the initiative forward, especially given domestic forces pushing for a more muscular, military-centered policy. Subsequently, the administration's plan to "lead from behind" to revise and develop an international code of conduct for responsible spacefaring nations began to unravel. For all intents and purposes, the code of conduct met its demise in July 2015 when Russia, China, Brazil, South Africa, India, and the NAM (nonaligned movement) nations joined forces to insist that any negotiating process be placed under an open-ended UN mandate. Negotiating through the United Nations was exactly what the European Union and the United States had been trying to avoid because consensus diplomacy is inherently slow and cumbersome.

In his November 2015 address to the ASEAN Workshop on Space Security in Beijing, Assistant Secretary of State Frank Rose stated US interest in debris mitigation, transparency, and confidence-building measures (TCBMs) through the United Nations as well as "participation in thematic workshops and conferences on space security issues."[10] But there was no mention of an international code of conduct for space. Whatever bargain the United States had been offering before in terms of limiting its own activities in space in return for others doing the same was now gone.

Though stalled early in 2016, efforts through the United Nations to establish long-term guidelines for the sustainability of the space environment are now progressing well again. But US attention seems now largely focused on options for fighting a war in space, and setting up organizations and processes for doing so. Even US diplomats are carefully shifting their rhetoric to be more in line with the Pentagon's drum beat. Beyond the Pentagon and the State Department, Congress has been involved in terms of sending signals regarding US willingness, or unwillingness, to cooperate in space as well.

Congressional action consequent to the Space Portfolio Review has come by way of funding. But even before that, a well-placed member had sent a clear signal to China that the United States had no interest in bargains or assurances in 2011.[11] President Barack Obama met with then Chinese President Hu Jintao in January 2011. Part of their joint statement addressed the desire for deepened dialogue and interaction in space, which many people interpreted as a renewed willingness on the part of the United States to work with China—a willingness that had been abated since the 1999 Cox Committee report.[12] But cooperation was not to be. In 2011, Congressman Frank Wolf (R-VA)—a vocal critic of China's human rights record and then Chair of the House Appropriations Commerce, Justice and Science Subcommittee, which funds NASA—inserted a clause into the NASA Appropriations Bill prohibiting any joint scientific activity between the United States and China involving NASA or coordinated by the White House Office of

Science and Technology Policy (OSTP). Congressman Wolf publicly stated the rationale behind the legislation in a 2011 interview: "We don't want to give them the opportunity to take advantage of our technology, and we have nothing to gain from dealing with them. ... And frankly, it boils down to a moral issue. ... Would you have a bilateral program with Stalin?"[13] A 2013 letter from Congressman Wolf to NASA Administrator Charles Bolden provides another rationale having to do with potentially using the promise of space cooperation as a means to seek meaningful progress in China on freedom of ideology.[14] In other words, if China wants space cooperation with the United States, then it should change its domestic policies on freedom of religion and human rights—a linkage that is unrealistic.

Congressman Wolf largely restated the reasons most often used for why the United States should not working with China on space issues—technology transfer concerns, different values, and there being nothing to gain—thus limiting US policy options necessary for achieving stated policy goals. Additionally, especially among those who grew up during the Cold War, there is a tendency to equate China with the Soviet Union, despite the vast difference between them in the context of today's globalized world versus the post-World War II world. Limiting US options has never been in the national interest and is not on this issue either. Varied options can enhance deter, defend, and defeat efforts. First, however, the counterarguments to each of Congressman Wolf's arguments deserve consideration. It should be noted as well that although Congressman Wolf retired in 2015, his successor to the Chair of the NASA appropriations subcommittee, Rep. John Culbertson (R-TX), has echoed Wolf's views on China and maintained the legislative ban on bilateral cooperation.[15]

Congressman's Wolf's perspective assumed that working with the United States would give China opportunities in terms of surreptitiously obtaining US technology otherwise unavailable to it. But we live in a globalized world. Attempting to isolate Chinese space activities has proved futile. In fact, US protectionism has encouraged, indeed pushed, China and other countries into developing indigenous space industries, totally beyond any US control, to a greater extent than they might have done otherwise. Further, those countries arguably reap more political and prestige benefits from indigenously developed technology than if they had gotten the same technology from partnering with the United States. The only outcome of the past two decades of strict export control evidenced by hard data is damage to the US commercial space sector,[16] as described in Chapter 3.

Second, Wolf's rationale assumes the United States has nothing to gain by working with the Chinese. On a technical level, it seems hubris to assume that the United States knows everything and could learn nothing from others, though that assumption was also made when launch technology was leased to Japan in the 1970s and while working with Europe on the Shuttle program in the 1980s. On a nontechnical level, the United States could learn a significant amount about how the Chinese work—their decision-making processes, institutional policies, and standard operating procedures. This is valuable information in accurately deciphering the intended use of dual-use space technology, long a weakness and so a vulnerability in US analysis. Working on an actual project where people confront and solve problems together builds trust, which is currently severely lacking, on both sides. It also allows each side to understand the other's cultural proclivities, reasoning, and institutional constraints with minimal risk of technology sharing. Perhaps most importantly, cooperation would politically empower Chinese individuals and institutions that are stakeholders in Chinese space policy to be more favorably inclined toward the United States. A cooperative civil and commercial relationship creates interests that could inhibit aggressive or reckless behavior, as opposed to the situation where Chinese space policy is untethered to any obligations, interests, or benefits it might obtain through cooperation with the United States—cooperation with increasing external support.

The National Academies of Science (NAS) 2014 report titled *Pathways to Exploration: Rationales and Approaches for a US Program of Space Exploration*[17] includes a specific recommendation that it is in the best interests of the United States to work with China. The NAS and the Chinese Academy of Science has conducted an annual Forum for New Leaders in Space Science since 2014. The Forum brings early career space scientists from China and the United States to meet over two workshops where they shared research results and discussed future research opportunities; two additional Forums were held subsequently. Linking space to other political issues, however, can sidetrack the ability to achieve US space goals.

Wolf further stated that the United States should not work with China based on moral grounds. While clearly the United States would prefer not to work with authoritarian and/or communist regimes, it has done so in war and in peacetime whenever it has served American interests and continues to do so today. The basis of realism is to serve American interests first. While the United States would prefer not to work with Stalin, we continue to work with Putin because it benefits us to do so. Were the United States not to work with authoritarian regimes, it would have few regimes to work with at all in the Middle East. Indeed, the United States provided support to Saddam Hussein's regime in the Iran–Iraq War of 1980–88.[18]

Chinese politicians are interested in the International Space Station for symbolic reasons—specifically, being accepted as part of the international family of spacefaring nations as a sign of regime legitimacy. But it is unrealistic to expect that withholding US cooperation on space issues will influence regime change in China. A similar approach was considered with the Soviet Union, and it failed. Further, in terms of the United States doing China a favor by working with it, perhaps ironically, many Chinese space professionals fear that cooperation with the United States would just slow them down. American politics are viewed as fickle and without the political will to see programs to completion. This view of the United States is reflected in changing European views regarding space leadership. A 2013 article in Germany's *Der Spiegel* suggested that Europe is thinking of redirecting its primary space alliance from the United States to China based on China's "rising power" status in space.[19] The German reassessment was not based on China as a space threat, but on it being able to execute a very visible human spaceflight program and lunar robotic program, whereas the US civil space program, especially NASA's Journey to Mars program, remains largely unknown to the public.

It is also important to note that other countries do not share the overall view of the United States that Chinese space activities are nefarious. The Chinese Academy of Sciences and the European Space Agency (ESA) have discussed plans for a robotic space mission,[20] and China has signed initial agreements with the Russian and European space agencies for cooperation on its planned space station; the ESA are already training their astronauts in Chinese.[21] The United States is alone in its intransigence toward China.

This rebuttal to Congressman Wolf's views assumes that the United States has a choice regarding whether or not to work with China. If, however, stability in space is to be maintained, the space debris issue alone requires that the United States not exclude diplomacy as a policy option. National security goals are being sacrificed to the unrealistic and seemingly hypocritical self-proclaimed moral stance of a very few individuals. Rather than "fixing" or even addressing any real issue, the Wolf amendment only creates them. This amendment is not the first time the personal ideology of a Member of Congress has been counterproductively imposed upon broader US foreign policy, but it is one that currently needs to be corrected. The issues it purports to tackle are likely best dealt with elsewhere.

> Clearly sensitive technologies need to be protected. But, protecting US intellectual property is not known to be a domain where the House Appropriations Committee of the US Congress has recognized expertise or where it has been invested with any specific authority. Additionally, NASA is a relatively tiny domain in the vast territory of advanced technology under development by the US. The Wolf Amendment, in fact, offers no protection of American technology but instead empowers members of a Congressional committee with no relevant expertise or authority to play a foreign policy role.[22]

The United States has been hamstrung by this ill-conceived congressional power play long enough.

The signals being sent to China—to all countries—from Congress, the State Department, and the Pentagon are clear. Whatever bargain the United States might have been willing to offer in the past, whatever assurances the United States might have been ready to give in return for some as yet undefined responsible behavior on China's part now appear gone. Yet as Christensen pointed out, without credible bargains and assurances, deterrence efforts carry little credibility. Analysts and observers without a vested interest in military programs who have considered the issues of space warfare continually emphasize multilayered deterrence, as outlined in Chapter 1, rather than reliance on deterrence by punishment without any associated bargains and accompanied by bellicose rhetoric.

Many of those asked to reflect on the Schreiver V space wargame emphasized the role of deterring activities before they reached the conflict stage. Wargame

"President" Terry Everett said the experience made two things clear to him: "First, we must have a strategy for space deterrence, and second, that strategy must effectively reflect the domestic and international politics of space."[23] Lockheed Martin Vice President Marc Berkowitz offered the industry perspective post Schreiver V.

> Actions taken during the pre-crisis or pre-hostilities phase are of course critical to deterrence, dissuasion, and prevention of armed conflict. The US must actively promote the peaceful uses of space and cyberspace, facilitate a code of conduct to establish norms of responsible spacefaring and cyber behavior, establish a leadership position in international deliberations of legal and regulatory matters affecting space and cyber activities, and protect our space- and cyber-related commerce, trade, and security equities within international regulatory bodies.[24]

Yet the actions supported by Everett and by Berkowitz seem continually de-emphasized in favor of those to "defend and defeat."

Space is referenced as a "domain" but, in many ways, it is territory as much as any piece of land. It is a commons[25] which all seek to use, and if that ability becomes perceived as jeopardized, according to Oxford University Professors Johnson and Toft in their 2014 policy brief "Grounds for Hope: The Evolutionary Science Behind Territorial Conflict," then "perceptions can directly upset the conditions for territorial equilibrium."[26] They state that aggression over territory will increase if actors underestimate the costs of conflict, feel cornered, see their alternatives as being worse, or see territorial preference being given to exclusive ethnic, cultural, or religious groups. In that regard, signals regarding the manageability of space conflict and US intentions to deny access to space form perceptions that increase, not deter, the likelihood of conflict.

Washington's preferred version of deterrence seems to be that of dissuasion. While, most simply, dissuasion is the French word for deterrence, Secretary of Defense Donald Rumsfeld gave dissuasion a more specific definition, one that was subsequently used in such US documents as the Quadrennial Defense Review. Dissuasion means to persuade other countries away from competing with the United States in terms of military capabilities by convincing a potential adversary of the futility of such competition. Rumsfeld described the logic of the concept in the May/June 2002 issue of *Foreign Affairs*, arguing that "[w]e must develop new assets, the mere possession of which discourages adversaries from competing."[27] This version of deterrence bypasses the deterrence requirements explained by Christensen, in favor of moving directly toward building more and more threatening capabilities. Deterrence in terms of attempts to prevent conflict through specified goals, signals, bargaining, and assurance is now largely dismissed. Dissuasion has become the preferred substitute for deter, under the guise of "defend."

## Defend

Because, as considered in Chapter 1, satellites are bright objects against a dark sky, traveling in relatively more predictable orbits than missiles in flight, they are vulnerable. They are also valuable. Efforts to defend these assets, and the language used to describe efforts to defend these assets, has become an exercise in deliberate doublespeak. In "The Battle Above," when *60 Minutes* correspondent David Martin asked Secretary of the Air Force Deborah Lee James if the United States had any weapons in space, she replied, "No, we do not."[28] In this case, ambiguity in defining space weapons worked in favor of the United States as while it is not developing anything it overtly calls space weapons, it is heavily engaged in development of "offensive counterspace" (OCS) capabilities, including those to be potentially used in preemptive and even preventive operations. Words are important for political and public consumption, and the terms preemption and prevention are sometimes inappropriately used synonymously; for example, the 2003 US invasion of Iraq has been referred to as a preemptive action though, in fact, it was preventive.[29] But the tyranny of distance inherent with space events makes determining intent and attribution—even what really happened—difficult. Consequently, preventive action is risky at best and, more likely, rapidly escalatory.

The open suggestion by US analysts of preventive strikes against space targets appears a new direction, largely emboldened by and in line with increasingly ham-fisted US government rhetoric. Space analyst Christopher Stone urged in February 2016 that strategists "be prepared to engage in military operations preventively when necessary to actively defend space infrastructure and maintain escalation dominance in crisis or conflict."[30] That recommendation assumes that both a first strike on space assets and escalation would work in favor of the United States, though multiple views to the contrary, many based on wargaming experience, were presented in Chapter 1. Further, it is based on an assessment that China has "the ability to conduct a first strike against the critical infrastructure of the homeland and the armed forces, while the US does not have a dedicated program or strategy to mitigate this threat."[31] That assessment raises some serious points and questions. Apparently the Chinese, with a fraction of the US military space budget and starting from much farther down the learning curve, has been able to (presumably, rapidly) achieve technical capabilities that the United States has not, and US strategists have missed this entirely. That seems highly unlikely.

Stone's analysis twice references the need to understand "the adversary decision calculus." Such an understanding is indeed critical to better assessments of "intent," long a weakness in US threat assessments. How that would be done, however, is left unstated. An assumption, however, might be through diplomacy—a once integral part of trying to achieve US space goals as opposed to war planning and consideration of preventive strikes.

So the United States is developing defensive capabilities that can be used to protect assets it believes to be in danger, not necessarily under attack or imminent threat, but not space weapons. The differentiation between offensive counterspace capabilities and weapons appears more rhetorical than actual. The problem is that other countries recognize that blurred line as well, which spins up a security dilemma. The virtue of the line still being blurred is that, officially, the space weapons Rubicon remains uncrossed, which still leaves the diplomatic door open for deterrence rather than after-the-fact, more difficult compellence.

The Pentagon has been allocated a budget increase for fiscal years 2016 to 2020 of more than $5 billion for what officials call space protection activities; though some industry sources say that amount could reach $8 billion, mostly for classified space protection projects.[32] The three unclassified Air Force programs known to be included in the space protection plans are: the Space Fence, a next-generation space surveillance radar; the Space-Based Space Surveillance satellite follow-on, intended to watch objects in geostationary orbit; and the Space Operations Center Mission System, a three-phase hardware and software upgrade to improve the precision and timeliness of SSA information.[33] Beyond these and other space systems, a new $16 million Joint Interagency Combined Space Operations Center (JICSPOC) is being built at Schriever Air Force Base in Colorado, intended as a joint military and intelligence space battle management center.

During a June 2015 speech, US Deputy Defense Secretary Robert Work commented that the $5 billion (likely closer to $8 billion) budget increase "doesn't sound like a lot, but it's a big, big muscle movement."[34] But by way of comparison, the Coast Guard, charged with missions related to transnational organized crime (TOC), securing the southern border, safeguarding maritime commerce, aspects of cybersecurity, and increasingly with challenges and opportunities related to the Arctic, has an entire annual budget of about $10 billion.[35] Clearly, space is big business.

Without question, while the challenges of operating in the Arctic, terrestrial battlespaces, and elsewhere are significant, the space environment and the technical challenges of space inherently make it an especially expensive domain in which to operate. But it is a domain where physics, technology, and cost limit feasibility— limitations not well understood by those beyond the technical communities. David Wright, Laura Grego, and Lisbeth Gronlund, in their 2005 reference manual *The Physics of Space Security*,[36] presented relevant information on the physics of space to better enable decision-makers to make sound policy decisions.[37] They discuss the importance of feasibility differences between physics, technology, and economics.

> The cost of operating in space is often high relative to the cost of operating in the air or on the ground. While cost will be important in considering development and deployment, it may not be decisive if the system could provide a unique capability that is deemed important. Available technology places important limits on what systems are currently feasible for a given country, but those limits can change over time and do not represent fundamental limitations. The space-based laser, for example, has so far achieved power levels well below what is required for a usable weapon, but there do not appear to be fundamental limits to increasing its power over time. Physics, on the other hand, places fundamental limits on space

operations that will not change with time. An example of a fundamental limit posed by physics is the fact that satellites in low orbits cannot remain stationary over a given location on Earth, so multiple satellites are required to ensure that one is always near that location.[38]

So while there is no limit to what *could* be spent on developing space assets, the question is how much *should* be spent relative to gains, limitations, and risk. If stability is the ultimate US goal, what is to be gained by increasing the ability to know what is going on in space relative to, for example, hypersonic missiles capable of traveling more than five times the speed of sound?

Knowing what is going on in space has been demonstrated as key to avoidance of mishaps, misinterpretations, and miscalculations and consequent escalatory responses, so advances in that area are largely supported by the entire space security community. The US military defines SSA as one of its mission areas.

> Space situational awareness (SSA) involves characterizing, as completely as necessary, the space capabilities operating within the terrestrial environment and the space domain. SSA is dependent on integrating space surveillance, collection, and processing; environmental monitoring, processing and analysis; status of US and cooperative satellite systems; collection of US and multinational space readiness; and analysis of the space domain. It also incorporates the use of intelligence sources to provide insight into adversary use of space capabilities and their threats to our space capabilities while in turn contributing to the JFC's [joint force commander's] ability to understand adversary intent.[39]

Even regarding SSA, however, unanswered questions remain. Certainly there is a need to know some things, but what constitutes "as much as necessary" and how much is enough before return on investments begin to decrease?

Currently, avoiding collisions is a key goal, and this is not just for the military, but for commercial space operators as well. Because collision avoidance inherently involves sharing information, often an anathema of the military, the commercial sector has, in some ways, led the way in this endeavor. The Space Data Association (SDA) was formed in 2009 by satellite operators Inmarsat, Intelsat, and SES as a formal, nonprofit association supporting the controlled, reliable, and efficient sharing of information critical to the safety and integrity of satellite operations. In April 2011, the Space Data Center began operation as SDA's "automated space situational awareness system designed to reduce the risks of on-orbit collisions and radio frequency interference."[40] When satellites of subscribing members appear to threaten each other, the two operators are notified. SDA international member and participant organizations and companies have increased to more than 20 since its inception, and these include NASA and NOAA.[41]

Military and intelligence organizations, however, are often reluctant to share what they know with others. Knowledge is power. Yet, counterproductively, in an inherently globalized environment such as space, there is often conflict in terms of not sharing information and yet needing information from others. Hence, the US security communities are doing all they can to gather the information needed without having to rely on others to provide it; doctrine has always held to trust only what is derived from your own sensors.

Space Fence is a second-generation program to replace the Air Force Space Surveillance System (AFSSS), originally the Naval Space Fence, which was in service from 1961 until it was mothballed in September 2013 due to budget constraints. Since then, the Air Force has been reliant upon other surveillance assets to provide SSA, including ground-based radars and optical sensors and satellites. The new system is intended to eventually allow for the detection of smaller microsatellites and debris than current systems and to track baseball-sized objects as far out as 1,900 kilometers in space. However, whether it will reach the capability of the former Naval Space Fence, which could detect everything up to 1,500 kilometers altitude, approximately 85 percent of the satellites in low Earth orbit, is debatable. Space Fence will utilize S-band ground-based radars, currently only from a site on the Kwajalein Atoll in the Pacific Ocean, with a possible second site planned for Western Australia. While it has an "uncued" mode to allow it to be able to detect and track objects without being specifically tasked to do so, that is only one of several modes of operation and they cannot be used simultaneously. The new Space Fence is also intended to significantly improve the timeliness with which operators can detect space events potentially threatening to GPS satellites or the ISS. Initial operating capability was originally scheduled for 2015, but delays have now pushed that to December 2018 at the earliest. Delays have been largely due to budget issues. If, however, this system will increase US capabilities by a significant amount and SSA is a priority, it is curious that it is not a higher up the list in the Air Force's regular space budget.

According to a 2015 Government Accounting Office (GAO) report,[42] the Air Force has already spent some $1.6 billion on the Space Fence program over a period of several years, largely on development of competing designs and prototypes from Lockheed Martin and Raytheon. The Air Force had originally planned to award a contract for Space Fence systems development in July 2012, but due to internal program reviews and budget re-prioritizations, the date was delayed to 2014.[43] The program was cut back, and in April 2014, Lockheed Martin was awarded a $914 million firm-fixed price contract. At a subsequent briefing, a Lockheed official said the Space Fence would track about 200,000 objects and make 1.5 million observations per day, about ten times the number made by previous systems.[44] The more observations obtained on orbital objects, the more accurate the prediction of future movement of those objects and the greater the precision in prediction of future conjunctions/collisions. But how much analysis is done with this increased cache of observations, beyond just gathering it, is a key consideration as well, and it is one where prudent stewardship of government funding becomes a consideration.

Space programs generally and military space programs in particular regularly cost more than originally estimated. According to the 2015 GAO report,

> current annual estimated costs for selected major space system acquisition programs have overrun and are projected to exceed original annual estimates by a cumulative $16.7 billion—186 percent—over fiscal years 2014 through 2019. The cost increases that DOD is dealing with today are partly the result of management and oversight problems.[45]

That makes stewardship of government funding imperative, stewardship based on a prudent assessment of need, viability, and consequences.

Also on the Air Force "must have" list of items to be paid for with the $5 billion budget boost is a new Space-Based Space Surveillance (SBSS) satellite, another aspect of SSA efforts. The first SBSS satellite, SSB Block 10, was launched in 2010 carrying an optical telescope to observe spacecraft in geosynchronous orbit. According to the Air Force, "the Space Based Space Surveillance Block 10 satellite operates 24-hours a day, 7-days a week collecting metric and Space Object Identification data for man-made orbiting objects without the disruption of weather, time of day and atmosphere that can limit ground-based systems."[46]

The SBSS Block 10 satellite is a follow-on to the successful Advanced Concept Technology Demonstration (ACTD) of the Space-Based Visible (SBV) sensor on the Midcourse Space Experiment (MSX) satellite. The MSX satellite was a late 1990s missile defense test satellite, and most of its sensors had failed by 2002. SBSS improved the ability to detect deep space objects by 80 percent over the course of using MSX/SBV system. But that satellite flies at an altitude of about 300 miles, thousands of miles from the satellites it observes. The SSBS system was designed to consist of three to eight satellites.[47] The SBSS Block 20 constellation was expected to include four satellites when fully developed, and the original expectation was that it would be operational in fiscal year 2013. Not surprisingly though, delays ensued.

In 2005, an independent review team found that the program's baseline was not executable; that the assembly, integration, and test plan was risky; and that the requirements were overstated. The SBSS was restructured in early 2006, considering cost growth and scheduling delays. The restructuring increased funding and schedule flexibility; streamlined the assembly, integration, and test plan; and relaxed requirements. The launch of the initial satellite was delayed and costs increased by about $130 million over initial estimates.[48] But Congress began cutting funding for the follow-on system in fiscal year 2011, and the Air Force canceled the program in April 2013. However, in Washington, few programs ever really die, and by fiscal year 2015, SBSS was back in the Air Force budget.

Meanwhile, in 2014, the Air Force revealed a previously classified initiative called the Geosynchronous Space Situational Awareness Program (GSSAP).[49] Not coincidentally, that revelation occurred shortly after China's May 2013 test of a missile nearly capable of reaching what had been considered the "safe haven" (or sanctuary) of geosynchronous orbit, out of reach of potential adversaries. The Air

Force announcement was another signal of sorts, telling the Chinese that the United States was watching its activities, increasing the risk of attribution for China if it attempted anything nefarious. That revelation was likely a more effective signal of US deterrent by denial capabilities than any battle plan pronouncement.

The GSSAP program is also intended to help track man-made orbiting objects in high-altitude orbits. Two GSSAP satellites acknowledged as capable of performing rendezvous and proximity maneuvers were launched in July 2015.[50] Given the crowded nature of the "near-geosynchronous orbit regime" where the satellites operate, they must be capable of not just maneuvering, but precision maneuvering. Two additional GSSAP satellites are scheduled for launch in 2016. While the need and desire for ever more SSA is clear, the cost of gathering that data largely autonomously is high, especially given all the other (unclassified) space defense requests. The United States is concerned about the Chinese ability to reach geosynchronous orbit with missiles potentially capable of acting as ASATs. Yet the close proximity maneuverability of the GSSAP satellites is exactly the kind of capability the United States worries could be used by other countries as ASATs. Understandably, other countries have concerns about US technology, just as the United States has concerns about theirs.

The XSS-10 and XSS-11 satellites developed by the Air Force Research Laboratory (AFRL) in the mid 2000s were also capable of close-in satellite inspection. The XSS-11 inspected the rocket body that placed it in orbit and another US satellite. The Air Force characterized those programs as satellite inspectors. However, one unidentified Pentagon official was quoted in 2003 as saying that "XSS-11 can be used as an ASAT weapon."[51] Further, the "single strongest recommendation" of an informal 1999 study of microsatellite technology and requirements prepared for Air Force Space Command was "the deployment, as rapidly as possible, of XSS-10-based satellites to intercept, image and, if needed, take action against a target satellite" based on technology from the Army's kinetic energy ASAT program.[52] The XSS programs were precursors to the Automated Navigation and Guidance Experiment for Local Space (ANGELS) program[53] involving satellites designed to escort other satellites in orbit to keep an eye on the environment. Their maneuverability offers the military a wide range of uses, including offensive counterspace.

Other space-based or related systems in the fiscal year 2015 US defense budget include: the Joint Space Operations Center Mission Systems (JMS); Evolved Expendable Launch Vehicle (EELV); Mobile User Objective System (MUOS); Advanced Extremely High Frequency Satellite (AEHF); Global Positioning System (GPS); Space-Based Infrared System (SBIRS); Wideband Global SATCOM; and Weather System Follow-On. Many, if not most, are follow-on systems to those already in place to allow for technical advancements. The JMS is predominantly a software effort, intended to allow an enhanced and modernized picture of the space environment, including through improved algorithms. The EELV budget covers the cost of launching the various planned satellites. MUOS is a military communications satellite system intended to augment the eight currently operating

Ultra High Frequency Follow-On (UFO) satellites currently providing narrowband tactical communications. AEHF is a satellite communications system intended to be used by all armed services to provide survivable, anti-jam, worldwide secure communications. The billion-dollar-plus budget for GPS covers upgrades, maintenance, new technology, and any and all support needed. The SBIRS program is intended to augment and then replace the aging Defense Support Program (DSP) satellite constellation that provides early warning for the United States and its allies in four areas: missile warning, missile defense, technical intelligence, and battlespace awareness. Wideband Global SATCOM (WGS) is the follow-on for the Defense Satellite Communication System (DSCS), which provides the military with command, control, communications, computers, intelligence, surveillance, and reconnaissance (C4ISR) execution capabilities as well as battle management and combat support information functions. Each WGS satellite delivers the equivalent capacity of the entire DSCS constellation as it now stands. Finally, the Weather System Follow-On will replace the Defense Meteorological Satellite Program (DMSP) to provide the Defense Department weather information.[54] These are just programs dependent on the budget boost. While these programs largely support force enhancement capabilities, the intent of other programs is more questionable.

Perhaps most infamously among Air Force programs considered a potential space weapon is the X-37B Orbital Test Vehicle. This unmanned, reusable space plane looks like a miniature Space Shuttle and has flown repeated test missions of increasing duration. Because little is known about the program goals or payloads,[55] speculation has been rampant. China, for example, suspects it may be a space weapon and part of a march toward space warfare.[56] Even the Brits have closely followed the X-37B test flights, speculating on intent.[57]

Nevertheless, officially and according to Secretary of the Air Force James, the United States has no weapons in space. Given the menu of US assets with capabilities that could be used as weapons though, it is easy to understand how and why some other countries might be skeptical and question US intent. The intent of other countries when they build similar capabilities is certainly questioned.

In January 2016, China announced that it too was building a space plane, called Shenlong, which looks very much like the X-37B and is described as being very similar. That announcement was translated in the American press as being "revealed" as part of a "growing space warfare program" and "likely to be deployed" as part of the Chinese "Strategic Support Force that is designed for high-technology warfare, including space, cyber and electronic warfare."[58] It is easy to see how this characterization would be viewed from a Chinese perspective as a hypocritical "do as we say not as we do" interpretation of their program activities. Further, there has been speculation about a Chinese spaceplane being under development since 2007 though nothing has been seen beyond models, making "deployment" far from imminent if it is built at all.

The US Defense Advance Research Projects Agency (DARPA) also develops space and space-related programs. According to the DARPA website, its MAgneto

Hydrodynamic Explosive Munition program, or MAHEM—a particularly bombastic acronym—uses explosively formed jets (EFJs) and fragments and self-forging penetrators (SFPs) for precision strike against targets such as armored vehicles and reinforced structures and can be packaged into a missile.[59] And then there is the XS-1 Space Plane, intended to provide fast, affordable access to space, specifically ten launches in ten days at a cost of less than $5 million per flight.[60]

The programs cited here are only exemplary. The roster of space-related programs being developed by various agencies is lengthy and expensive. The United States has the most robust, most technically advanced, best-financed, and most muscular military space program in the world. The way to stay ahead in technology is not to try to stifle others—because, at best, technology development can be slowed, not stopped, if there is determined intent—but to continually push the technological envelope. Be the country to develop the technology game changer. The challenge is to do that without sparking an arms race. Because of the dual-use nature of space technology, the imperative to offer assurances and place equal effort on deterring space warfare through diplomatic channels and on developing technology becomes even greater. While striving for that balance has not been the case, neither, apparently, has the notion of what an end state would look like if it came to "defeating" an enemy on the space battlefield.

## Defeat

After the 2007 Chinese ASAT test, MIT scientist and strategic weapons analyst Geoffrey Forden wrote a three-part article titled "How China Loses the Coming Space War" for *Wired* magazine. That article basically concluded that while China could degrade US capabilities in a space battle, it could not debilitate them.

> The short-term military consequences of an all attack by China on US space assets are limited, at most. Even under the worst-case scenario, China could only reduce the use of precision-guided munitions or satellite communications into and out of the theater of operations. They would not be stopped. China could destroy a large fraction of strategic intelligence gathering capabilities; but not all of it. With a greater than normal expenditure of fuel, the remaining US spy satellites could continue to survive their crosses over China and photograph Chinese troop movements, harbors, and strategic forces but, of course, at a reduced rate. The war would, however, quickly move into a tactical phase where the US gathers most of its operational photographs using airplanes, instead of satellites. US ships and unmanned vehicles might, theoretically, have difficulty coordinating, during certain hours of the day. Most of the time, they would be free to function normally. China's space strike would fail to achieve its war aims even if the United States failed to respond in any way other than moving its low Earth orbit satellites.[61]

Although Chinese capabilities have improved since 2008, it must be assumed that US capabilities and tactical, operational, and strategic considerations of a potential attack on space assets have not been stagnant during that period either. Also, Forden's scenario focuses on short-term impacts and assumes the use of space-debris-causing kinetic weapons.

More recently in 2014, Jaganath Sankaran, a research scholar at the University of Maryland, considered the "Limits of the Chinese Antisatellite Threat to the United States"[62] and came away with much the same conclusions as Forden. He argues that there is no evidence for the often-made presumption that the US military is "critically dependent" on satellites and, consequently, extremely vulnerable to disruption by Chinese ASAT attacks. Though some US satellites clearly are vulnerable, he says that "the limited reach of China's ballistic missiles and inadequate infrastructure make it infeasible for China to mount extensive ASAT operations necessary to substantially affect US capabilities."[63] While the 2013 Chinese launch apparently demonstrated a potential capability to extend that reach, both Forden and Sankaran raise issues about how much damage the Chinese could actually inflict. To that point, Sankaran recommends that the United States employ technical innovations including SSA, shielding, avoidance, and redundancies to deter an attack by denial. He further states that negotiation and arms control must be part of any coherent deterrence plan.

If the major space powers with offensive space capabilities can be assumed rationale actors not wanting to risk negating their own space assets as well as those of a competitor by using kinetic kill ASATs, then what would space war look like short of a kinectic attack on a satellite? The Army held a highly classified war game in August 2015 that was focused on electronic warfare drills. The concern to be addressed was whether Chinese or Russian jammers "could trick US missile defense networks into firing into an empty sky."[64] Beyond "tricking" US operators into taking ill-founded actions, planners are also concerned that control of space assets could be hijacked through cyberwar. Russian hackers have already demonstrated their ability to hack into satellite transmissions,[65] and Chinese hackers broke into NOAA weather and satellite systems in 2014.[66] Gen. Hyten has made countering jamming one of his priorities. A big part of that involves training troops to use the most advanced equipment and to operate in a potentially hostile environment.[67]

The use of lasers to incapacitate satellite sensors is also a possibility of space warfare. The United States and other countries routinely track satellites by "painting" the satellite with a laser beam. Military laser research in the United States is carried out at the Starfire Optical Range in New Mexico, with laser weapons already incorporated on ships and army trucks. Intentionally or unintentionally, a high-powered laser beam can "dazzle" the satellite, rendering it temporarily or permanently "blind." Reports that the Chinese attempted to blind a US satellite in 2006 have been cited for years.[68] The director of the Pentagon's National Reconnaissance Office, Donald Kerr, however, has said of that claim that, in fact, whatever happened "did not materially damage the US satellite's ability to collect information."[69] Further, Gen. James Cartwright, then in charge of

US military operations in space, indicated that the United States has seen no "clear indications that China had intentionally disrupted US satellite capabilities."[70] Differentiating between painting, dazzling, and blinding is another potential area of ambiguity that can lead to escalatory responses.

Characteristic of Vladimir Putin's regime, bombastic Russian rhetoric has focused on two areas regarding space: electronic warfare and hypersonic missiles. Russian media sources quote an official from the Russian Radio-Electronic Technologies Concern:

> If the United States starts developing and launching its battle stations into space, Russia will have to respond in kind – namely with the development of high-performance Electronic Warfare (EW) tools on different types of bases; the use of these tools will be a distinct advantage [for Russia].[71]

The hypersonic missiles cut into decision time, raising the risk of escalation. All considerations combined, the potential end state of a space conflict is not favorable to anyone.

If the Schriever wargames have demonstrated anything, it is that when things start to go poorly in the space battlefield, rapid escalation occurs. The chances of maintaining a space war at a limited level appear similar to those of fighting a limited nuclear war: not good. The development of technology intentionally designed to cut into an opponents decision-making time with often ambiguous dual-use technology continues to heighten already-high odds of space warfare escalating into a nuclear exchange or one that, at best, leaves the world back in the industrial age. Allison references the aftereffects of these catastrophic conflicts, drawing parallels to the end of World War I in order to make it clear that there are no real winners.

> When war ended four years later, Europe lay in ruins: the kaiser gone, the Austro-Hungarian Empire dissolved, the Russian tsar overthrown by the Bolsheviks, France bled for a generation, and England shorn of its youth and treasure. A millennium in which Europe had been the political center of the world came to a crashing halt.
> [...]
> Most such contests have ended badly, often for both nations ... .[72]

While history is replete with examples of the end states of war, there are none to draw from regarding a space war.

What does a termination phase look like in space war? The United States went into Iraq without having a clear military end state identified, and that did not work out well. That "lesson learned" must be applied to space as well. One of the goals of the 2015 Schriever Wargame was stated as "identifying ways to increase the resilience of space that includes our Intelligence Community, civil, commercial and Allied partners."[73] Whether that is during or after a conflict is not clear, and if it is afterward, it assumes escalation was avoided. Whether that is a reasonable assumption, however, requires further and more transparent consideration by the next administration.

## Notes

1 Paraphrase of an address made by Otto von Bismark to the Reichstag on February 9, 1876.

2 Original version published by Yale University Press.

3 Thomas Schelling, *Arms and Influence*, Princeton University Press, Princeton, NJ, 2009, new edition, pp. 2–3.

4 Thomas J. Christensen, *Worse Than a Monolith: Alliance Politics and Problems of Coercive Diplomacy*, Princeton University Press, Princeton, NJ, 2011, p. 3.

5 William J. Lynn III, "A military strategy for the new space environment," *The Washington Quarterly*, 34(3), Summer 2011, 7–16: p. 9.

6 Ibid., p. 11.

7 Hillary Rodman Clinton, Press Statement, "International Code of Conduct for Outer Space Activities," January 17, 2012. www.state.gov/secretary/20092013clinton/rm/2012/01/180969.htm

8 Sydney J. Greenberg, Jr., "Safe passage: why the Pentagon wants an 'International Code of Conduct' for space," *Breaking Defense*, March 22, 2012. http://breakingdefense.com/2012/03/safe-passage-why-the-pentagon-wants-an-international-code-of-c/

9 Michael Krepon, "Second-term blues for arms control," *Arms Control Wonk,* December 2, 2015. www.armscontrolwonk.com/archive/1200588/second-term-blues-for-arms-control/

10 Frank A. Rose, Remarks to Third ASEAN Regional Forum Workshop on Space Security, Beijing, China, November 30, 2015. www.state.gov/t/avc/rls/2015/250140.htm

11 The discussion on the NASA ban on bilateral cooperation is largely drawn from Joan Johnson-Freese, Testimony to the US-China Economic and Security Review Commission, February 18, 2015. www.uscc.gov/sites/default/files/Johnson%20Freese_Testimony.pdf

12 *Report of the Select Committee on U.S. National Security and Military/Commercial Concerns with the People's Republic of China*, 105th Congress, January 3, US Government Printing Office, Washington, DC., 1999.

13 Jeffrey Mervis, "Spending bill prohibits US-China collaborations," *ScienceInsider*, April 21, 2011. http://news.sciencemag.org/technology/2011/04/spending-bill-prohibits-u.s.-china-collaborations

14 Yudhijit Bhattacharjee, "U.S. Congressman asks NASA to disinvite Chinese participants from upcoming meeting," *Science*, March 5, 2013. www.sciencemag.org/news/2013/03/us-congressman-asks-nasa-disinvite-chinese-participants-upcoming-meeting

15 Dan Leone, "NASA spending panel chairman keeps focus on China," *SpaceNews*, February 25, 2015. http://spacenews.com/nasa-spending-panel-chairman-keeps-focus-on-china/

16 U.S. Department of Commerce, *U.S. Space Industry "Deep Dive" Assessment: Impact of U.S. Export Controls on the Space Industrial Base*, Bureau of Industry and Security,

Washington, DC, February 2014. www.bis.doc.gov/index.php/forms-documents/doc_view/898-space-export-control-report

17 National Academies of Science, *Pathways to Exploration: Rationales and Approaches for a US Program of Space Exploration*, National Academies Press, Washington, DC, 2014.

18 Ted Koppel reported in 1992 that the "Reagan/Bush administrations permitted—and frequently encouraged—the flow of money, agricultural credits, dual-use technology, chemicals, and weapons to Iraq," ABC *Nightline*, July 1, 1992.

19 Kevin Holden Platt, "ESA mulls new alliance as China becomes space leader," Der Spiegel, February 8, 2013. www.spiegel.de/international/europe/esa-mulls-new-alliance-as-china-becomes-space-leader-a- 882212.html

20 Mike Wall, "China and Europe will team up for robotic space mission," *Space.com*, January 22, 2015. www.space.com/28331-china-europe-space-mission.html

21 Peter de Selding, "China's space station planners put out welcome mat," *SpaceNews*, October 13, 2015. http://spacenews.com/chinas-space-station-planners-put-out-welcome-mat/

22 Vid Beldavs, "Prospects for US-China space cooperation," *The Space Review*, December 7, 2015. www.thespacereview.com/article/2878/1

23 Terry Everett, "Building the political consensus to deter attacks on our nation's space systems," *High Frontier*, 5(4), 3–8: p. 3.

24 Marc J. Berkowitz, "The Strategic Value of Schriever V: Policy and Strategy Insights for the Quadrennial Defense Review," *High Frontier*, 5(4), August 2009, 32–6: p. 33. www.afspc.af.mil/shared/media/document/AFD-101020-017.pdf

25 Joan Johnson-Freese and Brian Weeden, "Application of Ostrom's principles for sustainable governance of common-pool resources in near-earth orbit," *Global Policy*, 3(1), February 2012, 72–81.

26 Dominic D. P. Johnson and Monica Duffy Toft, *Grounds for Hope: The Evolutionary Science behind Territorial Conflict*, Policy Brief, Belfer Center for Science and International Affairs, Harvard Kennedy School, March 2014 (based on their article in *International Security*, Winter 2013/14). http://belfercenter.ksg.harvard.edu/publication/24074/grounds_for_hope.html

27 Donald H. Rumsfeld, "Transforming the military," *Foreign Affairs*, May/June, 2002. https://www.foreignaffairs.com/articles/2002-05-01/transforming-military

28 Transcript of "The Battle Above," *60 Minutes*, David Martin (correspondent), Andy Court(producer),April26,2015.http://spacenews.com/transcript-of-60-minutes-air-force-space-command-segment/

29 Nathan Gonzalez, "Iraq was not a preemptive war," *Huffington Post*, April 10, 2008. www.huffingtonpost.com/nathan-gonzalez/iraq-was-not-a-preemptive_b_96040.html

30 Christopher Stone, "Rethinking the national security space strategy: part 3," *The Space Review*, February 8, 2016. www.thespacereview.com/article/2918/1

31 Ibid., 2016.

32 Mike Gruss, "Hyten: continuing resolution would delay space protection efforts," *SpaceNews*, September 17, 2015. http://spacenews.com/hyten-continuing-resolution-would-delay-space-protection-efforts/

33 Ibid., 2015.

34 Cited in Mike Gruss, "US spending on space protection could hit $8 billion through 2020," *SpaceNews*, July 2, 2015. http://spacenews.com/u-s-spending-on-space-protection-could-hit-8-billion-through-2020/

35  US Coast Guard, Posture Statement, *2016 Budget in Brief*, US Coast Guard Headquarters, Washington, DC. https://www.uscg.mil/budget/docs/2016_Budget_in_Brief.pdf

36  David Wright, Laura Grego, and Lisbeth Gronlund, *The Physics of Space Security: A Reference Manual*, American Academy of Arts & Sciences, Cambridge, MA, 2005. www.amacad.org/publications/Physics_of_space_security.pdf

37  On technical issues related to space security, see also: Ashton B. Carter, "Satellites and anti-satellites: the limits of the possible," *International Security*, 10(4), Spring 1986, 46–98; Richard L. Garwin, "Space technology: myth and promise," for the Second International Scientists Conference, *From the Nuclear Threat to Mutual Security*, London, December 3, 1988. www.fas.org/rlg/myths-of-space.htm

38  Wright, Grego and Gronlund, *The Physics of Space Security*, p. 2.

39  Joint Chiefs of Staff, *Joint Doctrine for Space Operations*, Joint Publication 3-14, August 9, 2002, Office of the Joint Chiefs of Staff, Washington, DC, p. 22. www.dtic.mil/doctrine/new_pubs/jp3_14.pdf

40  "SDA overview," *Space Data Association*. www.space-data.org/sda/about/sda-overview/

41  "Members and Participants," *Space Data Association*. www.space-data.org/sda/about/membersandparticipants/

42  Testimony of Christina T. Chaplin before the Subcommittee on Strategic Forces, Committee on Armed Services, U.S. Senate, "Space Acquisitions," GAO-15-492T, April 29, 2015. p. 8. www.gao.gov/assets/670/669930.pdf

43  Testimony of Christina T. Chaplain before the Subcommittee on Strategic Forces, Committee on Armed Services, U.S. Senate, "Space Acquisitions," GAO-14-382T, March 12, 2014. p. 7. www.gao.gov/assets/670/661567.pdf

44  Mike Gruss, "Lockheed Martin lands $914m Space Fence contract," *SpaceNews*, June 2, 2014. http://spacenews.com/40776lockheed-martin-lands-914m-space-fence-contract/

45  Testimony of Christina T. Chaplin, GAO-15-492T, April 29, 2015, p. 2.

46  "Space Based Space Surveillance (SBSS)," Air Force Space Command Fact Sheet, March 26, 2013. www.afspc.af.mil/library/factsheets/factsheet.asp?id=20523

47  Jayant Sharma, Grant H. Stokes, Curt von Braun, George Zollinger, and Andrew J. Wiseman, "Toward Operational Space-Based Space Surveillance," *Lincoln Lab Journal*, 13(2), November 2002, p. 331.

48  "Space Based Space Surveillance (SBSS)," *Global Security*. www.globalsecurity.org/space/systems/sbss.htm

49  Stephen Clark, "Air Force general reveals new space surveillance program," *Spaceflight Now*, March 3, 2014. www.space.com/24897-air-force-space-surveillance-program.html

50  Mike Gruss, "New US Air Force space surveillance satellites require great precision," *SpaceNews*,January 12,2015.http://spacenews.com/new-u-s-air-force-space-surveillance-satellites-require-great-precision/

51  Elaine Grossman and Keith Costa, "Small, experimental satellite may offer more than meets the eye," *Inside the Pentagon*, December 4, 2003.

52  Matte Bille, Robyn Kane, and Mel Knowlin, "Military microsatellites: matching requirements and technology," American Institute of Aeronautics and Astronautics, AIAA-2000-5186, September 19–21, 2000; cited in Theresa Hitchens, Michael

Katz-Hyman, Jeffrey Lewis, "Space weapons: big intentions, little focus," *Nonproliferation Review*, March 2006. p. 40. http://cns.miis.edu/npr/pdfs/131hitchens.pdf

53 "Automated Navigation and Guidance Experiment for Local Space," *Kirtland Air Force Base*. www.kirtland.af.mil/shared/media/document/AFD-131204-039.pdf

54 The Space Foundation, US Defense Space-Based and -Related Systems, Fiscal Year 2015 Budget Comparison, Update 6. www.spacefoundation.org/sites/default/files/downloads/Update%206%20FY%202015%20DoD%20Space%20Budget%20Comparison.pdf; Mike Gruss, "Pentagon will decide future of two high-profile programs by year's end," *SpaceNews*, February 26, 2016. http://spacenews.com/pentagon-will-decide-future-of-two-high-profile-satellite-programs-by-years-end/

55 Leonard David, "US military's top-secret X-37B space plane mission nears 3-month mark," *Space.com*, August 13, 2015. www.space.com/30245-x37b-military-space-plane-100-days.html

56 Mike Wall, "China may be suspicious of US Air Force's X-37B space plane." *Space.com*, June 25, 2012. www.space.com/16283-china-x-37b-space-plane-concerns.html; Dean Cheng, "When the Chinese look at the US X-37B they see the future of space-based attack," *Foreign Policy*, October 23, 2014. www.space.com/16283-china-x-37b-space-plane-concerns.html

57 Sharon Weinberger, "X-37B: secrets of the US military space plane," *BBC*, November 18, 2014. www.bbc.com/future/story/20121123-secrets-of-us-military-spaceplane

58 Bill Gertz, "China's Shenlong spaceplane is part of growing space warfare program: Gertz," *Asia Times*, January 25, 2016. http://atimes.com/2016/01/chinas-shenlong-space-plane-revealed-as-part-of-growing-space-warfare-program-gertz/?utm_content=buffer54684&utm_medium=social&utm_source=facebook.com&utm_campaign=buffer

59 Jerome Dunn, "MAgneto Hydrodynamic Explosive Munition (MAHEM)," *DARPA*. www.darpa.mil/program/magneto-hydrodynamic-explosive-munition

60 Elizabeth Howell, "XS-1: DARPA's experimental spaceplane," *Space.com*, May 1, 2015. www.space.com/29287-x1-experimental-spaceplane.html

61 Geoffrey Forden, "How China loses the coming space war,'" *Wired*, January 10, 2008. www.wired.com/2008/01/inside-the-chin/ part 3

62 Jaganath Sankaran, "Limits to the Chinese antisatellite threat to the United States," *Strategic Studies Quarterly*, 8(4), Winter 2014, 19–46.

63 Ibid., p. 19.

64 "US Army held missile defense war games to subvert 'Russian jamming,'" *Space Daily*, August 18, 2015. www.spacedaily.com/reports/US_Army_Held_Missile_Defense_War_Games_to_Subvert_Russian_Jamming_999.html

65 Kim Zetter, "Russian spy gang hijacks satellite links to steal data," *Wired*, September 9, 2015. www.wired.com/2015/09/turla-russian-espionage-gang-hijacks-satellite-connec tions-to-steal-data/

66 Mary Pat Flaherty, Jason Samenow, and Lisa Rein, "Chinese hack US weather systems, satellite network," *The Washington Post*, November 12, 2014. https://www.washingtonpost.com/local/chinese-hack-us-weather-systems-satellite-network/2014/11/12/bef1206a-68e9-11e4-b053-65cea7903f2e_story.html

67 Tom Roeder, "Space Command general making changes to prep for the possibility of space war," *The Gazette*, November 16, 2015. http://gazette.com/space-command-general-making-changes-to-prep-for-possibility-of-space-war/article/1563440

68 Noah Shachtman, "Is this China's anti-satellite laser weapon site?" *Wired*, November 3, 2009. www.wired.com/2009/11/is-this-chinas-anti-satellite-laser-weapon-site/

69 Glenn Kessler, "Bachmann's claim that China had 'blinded' US satellites," *Washington Post*, October 4, 2011. https://www.washingtonpost.com/blogs/fact-checker/post/bachmanns-claim-that-china-blinded-us-satellites/2011/10/03/gIQAHvm7IL_blog.html

70 Ibid.

71 "Russia to engage US in space wars with new electronic warfare technology," *Sputnik International*, updated August 22, 2015. http://sputniknews.com/military/20150814/1025760955/russia-us-star-wars.html

72 Graham Allison, "The Thucydides Trap: are the US and China headed for war?" *The Atlantic*, September 24, 2015. www.theatlantic.com/international/archive/2015/09/united-states-china-war-thucydides-trap/406756/

73 "Schriever 2015 wargame set to begin," *Air Force Space Command*, December 9, 2015. www.afspc.af.mil/news/story.asp?id=123465068

# 5

# FEEDING THE BEAST

We must guard against the acquisition of unwarranted influence, whether sought or unsought, by the military–industrial complex. The potential for the disastrous rise of misplaced power exists and will persist.

Dwight D. Eisenhower[1]

In his seminal 1971 book *Essence of Decision*, Harvard Professor Graham Allison examined decision-making during the Cuban Missile Crisis from three different perspectives: Rational Actor, Organizational Behavior, and Government Politics. In summary, the Rational Actor model assumes internally consistent decisions based on clear goals. The Organizational Behavior model suggests that decisions are often based on planned, standard operating procedures of governmental organizations. The third model, Governmental Politics, begins from the assumption that decisions are made by players with no consistent set of strategic goals, "according to various conceptions of national, organizational and personal goals; players who make governmental decisions not by a single, rational choice but by the pulling and hauling that is politics."[2]

Similarly, elite power theorists in the C. Wright Mills tradition have long argued that the stew of interests and players that comprise the military–industrial complex have helped determine, shape, and refine the definition of "national interest" in order to maximize profits and protect access to resources. As such, the increasingly broad array of actors that comprise the military–industrial complex is an integral part of the "politics" that goes into decision-making regarding security policy generally and space policy specifically.

Retired Air Force officer and space analyst Bruce DeBlois suggested in 2003 that forces beyond national interest affect decisions on space policy.

In addition to the power of top-down policy leadership, forces outside the control of high-level policy makers will also drive the acquisition of space weapons. In some circumstances, the institutions involved in the planning processes – including scientific laboratories, administrative divisions and military consumers – apply significant pressure outside their formal areas of expertise or responsibility.[3]

As already considered, defense programs generally and space programs in particular are high-cost, high-profit programs for contractors, with cost overruns the norm. There is lots of money to be made and a bevy of military officers, contractors, government officials, think tanks analysts, research and development personnel, and industry associations who stand "at the lucrative nexus between the defense procurement system, which spends hundreds of billions of dollars a year, and the industry that feasts on those riches."[4] When he left the presidency in 1961, Dwight D. Eisenhower warned about undue influence of the "military–industrial complex" on Pentagon policy. Were he alive today, more than 50 years after that famous speech, he might well be stunned at how completely his prophetic warning was ignored.[5] Defense and aerospace contractors form a particularly large and influential industrial sector, different from many other sectors.

The industrial side of the military–industrial complex is comprised of corporations with common interests and distinguishable characteristics from other sectors of transnational capital. They are overwhelmingly dependent on military sales as a percentage of total sales revenue. As of 2012, arms sales accounted for over half of the total sales of Lockheed Martin (76 percent), BAE Systems (95 percent), Raytheon (92 percent), General Dynamics (66 percent), and Northrop Grumman (77 percent). Their products are not easily transferrable to consumer uses and so they are dependent on government contracts. At least 9 of the 25 largest US defense firms have a significant aerospace focus: CACI International, ManTech, Rockwell Collins, Exelis, Computer Science Corporation, Raytheon, General Dynamics, Boeing, and Lockheed Martin.[6] The political implications of this are stark. These companies inherently have a vested interest in maintaining and expanding systems, including weapons systems, which absent clear and direct external threats, may have limited political justification. Additionally, government counterparts to these for-profit companies have concurrently grown—some might even say, "become bloated"—and in many cases, a codependent relationship has developed between them.

Since the United States began maintaining a large standing military after World War II, the general attributes of US foreign policymaking have both expanded and intensified the influence of the military–industrial complex. Foreign policy decision-making is supported by a complex array of institutions whose very existence is predicated on and justified by the presence of a broad spectrum of threats from individual terrorists to be hunted down on the ground and with drones to near-peer competitors which must be countered with overwhelming air, naval, and space power. The government agencies and offices with a role in national security have expanded from inner circle policymakers to entire bureaucracies. The National Security Council staff has grown consistently since the Carter Administration from a small secretariat of less than 20 individuals to over 400 people during the Obama Administration. Post 9/11, the military created a Northern Command (USNORTHCOM) in 2002 to defend the homeland and the Department of Homeland Security (DHS) was stood up "to ensure a homeland that is safe, secure, and resilient against terrorism and other hazards"; these other hazards have come to include the safety hazards of deep-frying turkey and assuring that souvenir shirts sold at the Super Bowl are not Chinese knockoffs.[7] DHS is now the third-largest government bureaucracy, employing more than 240,000 people. There are 17 different intelligence agencies occupying 33 building complexes, the equivalent of almost 3 Pentagons or 22 Capitol Buildings, and the intelligence community continues to expand.[8] The Pentagon, with its some 23,000 military and civilian personnel, is only the hub of a Roman Empire-like division of the world into geographic military commands, the United States being the only country in the world brazen enough to create such commands.

The sheer numbers of individuals, institutions, organizations, bureaucracies, and companies with a vested interest in preserving the self-licking ice cream cone[9] that the ever-expanding military–industrial complex has become continues to expand. Government offices like the State Department's Bureau of Diplomatic Security hire private military contractors from such companies as DynCorp International, Tigerswan, Triple Canopy, and Blackwater to protect diplomats and perform security functions. Employees of these companies are often retired Special Forces operators. Companies like Kellogg, Brown and Root (KBR), formerly a subsidiary of Haliburton and where former Vice President Dick Cheney was once CEO and Chairman, is an engineering, procurement, and construction company doing everything from building embassies to supplying military bases. Think tanks, consulting firms, and lobbying firms focused on defense and security issues have proliferated as well in terms of both quantity and investments.

Members of Congress, traditionally elected largely according to the number of jobs they can bring home to their districts—and the campaign contributions they can raise—are part of the witches brew as well as they are largely supportive of defense contracts and the jobs those contracts bring. "Job loss" is among the first claims made by defense contractors in their appeals to Members of Congress when defense budget cuts or sequestration are threatened. Further, retired Members and their staffs are not immune to the lure of high-paying lobbying jobs.

## Defining Threats

There is a wide breadth of individuals and institutions with a vested interest in maintaining threats to the United States that justify a significant defense budget. During the transition to the post-Cold War period, the US military was faced with potentially substantial cuts to military spending: the "peace dividend." Consequently, the military suddenly found itself talking about taking on military operations other than war (MOOTWA), an acronym and job description that warriors found distasteful at best. Former Secretary of Defense Robert McNamara and other former Defense Department officials suggested that defense spending could safely be cut in half. Policy planning organizations with close ties to the military or military contractors—think tanks like RAND and the Center for Strategic and International Studies (CSIS)—were put to work to counter this claim and minimize budget cuts. They focused on the development of a new defense doctrine that would involve the retention of large-scale systems and big-ticket platforms like aircraft carriers, not just after the demise of the Soviet Union, but regardless of the short-term security environment. Contractors play an increasingly large part in the military–industrial complex as well.

Political economist Ronald Cox explains the role of defense contractors in shaping that doctrine and defining threats—how the fox guards the henhouse in terms of threat identification:

> Military producers have a sustained relationship with key US foreign policy bureaucracies, especially the Defense Department. … The extent to which military contractors are embedded within the decision-making framework of identifiable bureaucracies within the US federal government makes their profit-making margins a function of the political process by which those departments and agencies identify long-term strategic threats.[10]

Thus, as considered in Chapter 1, defense strategies reflect needs but not necessarily national needs. Bureaucratic and corporate needs also play into definition of threats. Writing about the impetus to acquire nuclear weapons, Scott Sagan said, "bureaucratic actors are not … passive recipients of top-down political decisions; instead, they create the conditions that favor weapons acquisition."[11] Bruce DeBlois later applied that premise to space weapons, suggesting that "with an absence of clear top-down policy guidance on space weapons … military doctrine can build an inertia of its own, and impact – or even become – the default policy."[12]

Also playing into the definition of long-term threats to US national security are think tanks—organizations often largely supported by the corporations themselves. Think tanks come in all varieties and sizes, some focused, some broad, some partisan, some not. The Heritage Foundation, for example, hosted a nine-city Defund Obamacare Town Hall Tour in 2013, headlined by Tea Party movement leader Jim DeMint, thereby clearly evidencing a partisan position. "Some [think] tanks on the left and the right of the ideological spectrum have grown so political that, to avoid losing their tax status as charitable organizations, they have established separate operations dedicated to lobbying and other advocacy work."[13] Some organizations, however, strive to be honest brokers of information in their areas of focus. The Secure World Foundation (SWF), for example, states its mission as "to work with governments, industry, international organizations, and civil society to develop and promote ideas and actions to achieve the secure, sustainable, and peaceful uses of outer space benefiting Earth and all its peoples."[14] Much of SWF's ability to be nonpartisan and beyond the reach of corporate influence stems from it being privately funded. That is not the case with many organizations though.

William Hartung and David Gibbs have written about the role of the largest defense contractors in the financing of conservative and neoconservative think tanks that have come to prominence in defense policy debates and discussions since the 1990s, and especially since 9/11; The Project for the New American Century (PNAC), the National Institute for Public Policy (NIPP), and the Center for Security Policy (CSP), for example.[15] The Center for Security Policy receives one-sixth of its funding from defense industries. CSP states on its website:

> The process the Center has repeatedly demonstrated is the unique ability that makes the Center the "Special Forces in the War of Ideas": forging teams to get things done that would otherwise be impossible for a small and relatively low-budget organization. In this way, we are able to offer maximum "bang for the buck" for the donors who make our work possible.[16]

While most think tanks declare their "intellectual independence," the reality is that, even if they do not specifically declare an offer of "maximum bang for the buck" to their donors, they largely rely on corporate donations for their existence. Donors rarely support organizations advocating opposition views or producing information counter to their best interests.

Relatively new on the block—and billing itself as "Bold. Innovative. Bipartisan."[17]—is the Center for a New American Security (CNAS), founded by Dr. Kurt Campbell and Michele Flournoy in 2007. Both Campbell and Flournoy formerly served as heavy-hitters in the Obama Administration, Campbell in the State Department and Flournoy in the Defense Department. CNAS lists Boeing, the Carnegie Corporation, the Government of Japan, Northrup Grumman Aerospace Systems, and the Smith Richardson Foundation on its "honor roll" of those who have contributed more than $250,0000.[18] Campbell and Flournoy are among the many former government employees who have gone on to create or work at think tanks. A strong overlapping relationship between the boards of directors of defense contractors, policy think tanks funded by these contractors, personnel in the Defense Department, and high-level cabinet executives is not uncommon.[19] Reports and analyses prepared by these think tanks can weigh heavily in government policy decisions.

The shaping of the post-Cold War defense posture, specifically in identifying new enemies, exemplifies the role of the expanded military–industrial complex to include influential corporations, think tanks, the Pentagon, and Members of Congress.

> Any doubt about the need for an identifiable enemy was firmly put to rest in March 1990 by Senator Sam Nunn, chairman of the Senate Armed Services Committee and an acknowledged ally of the military establishment. In a blistering attack on the Soviet-oriented military posture still officially embraced by Defense Secretary Cheney, Nunn charged that the Pentagon's

proposed spending plans were rendered worthless by a glaring "threat blank"—an unrealistic and unconvincing analysis of future adversaries.[20]

A 1988 CSIS report had warned against "maverick regimes," a warning that was resurrected and amplified in response to Nunn's charge. Reaching back to the Reagan Administration, these "maverick," soon to be renamed "rogue," regimes initially included Iran, Libya, North Korea, Cuba, and Nicaragua. Subsequently, the Rogue Doctrine was laid out in White House Fact Sheet in March 1990; it posited that the United States would continue to face considerable post-Cold War security threats, namely from states in the developing world that possessed or potentially would posses weapons of mass destruction and the capability to threaten vital US geostrategic interests in key regions.[21] Iraq was added to the list later in the 1990s.

Still, regardless of how dangerous they were, rogue states did not justify aircraft carriers and other big-ticket items. Large-scale Cold War weapons programs consequently declined by 17 percent under George H. W. Bush and by 12 percent during the first term of the Clinton Administration.[22] That problem had to be addressed.

Again, Sam Nunn led the charge to identify at least one worthy new opponent of the United States—one that could justify the retention of a large military structure, platforms, and expensive weapons systems. Concurrent to development of the Rogue Doctrine, Nunn had begun working toward that end with Chairman of the Joint Chiefs of Staff Colin Powell in 1988. Eventually, a new class of states called "emerging regional powers" was identified to include Argentina, Brazil, China, Egypt, India, Iran, Iraq, Israel, Libya, Pakistan, South Africa, Syria, Taiwan, Turkey, and the two Koreas. Each had different national interests and philosophical underpinnings that, for one reason or another, had justified large growth in their military structures and/or the development of weapons of mass destruction.[23] Some countries eventually became US allies and/or recipients of large amounts of US military aid. Others came to be considered as potential threats—more specifically near-peer competitors, particularly China—that the United States might at some point have to confront on the battlefield. Consequently, the United States moved almost seamlessly from the Cold War Containment Strategy to the Rogue Doctrine and identifying potential near-peer competitors.

## The Plethora of Players

Defense and aerospace contractors responded to post-Cold War reduced business opportunities through a mixture of economic and political strategies. Economically, corporate restructuring, layoffs, division sell-offs, and mergers and acquisitions of other firms were among the strategies used, with the Defense Department helping to arrange financing for those mergers and acquisitions from as early as 1993. Those tactics, in combination with the wider economic trends of the 1990s, "contributed to a defense sector whose top four firms were receiving a higher share of DOD contracts than had been true for most of the post-World War II period,"[24] even after the Cold War. Politically, however, a new enemy worthy of the United States, a near-peer competitor, still had to be identified.

In his 2011 book *Prophets of War: Lockheed Martin and the Making of the Military-Industrial Complex*, William D. Hartung considered the impact Lockheed Martin had on defense policy and the benefits the company and individual company leaders reaped from maintaining a high threat profile.[25] During the post-Cold War transition from containment strategy to the Rogue Doctrine and emerging regional powers focus, then Martin Marietta CEO Norman Augustine led the charge to build what he called a "super-company." While some companies tried to absorb defense spending "peace dividend" cuts by diversifying their base business, Augustine rejected that approach. He felt it was his patriotic duty to keep producing weapons for America and frequently referred to the weapons industry as "the fourth armed service."[26] Beyond acquiring a number of small companies, including the military division of General Electric, Martin Marietta and Lockheed merged in 1995. Martin was clearly the dominant partner as evidenced by Augustine being the new CEO, top management positions being filled by Martin employees, and the new headquarters being based at Martin's Bethesda, Maryland headquarters.

Augustine's political connections were unmatched. While still running the world's largest defense contractor, Augustine also served on the Defense Policy Advisory Committee on Trade (DPACT), a group advising the Secretary of Defense on arms export policies; was on the Defense Science Board (DSB), an advisory panel with the power to push forward or scrap emerging weapons programs based on performance; and was President of the Association of the United States Army, a politically robust interest group of retired military personnel and army contractors. Those political connections paid high returns during the transition. Augustine played a central role in convincing the Newt Gingrich-led, Republican-controlled Congress to allocate or add billions in funding to Lockheed Martin projects from the F-22 combat fighter to the "Star Wars" missile defense program. Perhaps his greatest coup, however, was persuading Congress to bankroll the major arms industry mergers that were occurring with taxpayer money for "restructuring costs," a policy that yielded hundreds of millions of dollars in government support to the creation of Lockheed Martin.

> As a result of an obscure policy change contained in a one-page memo from John Deutsch, then the Undersecretary of Defense (and a former Augustine business associate), the Pentagon authorized federal funding for closing plants, relocating equipment, paying severance to laid-off workers, and providing "golden parachutes" to board members and executives affected by the merger.[27]

The policy was not published in the *Federal Register*, the standard repository of virtually every important government action, and it was enacted without notification to Congress.

The benefits that accrued from that policy were both organizational and personal. Lockheed Martin, for example, benefited by almost $1.8 billion.

Personally, Augustine was promoted from being CEO of Martin Marietta to being CEO of Lockheed Martin. However, because he "left" Martin as a result of a consolidation merger, he was compensated in the amount of $8.2 million, approximately $2.9 million of that coming from taxpayer dollars.[28]

The incestuous link between the Pentagon, Congress, and defense companies is sold as being good for America based on the number one concern of voters. Jobs. No one is more sensitive to "jobs" arguments than Members of Congress, with those arguments often presented by lobbyists.

In 2015, corporations reported more than $2 billion in congressional lobbying expenditures. K Street in Washington, DC, where many lobbyists' offices are located, is sometimes known as the "road to riches" for retired Members of Congress, congressional staffers, and military officers who largely populate their ranks.

> Today, the biggest companies have upwards of 100 lobbyists representing them, allowing them to be everywhere, all the time. For every dollar spent on lobbying by labor unions and public-interest groups together, large corporations and their associations now spend $34. Of the 100 organizations that spend the most on lobbying, 95 consistently represent business.[29]

More often than not, the job of the lobbyist is to convince Members of Congress that cutting whatever program they are lobbying for will result in job losses in the Members' district. Unemployed voters aren't happy voters.

In 2011, the aerospace industry put out a report saying that chopping the defense budget would put over a million Americans out of work. Cuts that could total up to a trillion dollars over ten years would "devastate the economy and the defense industrial base and undermine the national security of our country," said Marion Blakeley, president of the Aerospace Industries Association (AIA), which sponsored and paid for the report.[30] While companies like Lockheed Martin and Boeing claim that the number of defense firm employees has dropped to about 10 percent from a peak of 14 percent in 2008, some of those job losses, as in the case of Boeing, have come through moving employees to the commercial side of the business. In other cases, jobs have been lost through divestitures such as Northrop's spin-off of Huntington Ingalls. Based on executive salaries though, job losses do not seem to come because companies are financially strapped. In 2010, Boeing's CEO Jim McNerney made $19.7 million while Lockheed Martin's CEO Robert Stevens took home $19.1 million.[31] Stevens made $25.3 million in compensation in 2011, which was more than all but two Wall Street CEOs.[32]

The revolving door doesn't just go between industry and the Pentagon, but includes Congress as well. In his 2014 book *This Town*,[33] chief national correspondent for the *New York Times Magazine* Mark Leibovich explains a lot about influence peddling with a simple statistic: In 1974, just 3 percent of retiring members of Congress became lobbyists; now, 50 percent of retiring Senators and 42 percent of retiring House members stay in DC and become lobbyists.[34] Websites like OpenSecrets.com, affiliated with the Center for Responsive Government, publish the names of former members and who they now lobby for, or become "senior advisors" to, which is basically the same thing.[35] Trent Lott, Dick Armey, Tom Daschle, Tom Foley, and Scott Brown are among the bipartisan former Members on their list.

President George W. Bush signed the Honest Leadership and Fair Government Act in 2007, intended to limit former Members' and staffers' immediate ability to cash in on their insider information in lobbying positions. President Barack Obama called it "the most sweeping ethics reform since Watergate."[36] A key provision required ex-Senators and administration executives to wait two years and representatives to wait one year as a "cooling off period" before becoming lobbyists. But loopholes seem to create more of a sieve than a barrier, and according to a 2015 report by the Center for Responsive Government and the Sunlight Foundation, encourage a culture of "shadow lobbying."[37]

> Of the 104 former congressional members and staffers whose "cooling off" period ends during the first session of the 114th Congress, which opens today, 29 are already in government relations, "public affairs," or serve as counsel at a firm that lobbies. And 13 of those are even registered as lobbyists, working to shape policy in Congress or the executive branch on behalf of paying clients.[38]

The door doesn't just swing only from government to the private sector. It swings both ways. In 2011, Ann Sauer left her position as a Lockheed vice president and lobbyist with a compensation package of $1.6 million. Senator John McCain hired her as the key Republican staffer on the Senate Armed Services committee in February 2012.[39]

Industry associations also advocate policy positions benefiting their large and continually growing memberships. For example, the National Defense Industrial Association (NDIA) is an organization with 9,000 corporate affiliates, 26,000 individual members, and no foreign membership. "The Association maintains close coordination with the DOD functioning though 56 chapters and 34 committees, each with direct access and a working relationship with the DOD. Divided up among these contractors is the largest single slice of the federal government's budget."[40]

There are also a multitude of industry organizations and associations specifically related to aerospace. The American Institute of Aeronautics and Astronautics (AIAA) with "more than 30,000 individual members from 88 countries, and 95 corporate members ... is the world's largest technical society dedicated to the global aerospace profession."[41] The Satellite Industry Association (SIA) bills itself as a unified voice on satellite industry policy, regulatory, and legislative issues. As a

> trade association representing the leading global satellite operators, service providers, manufacturers, launch service providers, and ground equipment suppliers ... [SIA] actively promotes the benefits and uses of commercial

satellite technology and its role in national security, homeland security, disaster relief and recovery, and the global information infrastructure and economy.[42]

There is an association or organization for every interest, oftentimes more than one.

Many of the individuals staffing and connecting this multitude of organizations are retired military officers, many of them three- or four-star generals and admirals. Their rank provides them with substantive knowledge of the defense field and a career's worth of Rolodex connections. For those seeking post-retirement consulting careers, that means access. According to retired Air Force General Gregory "Speedy" Martin, the practice of flag and general officers moving immediately to private sector jobs is both ethical and beneficial for American defense because it links private sector expertise with important Pentagon missions. "Access sounds sleazy, but it brings a value," says Martin. "I am interested in doing things that I think the Air Force or [Department of Defense] might benefit from."[43]

There is validity in what Gen. Martin says. Most Members of Congress and their staff have never served in the military and have little knowledge of, or even interest in, national security issues and needs unless it directly affects their district. While some staff and Members are or become very knowledge about national security and military issues, first-hand expertise from practitioners can be key to their education. Pentagon officials with broad portfolios of responsibility can also benefit from practitioner input on specific areas, especially technical areas like aerospace. The practice of exporting expertise from the military to the private sector is not inherently nefarious and, indeed, can serve the country. But the lines between education, advising, and persuasion are fine. That can be especially true when former flag officers, turned industry executives, visit the Pentagon.

Their rank carries with it a sense of respect, indeed awe, from former subordinates who they are now courting for contracts. "When a general-turned-businessman arrives at the Pentagon, he is often treated with extraordinary deference—as if still in uniform—which can greatly increase his effectiveness as a rainmaker for industry. The military even has a name for it – the 'bobblehead effect.'"[44] Retired generals and admirals with a practiced command voice understand the persuasive effect their authoritative presence can have on former employees. The sheer number of these retired flag officers working as defense consultants or executives—sometimes referenced as "rent-a-general" practice—tells a story, with a significant increase shown during the fat budget years of the Gulf War.

Between 2004 and 2008, 80 percent of three- and four-star officers joined defense firms upon retirement, up from less than 50 percent who followed that career path from 1994 to 1998. In some individual years, the move from senior military positions to the defense industry is a virtual clean sweep. In his 2010 investigative report for the *Boston Globe*, Bryan Bender found that 34 out of 39 three- and four-star generals and admirals who retired in 2007 went to work for defense firms—nearly 90 percent.[45] In some specialized commands, this feeder system of military officers into lucrative defense jobs is so powerful that the same companies have hired successive generations of flag officers. Bender reported, for example, that the last seven generals and admirals responsible for controlling international arms sales at the Pentagon went to work post retirement as contractors selling weapons and defense technologies overseas.

The rules governing post-retirement employment are part of federal statute 18 USC, section 207(c), that statute being known as the "revolving door" restriction. The Air Force explains this restriction in its post-retirement separation rules as follows:

- This means that for **one year** after their service terminates, senior employees may not knowingly make, with the *intent to influence*, any *communication or appearance* before an employee of the *agency in which they served* in the *year prior to their leaving*, if the communication or appearance is made on behalf of any other person and *official action* by the agency is sought.
- The purpose of this "cooling off" period is to allow for a period of adjustment for the former senior employee and personnel at the agency served and to diminish any appearance that government decisions are being improperly influenced by the former senior employee.
- This restriction does not apply to "behind-the-scenes" assistance. However, it does *not* require that the former senior employee was "personally and substantially" involved in the matter that is the subject of the communication or appearance.
- Instead, it applies to any representation back for the purpose of influencing employees at the agency that the employee just left.[46]

For two years after retirement, the Pentagon prohibits military officers from participating in "particular matters," meaning ongoing contracts greater than $10 million that were under their command. But due to another convenient loophole, "new editions of older weapons systems are not considered 'particular matters.'"[47]

Beyond loopholes, potential conflict of interest issues arise since these flag officers are often recruited for private sector employment well before they retire, raising questions about their independence in threat assessments, force planning, and general considerations of national interest versus the potential for post-retirement gain. Further, the revolving door—perhaps more a blender than a door—is actually promoted and facilitated by the government with taxpayer money. Taxpayer-funded career seminars on how to network into private industry are held, for example, for Navy and Air Force flag officers on Coronado Island near San Diego, sometimes two full years before their retirement.[48]

Other retirees have been more peripherally involved with linking Pentagon needs to industry desires to fill those needs, acting as what was called Pentagon "Senior Mentors." The Office of the Secretary of Defense defined a Senior Mentor as a retired flag, general or other military officer or senior retired military official who provides expert experienced-based mentoring, teaching, training, advice, and recommendations to senior military officers, staffs and students, as they participate in war games, warfighting courses, operational panning, operational exercises, and decision-making exercises.[49]

The Pentagon has stated that it increasingly needs and relies on these retired officer "mentors" to run war games and advise active duty commanders. But a series of media reports in 2010 raised issues about the program, specifically in terms of financial gains and conflicts of interest.

In some cases, for example, if payment was made to a retired military officer through a defense company rather than directly, the military services didn't even have to reveal the identity of the retiree. These were individuals who, in some instances, were making up to $440 an hour as mentors while drawing pensions as high as $220,000 per year and working full-time executive positions with defense companies.[50] *USA Today* reported that of the 158 Senior Mentors they identified, 80 percent had financial ties to defense contractors, including 29 being full-time executives of defense companies.

The Senate Armed Services committee took an interest in the Senior Mentors program, and soon thereafter, the Pentagon ordered a program overhaul.[51] Consequently, Secretary of Defense Robert Gates announced sweeping changes to the program in April 2010. Mentors were to be converted to Highly Qualified Expert (HQE) positions and, consequently, were held responsible for complying with all applicable federal personnel ethics laws and regulations. Those regulations included financial disclosure statements and imposed a salary cap. The financial disclosure part included revealing employers, earnings, and stocks. The salary cap meant that a HQE could only be paid up to a specific authorized amount, an amount equivalent to the salary authorized for a four-star general officer on active duty—the most they could have made before moving to the private sector. Further, mentors became subject to federal rules designed to prevent conflicts of interest, such as prohibiting mentors from divulging nonpublic information to defense contractors or taking actions that have "a direct and predictable"[52] effect on their private interests.

In October 2011, the DoD Inspector General reported on compliance with the new policy, focusing on the Navy, Marine Corps, Joint Forces Command, Special Forces Command, and Strategic Command. The Army and Air Force were omitted as they were conducting their own compliance studies.[53] Subsequent to the new rules being put into place, 98 percent of the retired officers from the Navy, the Marines, and three combatant commands left the Senior Mentor program. "It appears that, for at least some of the former military officers who dropped out the program, it's clear which choice they made when it came to patriotism or money."[54]

The kind of conflict of interest issue that had bothered the press and the Senate came up again in November 2011. Senator John McCain sent a letter to Defense

Secretary Leon Panetta expressing concern about retired Air Force General turned Boeing executive Charles Robinson's participation in a 2008 war game called Global Mobility "for a $51 billion aerial tanker contract Boeing was competing to win."[55] Boeing was later awarded the contract. McCain further criticized the Pentagon for taking two years to fulfill a FOIA request related to the subject.

It is not just the Pentagon and defense firms who are keen to hire retired general officers. According to retired Army General Wesley K. Clark, private equity firms and Wall Street investors are also increasingly interested in enlisting retired flag officers as consequence of a broader phenomenon: the increasing importance of the military to America's industrial base. "It's the militarization of the economy,"[56] Clark said; and he would know. Since leaving his position as NATO Supreme Allied Commander in 2000 and running for President from 2002 to 2004, Clark has worked for, often simultaneously, his own firm, Wesley K. Clark and Associates; the lobbying firm James Lee Witt Associates as Vice President and Senior Advisor; Rodman & Renshaw, eleventh largest investment bank in the United States, as former Chairman; Growth Energy, an alternative energy advocacy firm, as Co-Chairman; Geooptics LCC, an environmental data company, on the Board of Advisors; and the Blackstone Group, a private equity firm, as Senior Advisor. Clark is not alone in being sought after in the private equity, finance, and energy sectors. Retired Army General and former CIA Director David Petraeus was hired in 2013 by Kohlberg, Kravis, Roberts (KKR), a private equity firm specializing in leveraged buyouts, to head its KKR Global Institute.

The role of the media—specifically, paying former military members to act as advisors for the media and spokespersons for Pentagon policy—must also be considered as part of the supporting cast of the military–industrial complex. Retired General Jack Keane, for example, appeared on *Fox News* nine times over a two-month period in 2014 to advocate for air strikes and special forces to defeat ISIS, declaring that a bolder strategy was required. He made similar calls for more military action before Congress. What was left unsaid by the media, though, (and in congressional witness disclosure forms) was that Keane had a very personal interest in seeing military activity ramped up. Keane is a special adviser to Academi, the contractor formerly known as Blackwater; a board member to tank and aircraft manufacturer General Dynamics where he was paid over $245,000 in 2013; a "venture partner" to SCP Partners, an investment firm that partners with defense contractors, including XVionics, an "operations management decision support system" company used in Air Force drone training; and president of his own consulting firm, GSI LLC.[57] When the US military is involved in global conflicts, the firms that Keane is associated with benefit. Dean Ed Wasserman of the UC Berkeley Graduate School of Journalism was quoted in *The Nation* as saying, "I think an inclination to use military action a lot is something the defense industry subscribes to because it helps to perpetuate an overall climate of permissiveness towards military spending."[58] Those who profit from conflict certainly weren't going to argue against it.

The Pentagon has a track record of using the media for its own purposes as well. In 2002, during the run-up to the Iraq War, Assistant Secretary of Defense for

Public Affairs Victoria Clarke launched a program to recruit "key influentials" (retired military officers) to help sell the war to the public. More than 75 individuals were eventually signed up to appear on television and radio shows as military analysts and/or to pen newspaper op–ed columns. Many of these analysts were also lobbyists for defense contractors. The Pentagon held weekly meetings with the analysts, providing them "street credibility." The analysts benefited as the meetings indicated to their clients that they had personal access to the Pentagon, and they benefited the Pentagon by discouraging the analysts from questioning or criticizing Pentagon assertions. The arrangement worked well until *New York Times* reporter David Barstow reported on the program in 2008.[59] As part of the investigation leading up to Barstow's report, the newspaper sued the Defense Department and eventually gained access to 8,000 pages of e-mail messages, transcripts, and records describing years of private briefings, trips to Iraq and Guantánamo for the analysts, and an extensive Pentagon talking points operation. Barstow later won a Pulitzer Prize for his reporting. While issues regarding the military–industrial complex are evidenced across the board in defense policy and program decision-making, those that are space-related can be particularly noteworthy given their cost, endurance, and technical fatuity.

When all the wheels are turning in the right direction, a program can become one of those highly lucrative self-licking ice cream cones. Missile defense provides an illustrative example of what that looks like. Within that strategic program, there are multiple smaller, related programs. Many endure for years before collapsing. The $5 billion Airborne Laser, the $1.7 billion Kinetic Energy Interceptor, and the 700 million Multiple Kill Vehicle were all canceled after no, or failed, testing.[60] But yet the missile defense program lives on and is a testament to the persistence of its supporters.

## Missile Defense

The pedigree and growth of the US missile defense program exemplifies the expanse, influence, and confluence of military–industrial complex players on national security policy and programs and, specifically, space-related policy and programs. While once described by Air Force Lt. Gen. Henry Obering III, the Missile Defense Agency director, as operationally having a "better than zero"[61] chance of intercepting a warhead and considered by some deterrence experts as destabilizing, missile defense has unquestionably served an important strategic purpose. The tenacity and robustness with which missile defense was initially pursued by the United States convinced Soviet politicians to ignore the laws of physics that perplexed scientists and engineers in both countries and to spend the Soviet Union into oblivion trying to keep up with the United States in creating an operationally effective missile defense system. A soft ending to the Cold War was worth any price.

But the Cold War has been over for more than 20 years and missile defense lives on. The Ground-Based Midcourse (GMD) system largely intended to protect the continental United States against a nuclear missile attack was declared operational in 2004. Yet skepticism remains high regarding the operational viability of this system, once called "national" missile defense (NMD). But suspicion in other countries that, with modifications, those systems would be effective ASAT weapons is high as well.

Missile defense history goes back to World War II. *Washington Post* military affairs reporter Bradley Graham, in his 2001 book *Hit to Kill*, dates efforts back to the 1940s and German V-2 rockets.[62] According to Graham, the US Army wanted to immediately take up the gauntlet dropped by the V-2s and develop an anti-missile system. But a report issued by General Electric in 1945 indicated that such a defense system was, at that time, beyond technical reach. Since 1945 though, there have been advocates, and there have been debates regarding the technical and economic feasibility as well as the political wisdom of putting such a system in place even if it worked.

In the 1950s, scientists and engineers largely prevailed in the debates, arguing against missile defense based on offense being easier than defense as well as being more reliable and considerably less expensive. Graham notes that former Pentagon director of research and engineering Herbert York and President John Kennedy's science advisor Jerome Wiesner wrote a 1962 article in *Scientific American* also suggesting that development of a missile defense system would likely provoke an arms buildup in the Soviet Union and thus intensify the already existing arms race—an early warning of a security dilemma. Thus the technological implausibility of building an effective operational system and provoking an arms race and, consequently, political instability were raised as concerns early in the missile defense debate.

Graham also considers the role of scientists in the early missile defense debates as particularly noteworthy.

> As early as 1964, the Federation of American Scientists (FAS), a nationwide organization of about twenty-five hundred scientists and engineers concerned about the impact of science on national and international affairs, opposed any missile defense deployment. A 1968 article in *Scientific American* by Hans Bethe, a Nobel laureate professor of physics at Cornell University and member of the President's Scientific Advisory Committee, and Richard Garwin, a research scientist at IBM, outlined in public for the first time the technical vulnerabilities of ballistic missile defenses. Their article cited concerns about high-altitude detonations blinding radars on the ground and the prospect of decoys or multiple warheads overwhelming the system.[63]

Congress began seeking the advice of the scientific community in hearings as well.

Seeking advice from the science community was a new phenomenon as, previously, administration witnesses were almost exclusively called upon to testify on defense matters. It was during this time that the fundamental arguments against missile defense, that is was technically infeasible and encouraged an arms race, solidified and began to take root throughout the military establishment and on

Capitol Hill. While Congress and the military being opposed to missile defense seems implausible today, their views prevailed until the Reagan Administration. In the early years, it was the scientific community that was somewhat split.

A number of respected experts, including Freeman Dyson at the Institute for Advanced Study and Alvin Weinberg of the Oak Ridge National Laboratory, made the case for proceeding with a limited anti-missile system. Their argument was that a strong defense could undercut the value of intercontinental ballistic missiles (ICBMs) and end, rather than promote, an already existing arms race between the United States and the Soviet Union. Dyson wrote in the *Bulletin of the Atomic Scientists* that even in the absence of a defense that was 100 percent effective, benefit would accrue from saving most of a population.[64] RAND researcher Albert Wolhstetter was another supporter. He went so far as to accuse opponents of distorting operations research and data on the technical feasibility of a missile defense system. Not surprisingly, missile defense critics responded with accusations of their own. While most scientists doubted the technical veracity of missile defense, the existence of a few scientists who argued the merit nonetheless created the impression that for every expert declaring that missile defense would not work, another was prepared to argue it would. This is not an uncommon occurrence in areas of scientific research; witness a general scientific consensus on basic aspects of climate change science being weighted equally to the views of a small cadre of "doubters" in the science community,[65] especially when both sides are given equal media coverage.

Interestingly, Graham states that it was the general public weighing in that finally, though only temporarily, subdued the missile defense debate. In the last year of the Johnson Administration, the Army began to buy land for the missile defense sites.

> Opponents warned that cities near defensive missile sites would become "megaton magnets" for the Soviet Union. They also fanned fears by saying that the nuclear warheads of the Spartan and Sprint interceptors might detonate at low altitude during an attack, or accidentally in peacetime, thereby destroying the very cities they were intended to protect.[66]

This being the Vietnam era, public distrust of the military was particularly high. Therefore, Congress did not want to be on record as going against public wishes and missile defense was curbed, largely in favor of research and development activities. Further, the United States and the Soviet Union signed the Anti-Ballistic Missile (ABM) Treaty in 1972, restricting sites and tamping down testing opportunities under the premise that what couldn't be tested couldn't be relied upon as an operational system. In the treaty preamble, it was specifically stated that effective limits on anti-missile sites would be a substantial factor in curbing the race in strategic offensive arms. The treaty did allow theater missile defense (TMD) to protect against short- and medium-range missiles.[67]

Research eventually resulted in the Army combining the improved capabilities of infrared sensors with high-capacity computers to produce what has become known as "hit to kill" technology. This was considered the first major breakthrough in ballistic missile defense research since the 1940s. Hit to kill technology (kinetic weapons) was considered ready for demonstration in 1982. The Army called that demonstration the Homing Overlay Experiment (HOE).

> An experimental vehicle was launched from the Kwajalein missile range in the Marshall Islands using a modified Minuteman rocket. Once in space, the vehicle separated from its booster and homed in on a target missile that had been fired from an Air Force base in California. HOE succeeded in scoring a hit after three failures, but the credibility of the test was called into question years later when investigators at the Congressional General Accounting Office reported that the chances of intercepting the target warhead had been increased by heating it before launch and instructing it to fly sideways, thereby exposing a greater surface area to the interceptor's sensors. In any case, HOE was far too heavy and expensive for operational purposes.[68]

This was the first but not the last time that the veracity of missile defense tests would be called into question.

As it happened, the tests results didn't really matter. In March 1983, President Ronald Reagan gave his "Star Wars" speech announcing development of a system to protect the United States from nuclear weapons, though he never used the term "Star Wars" and, in fact, never specifically said it was to be a space-based program. Reagan clearly abhorred nuclear weapons. Whether he really believed that a technology system could be developed to protect the United States from nuclear weapons is a different question. Regardless, the actions taken following the speech through the Strategic Defense Initiative (SDI) program to develop such a system have become embedded in US security planning today, with dubious results[69] and a pricetag estimated at $274 billion in 2012.[70] with another $38 billion expected to be spent by 2019.[71] As scientist Freeman Dyson described in a 2007 interview, "Star Wars was basically just a source of money for all kinds of people with different ideas who came into the foreground to get their share."[72]

While Reagan claimed that he consulted with advisors before the speech, few in either the science or security communities had much faith in the technical feasibility of the program. Dyson explains his view thus:

> Well, I always believed in it politically, not technically. It was one of these things, I thought from a moral point of view and a human point of view, it was a good idea, that we should switch from an offensive to a defensive strategy. That was something that was, in the long run, very desirable. I still think so. Problem was, that the program was technically just – well, it was actually fraudulent. (laughs)[73]

Except for being potentially useful as a bargaining chip with the Soviets, National Security Advisor Robert (Bud) McFarlane regarded it primarily as a "pipe dream."[74] The military was supportive as long as the program would be accompanied by the necessary funding, and it came with buckets of money. Within the scientific community, there was a high correlation between the level of support and federal money being received or anticipated to make the next necessary breakthrough. Air Force Lt. Gen. James Abrahamson was picked to head the newly established Strategic Defense Initiative Organization (SDIO) in 1984 and the program was underway.

NATO members were unconvinced. The *Globe and Mail* (Canada) ran an article in 1985 voicing concerns about strife in NATO regarding the program, suggesting that "if the Soviets can't match the Americans—if they think the United States will develop a leak-proof umbrella—the danger of a preemptive strike grows."[75] Further, by 1987, physicist Edward Teller gave a speech at the American Defense Institute stating what, by then, most interested parties already knew; SDI would not be able to provide a leak-proof umbrella from nuclear attack. While Reagan had never promised such an umbrella, the perception of such a promise was generated nonetheless.[76] The program goals were being rolled back, though the science and engineering communities, not to mention the aerospace industries, were more than willing to continue to push full speed ahead.

Beyond physics and cost, it was the ABM Treaty that stood in the way of testing SDI technology. Rather than abrogate the treaty, though, the Reagan lawyers simply got creative and "reinterpreted" problematic parts. They asserted that technologies not in existence at the time the treaty was signed—like space-based Brilliant Pebbles designed to kinetically intercept and destroy warheads before they could reach their targets—were not covered. Further, the Reagan lawyers characterized SDI as a research program, not a program planned for deployment, and so not within the purview of the treaty anyway. The tortured logic of the ABM "reinterpretation" was politically resourceful. But the program continued to be a money sink in terms of progressing toward an operational viable technology. When George H. W. Bush took office in 1989, it was largely repackaged, being announced in his 1991 State of the Union address as Global Protection Against Limited Strikes (GPALS).

As the name indicates, GPALS' goals were much more limited than those of SDI. It aimed to stop a small ballistic missile attack on America and to thwart limited strikes against US troops by theater ballistic missiles. The idea of defending the US homeland from an all-out Soviet ICBM assault was dropped. While elements of GPALS have endured as part of US missile defenses today, many of the GPALS programs never came online.[77] Nevertheless, the idea of missile defense had received a huge public boost from the deployment and use of Patriot missiles during the 1990–91 Gulf War. Unfortunately, the television imagery of the Patriots being fired was far more effective in convincing people of the value of missile defense than the actual missile defense performance was succesful.

The Pentagon heralded the Patriot missiles as instrumental in defending civilian and military targets against Iraqi Scud missiles. But MIT scientists Ted Postol and

George Lewis challenged that assertion in 1992, based on studying Army videos that had been used to assess Patriot effectiveness.

> We found no convincing evidence in the video that any Scud warhead was destroyed by a Patriot. We have strong evidence that Patriots hit Scuds on two occasions, but in both cases the videos also show that the Scud warheads fell to the ground and exploded. These clips provide strong evidence that even when Patriots could hit Scuds they were still not able to destroy Scud warheads.[78]

Originally, Postol and Lewis were ridiculed for their contentions. Eventually, however, in 2001, Clinton Administration Defense Secretary William Cohen admitted that the Patriot had not worked.[79] Missile defense advocates remained stalwart nevertheless.

When Gen. Abrahmson was preparing to leave SDIO in 1989, to be replaced by Henry Cooper, he stated that an entire space-based missile defense system based on the Brilliant Pebbles concept could be deployed in no more than five years for a cost of no more than $25 billion. Bush was still strongly committed. But it became evident even during the campaign that Bush and candidate Clinton had very different views on missile defense. Clinton came out against a space-based missile defense plan and in support of theater missile defense and the ABM Treaty, as originally interpreted, but willing to consider a limited national missile defense system within ABM parameters. It is important to note that at this time, missile defense was still differentiated as being theater (Patriot-like systems) and strategic or national (the GMD system). It was only strategic missile defence that was prohibited by the ABM. When Clinton won the election and became president, there was an almost immediate shift in emphasis from strategic to theater missile defense efforts. SDIO was renamed the Ballistic Missile Defense Organization (BMDO) toward that end. In line with the emerging Rogue Doctrine, the rationale was that with the demise of the Soviet Union, there was no need for an SDI-like program, but the United States and its missile defense approach needed to focus on the threat from Third World dictators.

Strategic missile defense advocates, however, remained adamant that a layered system, involving multiple types of missile defense, was needed; they became zealots. Henry Cooper joined High Frontier, a missile defense advocacy organization, when he left SDIO and began advising CSP and the Heritage Foundation, all toward pushing layered missile defense. Three hundred and fifty Republican candidates for the House of Representatives signed pledges to develop and deploy a strategic missile defense system as part of their 1994 Contract with America. Only by a very narrow margin was a portion of the Contract requiring deployment of a strategic missile defense system "as soon as practical" defeated.

But the 1995 National Intelligence Estimate (NIE) didn't work in missile defense advocates favor. It found that no country could develop a missile to threaten the continental United States within the next 15 years. Further, in that year, the United States and Russia came to an understanding regarding a line differentiating allowable TMD activities from prohibited ABM-banned activities. There was no discernable threat for a NMD program to counter.

Nevertheless, the Defend America Act was introduced in both houses of Congress in March 1996, declaring it US policy to deploy a limited missile defense system by 2003. Recognizing the train that was rolling and trying to slow it down, Clinton agreed to a "3+3" plan for national (strategic) missile defense that allowed three years for development and, if then warranted, three more years to deploy the system. The Pentagon, by now fully on board and at least partly driving this train, changed the purpose of the then NMD plan from a technology readiness program to a deployment readiness program.

William Hartung explains how Bruce Jackson's career typifies the revolving door that serves the military–industrial complex, and the role of the military–industrial complex in the missile defense saga.[80] An Army Intelligence Officer from 1979 to 1990, Jackson left the military in 1990 and joined Lehman Brothers investment bank in New York as a proprietary trading operations strategist. Then in 1993, he joined Lockheed Martin as Vice President for Strategy and Planning, a position he held until 2002. Strategy and behind-the-scenes maneuvering was, unquestionably, his forte. Beginning in 1997, Jackson served as a director for the Project for the New American Century (PNAC). Jackson was also on the advisory board of Frank Gaffney's Center for Security Policy, offering donors "maximum bang for the buck."

While exactly how much Gaffney received from Lockheed is unclear, "it was enough for Gaffney to thank the company in its 1998 annual report."[81] CSP was and continues to be a strong advocate for missile defense. Other CSP board members included Senator Jon Kyl (R-AZ) and Representative Curt Weldon (R-PA), both influential in nuclear and missile defense policies; Senator Bob Smith, who would sponsor a bill that created the Outer Space Commission chaired by Donald Rumseld and which produced the "Space Pearl Harbor" warning; Air Force Generals Howell Estes and Thomas Moorman who had joined Aerospace Corporation after retirement; former Air Force Chief of Staff Larry Welch who became President of the Institute for Defense Analysis (IDA); and retired Army General Jay Garner from SY Technologies, a small missile defense contractor based in Huntsville, Alabama. It was Weldon from the CSP board who proved most important in revitalizing missile defense plans and spending as he sponsored an amendment that created the Commission on the Ballistic Missile Threat to the United States (CABMTUS), to be chaired by Donald Rumsfeld and so also known as the Rumsfeld Commission. Advocates were plentiful and committed, and they often networked through think tanks.

If the missile defense program was to avoid serious budget cuts, a threat had to be found, and that became the job of CABMTUS.

The commission – which one veteran missile defense watcher described as "something Curt Weldon dreamed up in the shower one morning" – emerged as a critical weapon in the conservative drive to reshape the debate over missile defense and create a sense of urgency for the deployment of a missile defense system. In painting the ultimate worst-case scenario, the report systematically ignored all the real-world obstacles that a country like North Korea would face in trying to achieve a long-range ballistic missile capability and played up to any factors (however remote) that might increase North Korea's chances of getting such missiles in a shorter time frame. As a result, the Rumsfeld Commission gave missile defense advocates in Congress the quasi-official endorsement they needed to effectively move forward on the issue.[82]

In other words, the commission was one of those beehives of mischief intended to find a threat, not to determine if there was one.

As well as serving on the Rumsfeld Commission, Air Force General Larry Welch also chaired an annual review panel on existing missile defense programs. The first of the review reports was issued in 1998, and in it, the panel criticized what they saw as overly ambitious program timelines. In some cases, these timelines were considered tantamount to a "rush to failure."[83] Needless to say, these findings were not well received by missile defense supporters.

The Rumsfeld Commission findings[84] were, not surprisingly, more threatening than those of past NIEs. Further, with Rumsfeld moving directly to his position as Secretary of Defense, the methodology used by the commission was adopted for future intelligence estimates. Three specific aspects of that methodology were particularly important. First, the commission employed what has been referred to as a hypothesis-based threat assessment, or a "could" standard, as opposed to whether the threat was likely or, even, more likely than something else. That is, some hypothetical "could" (if, for example, North Korea were given missile technology, *could* it adapt it?) was considered an acceptable basis from which to speculate. Second, the travel distance required for a missile to be considered an Intercontinental Ballistic Missile (ICBM), rather than an Intermediate-Range Ballistic Missile (IRBM) was shortened by 5,000 miles. Since there were more IRBMs than ICBMs globally, this meant that with no change to the global missile inventory whatsoever, the numerical threat from ICBMs went up considerably. And third, whereas past intelligence estimates had considered how long it would take a country to *deploy* a long-range missile, the metric for future assessments became how long it would take a country to *develop* a long-range missile, which is usually about five years or less.[85] As a result of adopting this methodology, not only did the Rumsfeld Commission find a nearly histrionic missile threat to the United States, but the 1999 NIE did as well.

According to Bradley Graham, the testimony of Lockheed Martin engineers was also central to the Rumsfeld Commission's finding that a nation with short- to medium-range missile technology—"Scud-based" technology such as possessed by both Iraq and North Korea—could achieve "first flight" of a long-range ballistic missile within five years of a decision to do so. According to Graham, Rumsfeld scribbled a sentence on a piece of paper during the engineers' briefing (apparently he often scribbled notes regarding what direction the discussion should take) and then said, "Let me read something to you and see if this is what you're saying: using Scud technology, a country could test-fly a long-range missile within about five years. Is that what you're saying?"[86] When Lockheed engineers agreed with Rumsfeld's summary of their remarks, the commission proceeded to adopt a modified version of Rumsfeld's statement as the central finding of their report. "As a result," said William Hartung in his analysis, "the opinions of employees of a company that stood to benefit from the perception of a greater missile threat were allowed to overrule the consensus of the US intelligence community."[87] After the report was issued in the fall of 1998, Rumsfeld was presented with the Keeper of the Flame award at a gala dinner sponsored by CSP. Perhaps ironically, Dick Cheney was given that award in 2009 though he had referred to SDI as "oversold" at the end of the Reagan presidency.[88]

By the time the 1999 NIE and the Rumsfeld reports came out, however, they were largely just icing on the cake as North Korea's August 31, 1998 Taepo Dong-1 missile launch was all that was really needed to make a case to the public and Congress to push NMD forward. The intelligence communities also now seemed aligned or at least accepting of the need for a NMD system. During Clinton's second term, missile defense funding went from about $3 billion annually to over $5 billion. This increase led to well over $1 billion in missile defense contracts to Lockheed Martin alone.[89]

Clinton tried to keep the now fast-moving NMD locomotive from becoming a runaway train, but with only marginal success. After the North Korean launch, Congress passed the National Missile Defense Act committing the United States to deploy a NMD system "as soon as technically possible," which at that time was being stated as 2005. But when Clinton signed the legislation in July 1999, he gave four criteria to be used before a decision to deploy was made: threat, cost, the technical status of the NMD program, and adherence to the ABM Treaty.

Meanwhile in September 1999, the Welch panel took its second look at the NMD development timelines and again concluded that the program was high risk. The Welch panel recommended that the President again consider the "feasibility" of the system rather than if it was "ready to deploy." That assessment was countered by a new NIE, using the new methodology from the Rumsfeld Commission, which found a threat and, therefore, again supported the needs of missile defense advocates. Specifically, it found that within 15 years, the United States would likely face ICBM threats from Russia, China, and North Korea and probably from Iran and possibly Iraq. Advocates were pushing hard and there was a great deal of money at stake.

In February 2000, the Director of the Pentagon's Office of Operational Test and Evaluation, Philip Coyle, testified before Congress on the NMD program. He stated that "[u]ndue pressure has been placed on the [NMD] program by artificial goals for deployment in 2005."[90] Concurrently, a third Welch panel was issued, still asserting that deployment timetables were "high risk." This time as well the report also pointed out that the flight tests undertaken so far represented only "a limited part of the required operating envelope."[91] That comment foreshadowed an enduring controversy regarding the veracity of the missile defense testing[92] and whether it would translate into a viable operational capability. In September 2000, President Clinton decided not to authorize further work toward NMD deployment. Shortly thereafter in January 2001, the *other* Rumsfeld-led Commission, the Commission to Assess United States National Security Space Management, released its findings. That report provided the "Space Pearl Harbor" warning. Together, the Rumsfeld Commission reports provided the space blueprint for the George W. Bush Administration.

Candidate George W. Bush made his position on missile defense clear in his acceptance speech at the Republican Convention: "My administration will deploy missile defenses to guard against attack and blackmail. Now is the time, not to defend outdated treaties, but to defend the American people."[93] While pre-9/11 public opinion polls and intelligence estimates both clearly saw a higher risk from terrorist attacks than a missile attack, missile defense was the higher administration priority. It was prioritized as a "moral imperative," a reference used in conjunction with missile defense dating back to the Clinton years. Family Research Council President Gary Bauer included it in a 1998 Heritage Foundation lecture, even before the Taepo Dong launch:

> The evidence is overwhelming that ballistic missiles pose a very real threat to the United States and that the technology to defend America exists and is affordable. Incredibly, however, the country remains unprotected. Reversing this intolerable situation is a moral imperative as powerful as the defense of the unborn and the fostering of the family.[94]

Subsequently, references to the moral imperative are found in speeches by individuals such as Heritage Foundation President Edwin Feulner,[95] House Republican leader Dick Armey,[96] and Donald Rumsfeld. Said Rumsfeld:

> No US President can responsibly say that his defense policy is calculated and designed to leave the American people undefended against threats that are known to exist. ... It is not so much a technical question as a matter of a president's constitutional responsibility. Indeed it is in many respects ... a moral issue.[97]

Establishing NMD as a moral imperative served the administration well in quashing questions regarding cost and feasibility.

Further, perhaps more than any of the other post-Cold War think tanks created to keep the defense budget strong, PNAC members, including Paul Wolfowitz, Donald Rumsfeld, and Dick Cheney, moved directly into high-level national security jobs in the George W. Bush Administration. Individuals affiliated with Lockheed Martin, and sometimes overlapping with PNAC, also populated the Bush Administration. Former Lockheed Chief Operating Officer Peter Teets, for example, became Undersecretary of the Air Force and Director of the National Reconnaissance Office, responsible for decision-making on a range of areas from surveillance satellites to space-based elements of missile defense.

If all of the planets were still not fully aligned in support of missile defense before 9/11, specifically regarding public support, they were after. The Bush Administration got carte blanche from the American people and pushed forward generally on policies that had been slow or hard sells previously, but on space-related ones specifically. After 9/11, terrorist attacks were spuriously linked to the threat of missile attacks, a tactic that effectively gave the boost to the public support for missile defense that pollsters had been looking for and previously lacking.

> The decision to expand National Missile Defense as part of the war on terror proceeded after 9/11 namely due to the influence and recommendations of members of this conservative think tank [CSP], several of which were represented in the Bush Administration and gained increasing influence in policy recommendations after 9/11. The missile defense program continued to be expanded and justified even though the National Intelligence Estimate argued that it was highly unlikely that the terrorist threat could be effectively countered by the development of a missile defence program.
>
> [...]
>
> The lack of fit between the recommendations of the right-wing groups heavily financed and staffed by the military-industrial complex and the recommendations made by the 9/11 Commission to most effectively fight the war on terror are worth noting.[98]

Consequently, post 9/11, it was full speed ahead with a NMD system.

Toward that goal, several organizational and structural changes were made in the missile defense program. Differentiations between TMD programs and NMD programs were dropped. All efforts were simply categorized as "missile defense," which allowed for shifting budget priorities away from what had been TMD to NMD without explanation. The Ballistic Missile Defense Organization was renamed the Missile Defense Agency (MDA) in 2002, and it was positioned as an independent agency beyond the purview of DoD oversight. Also in 2002, the United States withdrew from the ABM Treaty so that any and all missile defense systems could be tested and deployed. The cautions of past years regarding technical and economic feasibility, and spurring an arms race, were dismissed with a hand wave.

When President Bush declared GMD operational in 2004, it was largely for political reasons as a show of confidence. But technically there was nothing different about the program after the declaration than the day before, when it was known largely for being plagued by test failures, even when the tests were scripted. There was a moment in 2006, however, that threatened to expose that the Emperor had no clothes.

In July 2006, North Korea launched another Taepo Dong missile, which failed in its first stage. For the second time in as many launches, North Korean rockets met an inglorious end. The test seemed another example of a North Korean propensity for adolescent attention-seeking behavior rather than an ability to demonstrate technical prowess. But the United States was put in the uncomfortable position of potentially having to put up or shut up, using its long-vaunted and chokingly expensive missile defense system against the North Korean missile. Fortuitously, Northern Command was quickly able to determine that the North Korean launch posed no threat to the United States and therefore did not have to fire an interceptor to attempt to stop it, which might have led to a very embarrassing "miss." President Bush stated that he thought the United States had a "reasonable" chance of a successful intercept.[99] But the North Korean test did provide further impetus for the administration to boost the missile defense budget, which by this time, annually exceeded the budgets of both the US Border Patrol and the US Coast Guard. Meanwhile, the veracity of missile defense tests continued to be questioned by technical experts, with some familiar figures involved.

Norm Augustine was retained as a consultant by the DoD in March 2006 to oversee an investigation of potential fraud in missile defense research at the Massachusetts Institute of Technology. The investigation concerned allegations by MIT Professor Theodore Postol—one of the two individuals who had debunked exaggerated claims of the effectiveness of the Patriot missile in the 1991 Gulf War—that well-funded MIT researchers had "cooked the books" by endorsing a 1997 test of a missile defense sensor that was in fact deeply flawed. Postol had been calling for an independent investigation of the incident for years and was outraged that when an investigation was finally started, MIT decided to let the Pentagon and Augustine oversee the work. He said: "It's hard to see how people can be so clumsy and dishonest. ... What MIT is in effect doing is turning over the responsibilities for oversight of its own academic operations to the Department of Defense."[100] Beyond the Patriot missile, Lockheed Martin was, at the time of the investigation, one of the Pentagon's top missile defense contractors. Not surprisingly, Augustine's investigation found that there had been no wrongdoing by MIT researchers.[101]

Since the Bush Administration, missile defense plans have been reconfigured, but spending has continued at about $8 billion annually, which is considered "stable" given budget cuts in many other areas of the federal and even defense budget.[102] While the MDA warned in 2015 that budget cuts due to sequestration would put US security in "serious jeopardy,"[103] its budget request for 2017 was $7.5 billion[104]—still a very healthy amount. Nevertheless, test results for the GMD system have consistently remained tenuous at best.[105]

And yet after the North Korean missile test in 2016, missile defense was again lauded, the *Wall Street Journal* proclaiming that the test "vindicated the long campaign for missile defense."[106] But, despite billions spent over decades, GMD still has no demonstrated capability to defend against a North Korean long-range missile. At least some in the science community feel the problems with missile defense harken back to the same issues raised by the 1998 Welch panel, which referred to missile defense as a "rush to failure." In response to the *Wall Street*

*Journal*, which claimed that operational missile defense issues were attributable to arms control efforts, physicist Laura Grego at the Union of Concerned Scientists argued instead that the rush to failure continues.

> The failure has its origins in the approach the George W. Bush administration took to hustle a system into the field, and to exempt it from normal oversight and accountability. This approach has been largely retained by the Obama administration, and Congress hasn't really challenged it. That approach has been a particular problem since strategic missile defense is really a very difficult physics and engineering problem.[107]

Missile defense is often seen as either a moral imperative or a solution that won't work to a problem that doesn't exist. If a moral imperative, then not just North Korea but Iranian missile tests in 2016 would presumably increase the imperative to have a proven system. If missile defense is to be pursued, the significant technical challenges involved ought to be addressed with the same kind of oversight and accountability that other significantly less expensive programs are subject to.

And while technical issues continue, it is the political issues associated with "sharing" missile defense that gets the most public attention. Specifically, missile defense creates considerable political angst between the United States and several other countries—China and Russia in particular—over its potential threat to nuclear deterrence and it being potentially better suited technically to use as an ASAT. In terms of the military–industrial complex, however, it remains the goose that laid the golden egg.

The revolving door of government officials who traverse between the public and private defense sector is a reality, and few have escaped involvement of some sort with missile defense. Even Defense Secretary Ashton Carter has a long history of involvement with missile defense issues. While serving on a board that advised the State Department on missile defense, Carter received $10,000 in 2008 from missile defense contractor Raytheon for provision of technical advice. When Carter became the Under Secretary of Defense for Acquisition, Technology and Logistics in 2009, he appropriately disclosed his work for Raytheon and, per ethics regulations, agreed to wait the required year before participating in Defense Department matters involving Raytheon. His support for missile defense and Raytheon products then quickly recommenced.

> In a 2010 *Wall Street Journal* op-ed, then-Under Secretary Carter wrote that an "essential element" of the program is the Standard Missile 3 (SM-3) interceptor, which is manufactured by Raytheon. The company also makes the Patriot missile defense system and the Exoatmospheric Kill Vehicle, a key component of intercontinental ballistic missile defense. In 2013, the MDA presented Carter with the Ronald Reagan Missile Defense Award. "Dr. Carter has been instrumental in defining the relationship between the Missile Defense Agency, the developer, and the Services," according to a DoD press release.[108]

Raytheon has received more than $11 billion in contract obligations from the MDA alone over the past decade.

## Things Change?

While most indicators see the military–industrial complex as healthy and a still-expanding stew of linkages, personal and corporate financial interests, and threat assessments to justify feeding the beast, there is another view. Innovation coming from the private sector, along with globalization, may change the future picture. Former Deputy Secretary of Defense William Lynn suggested in a 2014 *Foreign Affairs* article[109] that companies like Google—with a market value more than double that of General Dynamics, Northrop Grumman, Lockheed Martin, and Raytheon put together—are buying military suppliers and might not pursue further work for the military. In that article, Lynn explains:

> The Defense Department should be courting commercial companies, many of which will not seek out defense contracts themselves. Instead, the Pentagon has made it so difficult to bid on defense contracts that many companies shy away, finding the process unfamiliar and daunting. Some also avoid bidding because they have little interest in complying with what they see as unnecessary Pentagon requirements.[110]

Yet in 2016, Eric Schmitt, executive chairman of Google's parent company Alphabet, agreed to head a new Defense Innovation Advisory Board. A Pentagon press release stated that the board will "provide advice on the best and latest practices in innovation that the department can emulate."[111] So time will tell what relationship companies like Google work out with the Pentagon.

Perhaps it will be the reluctance of these new(er) private sector companies to become involved with the Byzantine world of the Pentagon and defense acquisitions that will allow the military–industrial behemoth to survive and thrive. Clearly, the cast of thousands, with a vested interest in its survival will not go down without a fight. But these new players with their innovation, and money, will play an important role in the future. Whether they remain aloof or join the crowd, they and their NewSpace private sector friends, along with long-suffering space diplomats, have a vested interest and a voice in keeping the space environment stable.

## Notes

1  Eisenhower's farewell address to the nation, January 17, 1961. http://avalon.law.yale.edu/20th_century/eisenhower001.asp
2  Graham Allison and Philip Zelikow, *Essence of Decision*, 2nd edition, Addison-Wesley Publishing, New York, 1999, p. 255.
3  Bruce DeBlois "The advent of space weapons," *Astropolitics*, 1(1), p. 7.

4 Bryan Bender, "From the Pentagon to the private sector," *Boston Globe*, December 26, 2010. http://archive.boston.com/news/nation/washington/articles/2010/12/26/defense_firms_lure_retired_generals/

5 Bryan Bender, "Seminars teach senior officers how to land industry jobs," *Boston Globe*, December 26, 2010.

6 Eloise Lee and Robert Johnson, "The 25 biggest defense companies in America," *Business Insider*, March 10, 2012, citing SIPRI data.

7 Joan Johnson-Freese and Thomas M. Nichols, "DHS: the department of everything," *Breaking Defense*, March 27, 2015. http://breakingdefense.com/2015/03/dhs-the-department-of-everything/

8 Tom Engelhardt, "Why does the United States have 17 different intelligence agencies?" *The Nation*, August 4, 2014.

9 S. Pete Worden, "On self-licking ice cream cones," Proceedings of the 7th Cambridge Workshop on Cool Stars, Stellar Systems and the Sun, ASP Conference Series, 26, 1992.

10 Ronald W. Cox, "The military-industrial complex and US military spending after 9/11," *Class, Race and Corporate Power*, 2(2), 2014, 2–3.

11 Scott Sagan, "Why do states build nuclear weapons: three models in search of a bomb," *International Security*, 21(3), Winter 1996–97, p. 64

12 Deblois, "The advent of space weapons," p. 7.

13 Bryan Bender, "Many D.C. think tanks now players in partisan wars," *Boston Globe*, August 11, 2013.

14 "Who we are," *Secure World Foundation*. http://swfound.org/about-us/who-we-are/

15 David Gibbs, "Pretexts in US foreign policy: the war on terrorism in historical perspective," *New Political Science*, 26(3), 2004, 293–321; William Hartung and Michelle Ciarrocca, "The military-industrial think tank complex," *Multinational Monitor*, January–February 2003, 17–20.

16 "About us," *Center for Security Policy*. www.centerforsecuritypolicy.org/about-us/

17 See Center for a New Security home page. www.cnas.org

18 "Honor roll of contributors," *Center for a New Security*. www.cnas.org/content/cnas-supporters

19 Cox, "The military-industrial complex," p. 9.

20 Michael Klare, *Rogue States and Nuclear Outlaws: America's Search for a New Foreign Policy*, Hill and Wang, New York, 1996, p. 14.

21 Cox, "The military-industrial complex," p. 6.

22 Ibid., p. 7.

23 Klare, *Rogue States and Nuclear Outlaws*, pp. 16–18.

24 Cox, "The military-industrial complex," p. 7.

25 William D. Hartung, *Prophets of War: Lockheed Martin and the Making of the Military-Industrial Complex*, Nation Books, New York, 2011; see Chapter 8, "Saint Augustine's laws," pp. 163–90.

26 Ibid., p. 167.

27 Ibid., p. 171

28 Ibid., pp. 169–74.

29 Lee Drutman, "How corporate lobbyists conquered American democracy," *The Atlantic*, April 20, 2015. www.theatlantic.com/business/archive/2015/04/how-corporate-lobbyists-conquered-american-democracy/390822/

30 Spencer Ackerman, "Keep paying us or the economy dies," *Wired*, October 26, 2011. www.wired.com/2011/10/defense-industry-cuts-economy/
31 Ibid., 2011.
32 William Hartung and Stephen Miles, "Pentagon contractors play a disturbing game," *The Huffington Post*, August 25, 2012. www.huffingtonpost.com/william-hartung/lockheed-martin_b_1625183.html
33 Mark Leibovich, *This Town*, Blue Rider Press, New York, 2014.
34 Ibid., p. 330.
35 Revolving Door, "Former members", *Open Secrets*. https://www.opensecrets.org/revolving/top.php?display=Z
36 Cited in Michael Hiltzit, "The revolving door spins faster: ex-Congressmen become 'stealth lobbyists.'" *Los Angeles Times*, January 6, 2015. www.latimes.com/business/hiltzik/la-fi-mh-the-revolving-door-20150106-column.html
37 "All cooled off: as Congress convenes, former colleagues will soon be calling from K Street," *Open Secrets*, January 6, 2015. www.opensecrets.org/news/2015/01/coming-out-of-the-cool-as-congress-convenes-former-colleagues-will-soon-be-calling-from-k-street/
38 Ibid.
39 Justin Elliott, "Key Senate Staffer on Military Issues Got Big Payout From Lockheed Martin," *Pro Publica*, July 26, 2012. www.propublica.org/article/key-senate-staffer-on-military-issues-got-big-payout-from-lockheed-martin
40 Jerry Harris, *The Dialectics of Globalization*, Cambridge Scholars Publishing, Newcastle, UK, 2006, pp. 128–9.
41 "About AIAA'" *AIAA*. https://www.aiaa.org/AboutAIAA/
42 SIA home page. www.sia.org
43 Brian Bender, "From the Pentagon to the Private Sector."
44 Ibid.
45 Ibid.
46 The Department of the Air Force General Counsel, *Pre- and Post Retirement Restrictions for Separating and Retiring Air Force Personnel*, Air Force Ethics Office, The Pentagon, December 2013, p. 7. www.safgc.hq.af.mil/shared/media/document/AFD-131227-008.pdf
47 Bryan Bender, "Seminars teach senior officers how to land industry jobs."
48 Ibid.
49 Secretary of DefenseMemorandum, "Policy on Senior Mentors," April 1, 2010. www.acq.osd.mil/dpap/dars/docs/SeniorMentorPolicy.pdf
50 Tom Vanden Brook, "Pentagon revises military mentor rules," *USA Today*, September 8, 2010. www.usatoday.com/news/military/2010-08-09-1Amentors09_ST_N.htm
51 Dana Liebelson, "98 percent of former military officers drop out of Pentagon program after financial disclosure," *The Project on Government Oversight (POGO) Blog*, November 9, 2011. http://pogoblog.typepad.com/pogo/2011/11/98-percent-of-former-military-officers-drop-out-of-pentagon-program-after-financial-disclosure-.html
52 Ibid.
53 Inspector General, *DoD complied with policies on converting senior mentors to highly qualified experts, but few senior mentors converted*, Report no. D0DIG-2012-009, Department of Defense, Washington, DC, October 31, 2011. www.dodig.mil/audit/reports/fy12/audit/dodig-2012-009.pdf

54 "Financial disclosure rules repels Pentagon advisors," *Defense-Aerospace*, November 9, 2011. www.defense-aerospace.com/article-view/release/130229/financial-disclosure-rules-repels-pentagon-advisers.html

55 Tom Vanden Brook and Ray Locker, "McCain blasts Air Force on mentor use," *USA Today*, December 2, 2011. www.usatoday.com/news/military/story/2011-11-28/air-force-mentor-conflict/51451582/1

56 Bryan Bender, "From the Pentagon to the Private Sector."

57 Lee Fang, "Who's paying the pro-war pundits?" *The Nation*, September 16, 2014. www.thenation.com/article/whos-paying-pro-war-pundits/

58 Ibid.

59 David Barstow, "Behind TV analysts, Pentagon's hidden hand," *New York Times*, April 20, 2008. www.nytimes.com/2008/04/20/us/20generals.html?_r=0

60 David Willman, "The Pentagon's $10 billion bet gone bad," *Los Angeles Times*, April 5, 2015. http://graphics.latimes.com/missile-defense/

61 Cited in Ann Scott Tyson, "US missile defense being expanded, general says," *Washington Post*, July 22, 2005. www.washingtonpost.com/wp-dyn/content/article/2005/07/21/AR2005072102356.html

62 Bradley Graham, *Hit to Kill: The New Battle Over Shielding America From a Missile Attack*, Public Affairs, New York, 2001.

63 Ibid., pp. 8–9.

64 Freeman Dyson, "Defense against ballistic missiles," *Bulletin of the Atomic Scientists*, 20(6): 12, 1964.

65 "Scientific consensus on global warming," *Union of Concerned Scientists*. www.ucsusa.org/global_warming/science_and_impacts/science/scientific-consensus-on.html#.VwUlc6v1elI

66 Graham, *Hit to Kill*, p. 10.

67 "The Anti-Ballistic Missile (ABM) Treaty at a glance," *Arms Control Association*. https://www.armscontrol.org/factsheets/abmtreaty

68 Graham, *Hit to Kill*, p. 13.

69 Steven Pifer, "The limits of US missile defense," *Brookings Institute*, March 30, 2015. www.brookings.edu/research/opinions/2015/03/30-us-missile-defense-limits-pifer

70 Stephen Schwartz, "The real price of ballistic missile defense," *WMD Junction*, April 13, 2012. http://wmdjunction.com/120413_missile_defense_costs.htm

71 Government Accountability Office, *Missile Defense: Opportunities Exist to Reduce Acquisition Risk and Improve Reporting on System Capabilities*, GAO-15-345, GAO, Washington, DC, May 2015. www.gao.gov/assets/680/670048.pdf

72 Tim Nunan, "Exclusive interview with Freeman Dyson," *Nassau Weekly*, February 7, 2007. www.nassauweekly.com/exclusive_interview_with_freeman_dyson/

73 Ibid.

74 Cited in Geoffrey Smith, "Who won the war?" *National Interest*, Spring 2005, 119–25.

75 Jeffrey Simpson, "NATO and Star Wars," *Globe and Mail* (Canada), January 12, 1985.

76 Keith B. Payne and Colin S. Grey, "The Star Wars debate: nuclear policy and the defensive transition," *Foreign Affairs*, Spring 1984.

77 Steven Pifer, "The limits of US missile defense," *Brookings Institute*, March 30, 2015. www.brookings.edu/research/opinions/2015/03/30-us-missile-defense-limits-pifer

78 Postol/Lewis Review of Army's Study on Patriot Effectiveness, September 8, 1992. http://fas.org/spp/starwars/docops/pl920908.htm

79 Cited in William J. Broad, "MIT studies accusations of lies and cover-up of serious flaws in antimissile system," *New York Times*, January 2, 2003. www.nythimes. com/2003/01/02/national/02MISS.html?pagewanted=all

80 Hartung, *Prophets of War*, pp. 191–2.

81 Ibid., p. 198.

82 Ibid., p. 200.

83 Council for a Livable World, "Pentagon panel faults national missile defense 'rush to failure,'" *Global Beat*, April 1998. www.bu.edu/globalbeat/usdefense/clw0498.html

84 *Report of the Commission to Assess the Ballistic Missile Threat to the United States: Executive Summary*, Pursuant to Public Law 201, 104th Congress, July 15, 1998. http://fas.org/ irp/threat/missile/rumsfeld/index.html

85 Joseph Cirincione, "Political and Strategic Imperatives of National Missile Defense," *Carnegie Endowment for International Peace*, October 12, 2000. http://carnegieendowment. org/2000/10/12/political-and-strategic-imperatives-of-national-missile-defense

86 Cited in Graham, *Hit to Kill*, pp. 43–4.

87 Hartung, *Prophets of War*, p. 202.

88 Andrew Rosenthal, "Missile Shield Must Be Balanced Against Other Goals, Cheney Says," *New York Times*, January 27, 1989.

89 Hartung, *Prophets of War*, p. 203.

90 "The Coyle report", *Arms Control Association*. www.armscontrol.org/print/619

91 Larry D. Welch, *National Missile Defense Independent Review Team Executive Summary*, June 13, 2000. http://fas.org/spp/starwars/program/news00/welch2000.htm

92 Gary Taubes, "Postol vs. the Pentagon," *MIT Technology Review*, April 1, 2002. www. technologyreview.com/featuredstory/401412/postol-vs-the-pentagon/;       Thom Shakner, "Missile defense interceptor misses target in test," *The New York Times*, July 5, 2013. www.nytimes.com/2013/07/06/us/missile-defense-interceptor-misses-target-in-test.html?_r=0

93 "Text: George W. Bush accepts nomination," *washingtonpost.com*, August 3, 2000. www.washingtonpost.com/wp-srv/onpolitics/elections/bushtext080300.htm

94 Gary Bauer, "The moral foundations for strong national defense," Lecture at 21st Annual Heritage Foundation Resource Bank Meeting, Oak Brook, Il, April 24, 1998. www.heritage.org/research/lecture/ the-moral-foundations-for-strong-national-defense

95 Edwin J. Feulner, "Missile defense, the stakes couldn't be higher," *The Heritage Foundation*, September 8, 1998. www.heritage.org/research/commentary/1998/09/ missile-defense-the-stakes-couldnt-be-higher

96 Cited in Brian Knowlton, "Battle on missile-defense funds heats up," *International Herald Tribune*, September 10, 2001.

97 Cited in Robert Burns, "Rumsfeld assures Russia over arms," *New York Times*, February 3, 2001.

98 Cox, "The military-industrial complex," pp. 12–13.

99 Cited in David E. Sanger, "Bush says US may have been able to intercept North Korean missile," *New York Times*, July 7, 2005, p. 5.

100 Postol, cited in Hartung, *Prophets of War*, p. 189.

101 Angela Wang, "Lincoln Lab not guilty of fraud, DoD says," *The Tech*, 127(15), April 3, 2007. http://tech.mit/V127/N15/dodreport.html

102  Eric Auner, "Missile defense budgets hold steady," *Arms Control Association*, April 1, 2014. https://www.armscontrol.org/act/2014_04/Missile-Defense-Budget-Holds-Steady%20

103  Andrea Shalal, "US Missile Defense Agency warns of jeopardy from budget cuts," *Reuters*, March 13, 2015. www.reuters.com/article/usa-military-missiledefense-idUSL2N0WL25F20150319

104  Missile Defense Agency,      Fiscal Year (FY) 2017 Budget Estimates: Overview, Department of Defense, Washington, DC. www.mda.mil/global/documents/pdf/budgetfy17.pdf

105  George N. Lewis and Theodore Postol, "A flawed and dangerous missile defense plan," *Arms Control Association*. https://www.armscontrol.org/act/2010_05/Lewis-Postol; Theresa Hitchens (with Victoria Samson), "Technical hurdles in US missile defense agency programs," in *New Challenges in Missile Proliferation, Missile Defense, and Space Security*, Occasional Paper, No. 12, ed. James Clay Moltz, Center for Non-Proliferation Studies, Monterey, CA, July 2003, pp. 10–17. http://cns.miis.edu/opapers/op12/op12.pdf; Testimony of Philip Coyle before the Strategic Forces Subcommittee of the House Armed Service Subcommittee, February 25, 2009. https://www.gpo.gov/fdsys/pkg/CHRG-111hhrg51659/html/CHRG-111hhrg51659.htm

106  "The rogue-state nuclear missile threat," *The Wall Street Journal*, February 11, 2016. www.wsj.com/articles/the-rogue-state-icbm-2455237938

107  Laura Grego, "Missile defense folly," *All Things Nuclear*, March 9, 2016. http://allthingsnuclear.org/lgrego/missile-defense-folly

108  "Ashton Carter takes revolving door to higher level," *Project on Government Oversight*. January 6, 2015. www.pogo.org/blog/2015/01/ashton-carter-takes-revolving-door-to-higher-level.html

109  William Lynn III, "The end of the military-industrial complex: how the Pentagon is adapting to globalization," *Foreign Affairs*, November–December 2014, 104. https://www.foreignaffairs.com/articles/united-states/end-military-industrial-complex

110  Ibid., pp. 107–8.

111  Statement by Pentagon Press Secretary Peter Cook on the Establishment of the Defense Innovation Advisory Board, March 2, 2016. www.defense.gov/News/News-Releases/News-Release-View/Article/684201/statement-by-pentagon-press-secretary-peter-cook-on-the-establishment-of-the-de

# 6

# SPACE DEVELOPMENT AND GOVERNANCE

> More important than the material issue … the opening of a new, high frontier
> will challenge the best that is in us … the new lands waiting to be built in space
> will give us new freedom to search for better governments, social systems, and
> ways of life.
>
> Gerard K. O'Neill, *The High Frontier*, 1976.

There are individuals, many individuals, who think about space in terms of inevitability, but not the inevitability of warfare. Instead they think about the inevitability of the development of space, much like the development of the American West or development of the automobile or computer industries. They believe that space offers untold commercial and resource opportunities that will inevitably be tapped. Private sector entrepreneurs are working independently and in partnerships with government agencies in unprecedented ways toward the development of space as both a geographic domain and an industrial sector, ways that had been anticipated decades ago but did not begin to materialize on a broad scale until recently. Currently, "private commercial space activities have eclipsed government activities in economic value."[1] The needs of these space developers, however, are somewhat contradictory.

While a stable space environment is required to develop areas like tourism and to assure the safety of spacecraft, space entrepreneurs and developers often shun too many rules or regulations toward maintaining that stability, fearing those rules could impede the full exploitation of opportunities. On the other hand, new regulations or interpretations of regulations are needed at times in areas like property rights and patents to assure they are able to reap the rewards of their efforts. Consequently, domestic and international law, and politics, inherently affect space development.

No environment is free from conflict, but there are ways to address those conflicts other than with threats and warfare as the starting point. In that vein, global politicians are working multilaterally toward setting and maintaining the conditions—sustainability through stability—to allow space development and access to space for all to occur, though often with significant and raucous disagreement among them regarding "how." Additionally, there are ethical issues being raised by developing countries regarding where the ability to profit should end in favor of equity.

## Space Development

Princeton physicist Gerard K. O'Neill published his award-winning post-Apollo book *The High Frontier* in 1976, anticipating the colonization of space by 1995 and providing a blueprint for doing so.[2] He died in 1992 with humans no closer to space colonization than they had been in 1977. Instead of the real thing, humanity seemed to settle for multiple versions of *Star Trek* and *Star Wars*.

The Apollo program, while wildly popular among the public as a symbol of America's can-do spirit and technical prowess during the Cold War—American exceptionalism at its best—did not inspire public support for space travel or colonization. According to Roger Launius, space curator at the Smithsonian's National Air and Space Museum, the only time more than half of the public believed the Apollo Program worth the expense was at the time of the 1969 Apollo 11 landing as they watched Neil Armstrong walk on the Moon, and even then, only 53 percent of the public was supportive.[3] While the last three Apollo missions were canceled due to NASA budgetary restraints, the public's attention was drawn to turmoil elsewhere, including the civil rights movement and Vietnam. The public had already experienced the thrill of seeing Americans walking on the Moon. They "had the tee shirt" and their attention had gone elsewhere. Even during Apollo, much of the American public had shown reluctance to spend their government tax dollars on sending astronauts to the Moon;[4] though, the public routinely overestimates government expenditures for space programs.

In the 1970s, NASA began to consider ways to create a supplement to public funding for space activities through the private sector. A 1977 NASA-funded study by the Hudson Institute projected 100-year future space activities ripe for development.[5] In the 1980s, during the Reagan Administration, the Department of Commerce encouraged the development of space commerce through NASA public–private partnerships. Sometimes wildly optimistic projections of up to $60 billion in space commerce within 15 years (of the mid 1980s) spurred considerable interest but showed little results in other than selected areas, such as communications. High launch costs were partly responsible for stifling most private sector activities, except in specific areas like communications that flourished because government and commercial consumer demand, among very large consumer populations, steadily grew to where these costs could be offset. Other fields, such as remotely sensed imagery, took much longer to prosper and needed government and monopoly-like support for a decade before the market started to expand. Private companies made decisions regarding space commerce based on whether a business case could be made for development, not for the thrill of space development.

Nevertheless, efforts to expand space commerce continued, including consideration of various development analogs over the years. The transcontinental railroad, the telephone industry, the aerospace industry, supporting scientific research in Antarctica, advancing public works, and making accessible scenic and cultural conservation sites were all studied as models for space development.[6] But the high cost of launch continued to be a factor in business decisions on space development. Not surprisingly, therefore, it is likely that much of the more recent success of NewSpace actors stems from their attempts to bring down launch costs and make access to space more affordable.

## The Risk Takers

Companies that have become known as NewSpace actors are those largely financed by individuals operating with their own money and so willing—and able—to take risks. South African entrepreneur and co-founder of PayPal Elon Musk created Space Exploration Technologies Corporation (SpaceX), and Amazon founder Jeff Bezos started Blue Origin—both NewSpace launch companies. The politics of blame for any kind of failure makes risk-taking nearly impossible with government money. But these NewSpace actors have taken up O'Neill's dream, his expectation, to develop and colonize space. The SpaceX mission statement on its website says: "SpaceX designs, manufactures and launches advanced rockets and spacecraft. The company was founded in 2002 to revolutionize space technology, with the ultimate goal of enabling people to live on other planets."[7] Musk has been quoted as saying: "I would like to die on Mars. Just not on impact."[8]

SpaceX has focused on the development of a family of launchers and prides itself on having accomplished a number of "firsts." In December 2010, it became the first private company to return a spacecraft to Earth after completing nearly two orbits. Then in May 2012, its Dragon spacecraft attached to the International Space Station (ISS) exchanged cargo payloads and returned safely to Earth. That technically challenging feat had previously only by accomplished by governments. SpaceX thereby effectively demonstrated that space was no longer just a domain of nation-states. On December 21, 2015, the SpaceX Falcon 9 rocket carried 11 communications satellites to orbit and then returned and landed the first stage at its Landing Zone 1—the first-ever orbital-class rocket landing—with control room excitement reminiscent of the Apollo days.[9] SpaceX extended its line of "firsts" in April 2016 when—after several prior explosive failures—a Falcon 9 rocket delivered its payload to the ISS and then returned and landed on a sea-based drone platform.[10] Musk named the first SpaceX platform "Just Read the Instructions" and the second "Of Course I Still Love You."

SpaceX is one of several private companies that could someday launch humans into space. With the Space Shuttle's last flight in July 2011, the United States lost its independent human spaceflight capability. The United States became dependent upon Russia to carry astronauts and supplies to the ISS, a situation uncomfortable and alien to the United States. Consequently, NASA began or accelerated plans with the private sector to develop human transportation capabilities. Basically, the private sector was to take responsibility for low Earth orbit (LEO) activities so that NASA funds could be used to reach beyond.

It is important to recognize that there is a stark difference between commercial aerospace companies the likes of Boeing and Lockheed and those deemed part of the NewSpace genre because, although they are both privately owned, they operate under very different premises. Boeing, Lockheed, Northrop, etc. are "commercial" in that they are publicly traded, must respond to shareholders, and hope to make a profit. However, they all live, primarily, in a space environment that is dominated by government acquisition rules—Federal Acquisition Regulations (FAR), Part 15, Contracting by Negotiation—and classified projects. As a result, the organizations are structured—from accounting, to legal, to security—to respond to the government's slow-motion, primarily "cost-plus" approach to funding large defense projects. This structure is very complex and expensive and requires a large overhead of talented humans to meet the government's requirements.

NewSpace companies are not structured in the same fashion. They tend to be thinly self-funded or funded by venture capitalists. Most have a single product or solution that they are trying to sell in the commercial marketplace. They are not depending on the government for their survival although many or some would like to sell to the government. They do not have accounting systems that are compliant with government rules and regulations. Most do not have, or cannot obtain, facilities clearances so there is limited possibility to do classified work. Most do not expect to do cost-plus work and would prefer to do "firm fixed-price contracting"— preferably under FAR Part 12 (the way the DoD buys pencils) or a flexible method specifically designed to accommodate commercial vendors called Other Transactional Authority (OTA).[11] Most NewSpace companies do not have the legal staffs necessary to fight the interminable contract protest battles that inevitably result from large defense procurements.

By and large, the DoD, especially the Air Force, has looked at these NewSpace companies and responded with distrust and confusion. It is difficult and outside the bounds of standard operating procedures for the Air Force to accommodate all the paperwork necessary to contract for a low-cost launch vehicle. Consequently, the DoD does not want to change the way they do things and buy from NewSpace companies because doing so is, quite simply, hard. Doing things differently also opens the DoD to challenge and congressional oversight that can be avoided simply by adhering to the status quo—an approach that also benefits the military–industrial complex. But the result is that the DoD relies on the big prime contractors almost exclusively and cannot figure out how to work with the smaller and less sophisticated but potentially more economical companies.

That said, NASA and the DoD, mostly NASA, are selectively employing or saying they will employ new approaches toward development and utilization of space capabilities. The Air Force, for example, says it will make much-needed changes to the lengthy, burdensome government acquisition process[12] toward more efficiency. More concretely, NASA's Commercial Crew and Cargo Program represents a departure from the past model of NASA owning and operating its own vehicles and is intended to facilitate space development through the use of FAR firm fixed-price contracts with commercial vendors.[13] "Because all space activity requires transportation to space, NASA's Commercial Crew and Cargo Program is the critical enabler for further American space economic development—the equivalent to roads, railroads, canals, and other national investments that expended our frontiers."[14] NASA awarded a series of Phase 1 Commercial Resupply Services contracts (CRS1) in 2008 for delivery of cargo and supplies to the ISS on commercially operated spacecraft. SpaceX was awarded $1.6 billion for 12 cargo transport missions while Orbital Sciences was awarded $1.9 billion for 8 missions, extending to 2016. CRS2 contracts to cover transport flights from 2019 until 2024 were awarded in January 2016 to SpaceX, Orbital ATK, and the Sierra Nevada Corporation.[15, 16] The most recent competition for five follow-on cargo supply missions were all awarded to SpaceX in December 2015. These were awarded under the CRS1 contract. CRS2 contracts are priced slightly higher, so NASA, not surprisingly, purchased as many of the less expensive missions as possible under CRS1 before it expired.

NASA's human spaceflight corollary program to CRS is the Commercial Crew Program (CCP), with firm fixed-price Commercial Crew Transportation Capability (CCtCap) contracts awarded to both Boeing and SpaceX.[17] In September 2014, Boeing received a $4.2 billion contract to complete development and manufacture of the CST-100 "space taxi," recently renamed "Starliner." The first tests for Starliner were originally scheduled for 2016 with a first operational flight in 2017; however, dates are always subject to delay, due as often to budget issues as to technology development. SpaceX was also awarded a $2.6 billion contract by NASA, toward development of its Crew Dragon spacecraft. Crew Dragon is expected to be able to dock to the ISS for up to 210 days and provide a safe haven for the crew in times of emergency.[18] Private companies are also working with NASA toward development of capabilities for NASA's Journey to Mars program.[19] Other companies are working to develop human spaceflight capabilities in conjunction with space tourism.

SpaceX isn't alone in its risk-taking approach to development of new space launch vehicles. Sir Richard Branson, the British entrepreneur behind Virgin Atlantic airlines, is also behind Virgin Galactic, which bills itself as the "world's first commercial spaceline" and states its purpose as "democratizing access to space for the benefit of life on Earth."[20] The Virgin Galactic plan to open space to a larger cadre of individuals than those selected by governments for space travel will initially involve two aircraft. The first, called WhiteKnightTwo, is a double-hulled piloted plane that resembles a catamaran and is designed for high altitudes. It is used to lift the second craft, which is manned by two pilots and carries six passengers. At an altitude of about 50,000 feet, WhiteKnightTwo drops the smaller craft, which fires a rocket that sends it to the very edge of the atmosphere. Passengers would then experience four minutes of weightlessness before the spacecraft re-enters the atmosphere. The first model of Virgin's passenger-carrying crafts is called SpaceShipTwo.

The first SpaceShipTwo craft suffered a catastrophic accident during a test flight on October 31, 2014. The National Transportation Safety Board (NTSB) declared pilot error as the cause. SpaceShipTwo uses an unusual feathered tail system to change position from one phase of flight to the next and the craft can safely coast back to Earth and land as a glider. On the day of the accident, pilot Peter Siebold called out a speed of Mach 0.8 at which point co-pilot Michael Alsbury moved a handle controlling the feathering mechanism from lock to unlock even though that shouldn't have been done until the spacecraft achieved a speed of Mach 1.4. Alsbury didn't, however, activate the feather system. Nevertheless, aerodynamic load overpowered the actuators holding it in place, forcing it to open. Consequently, SpaceShipTwo broke up in flight, killing Alsbury and seriously injuring Siebold.[21]

According to the NTSB report, the "lack of consideration for human error" in the design of the spacecraft contributed to the scenario that occurred that fateful day. First, "the system was not designed with safeguards to prevent unlocking feather"; additionally, "manuals/procedures did not have a warning about unlocking [the] feather early."[22] In other words, human error had not been anticipated.

Following the accident and much to his credit, after sober reflection on the wisdom of moving forward with something "that could result in such tragic circumstances,"[23] Branson decided that the company would move forward; the goal was worth the risk. Spaceflight is inherently risky, but progress always involves taking risks. NASA returned the Space Shuttle to flight after two catastrophic accidents, but on taxpayer funds and not without facing resistance. NewSpace private companies are now the ones taking the risk, using their own funds.

In February 2016, Virgin Galactic unveiled a replacement SpaceShipTwo model, this one called Virgin Spaceship (VSS) Unity, named by none other than physicist Stephen Hawking. Hawking's accompanying message stated, "I would be very proud to fly on this spaceship."[24] Though Virgin Galactic is reticent about specific dates when space tourists might expect a ride, more than 700 people have signed up for a ticket, including such celebrities as Ashton Kutcher, Katy Perry, Leonardo DiCaprio, and Kate Winslet, paying $250,000 in advance for a seat. Though a new system has been implemented that would prevent an accident like the one in 2014 from occurring again, the Virgin Galactic approach is reliant on pilots. Virgin Galactic says their piloted approach keeps the design simple with fewer systems likely to fail.[25] Included in Virgin Galactic's new group of test pilots is Kelly Latimer who formerly held the distinction of being NASA's first-ever female test pilot.[26]

The challenges Virgin Galactic faces are technical and economic, and typical of NewSpace firms. Beyond the development of an operational vehicle, the company must also train their pilots to fly the vehicle in both suborbital and sea level conditions, which is not an inconsequential undertaking and takes time. But it must also start flying customers and continue flying them at a fairly rapid pace to make the money necessary to continue research and development—it can't spend passengers' deposit money and Branson cannot self-finance indefinitely. Consequently, the pressure on these companies and the need to be innovative can be intense.

There is no shortage of approaches and goals for the NewSpace companies. XCOR's Lynx spacecraft is another entry into the suborbital market, intending to carry one pilot astronaut, one participant, and scientific payloads to the edge of space.[27] New Shepard, a competitor ship being built by Bezo's company Blue Origin, is aiming for the space tourism market. The company website advertises room for six passengers in a capsule "large enough to float freely and turn weightless somersaults," as well as "the largest windows in space."[28] Blue Origin successfully completed its third (uncrewed) test flight in April 2016.

NewSpace companies outside the United States are also involved in the development of innovative launch systems. These include zero2infinity, a high-altitude balloon company based in Spain that aims to deliver small satellites to LEO using a combination of a balloon and a rocket. The vehicle, called Bloostar, has its first orbital mission scheduled for late 2018.[29] Rocket Lab, a US–New Zealand venture, is developing the Electron small launch vehicle and plans to begin launches in 2016 from New Zealand's North Island. "Rocket Lab has emphasized the advanced technology used in the development of the engine. Elements of the engine are 3-D printed, and the engine uses electric motors to power its turbopumps."[30] With affordable and high-frequency launches, Rocket Lab says its mission is to "make space open for business."[31]

A Russian private company says it plans to be involved in the space tourism business. CosmoCourse says it will develop and build a spacecraft capable of suborbital space tourism flights. The developers—many, former employees of Russia's Khrunichev State Research and Production Space Center—say they will be up and flying by 2020.[32] Previously, Russian space tourism activity has been largely limited to accepting paid customers as visitors to the ISS, transported on Soyuz spacecraft via the American-based private company Space Adventures.

While spacecraft reusability has been the mantra for many companies seeking to bring down launch costs and so open space for development, other companies are taking a different approach. Orbital ATK Chief Executive David Thompson recently voiced skepticism over the drive toward reusability. "It may be intuitively appealing. We don't throw airplanes away and so on. Past experience with launch reusability has been mixed at best in terms of achieving sustainable cost reductions. So I am a skeptic."[33] Instead, Orbital is investing its own capital on the development of a satellite servicing spacecraft that is capable of refueling and conducting minor repairs on geosynchronous satellites.

Initially, the Orbital spacecraft will mechanically dock with a GEO spacecraft and take over guidance, navigation, and control (GNC) for pointing, station-keeping, and orbital transport (such as adjusting inclination and orbit location or moving to disposal orbit) purposes. For that reason, it is named the Mission Extension Vehicle (MEV). Only later will it take on tasks including refueling, repair, and mission enhancement capabilities. Orbital is investing heavily in those technologies, but also working on technology transfers with NASA through "unfunded" Space Act Agreements (SAA). Accomplishing these tasks will require autonomous rendezvous technology, a capability the United States expresses angst about when developed in other countries.

Bigelow Aerospace, founded by Robert Bigelow, the billionaire owner of the hotel chain Budget Suites of America, is another of the many NewSpace actors. The Bigelow banner on its website proclaims its mission.

> Since 1999 our mission has been to provide affordable destinations for national space agencies and corporate clients. In 2006 and 2007, we launched our orbiting prototypes Genesis I and Genesis II. We seek to assist human exploration and the discovery of beneficial resources, whether in Low Earth Orbit (LEO), on the Moon, in deep space or Mars.[34]

Bigelow designs and builds expandable, modular, pressurized space habitats. The habitat, called B330, can be deployed by multiple launch vehicles. A SpaceX Dragon capsule carried aloft on a Falcon 9 rocket delivered a Bigelow expandable habitat to the ISS in April 2016 for testing. Bigelow intends to operate free-flying orbital outposts for paying customers, including tourists. Ultimately, however, the goal is to deploy these portable habitats on the Moon beginning in 2025. Toward that end, Bigelow sought and received assurance from the US Federal Aviation Administration (FAA) in 2015 that they could conduct commercial activities on the lunar surface on a non-interference basis.[35] That permission was a precursor to further US actions to encourage the commercial development of space.

President Obama signed the US Commercial Space Launch Competitiveness Act (or US Space Act) in 2015. One of the key provisions protects private spaceflight from regulatory oversight for at least the next eight years. Some congressional space supporters felt the 2015 US Space Act went too far beyond addressing the legitimate needs of the industry and was, instead, heavily skewed toward fulfilling an industry wish list.[36] Eric Stallmer, president of the industry group Commercial Spaceflight Federation, saw it otherwise; he said, "It's a real vote of confidence from Congress that commercial space matters, and we can shape and grow the industry without the burdens of the federal government."[37] Another key aspect of the Space Act dealt with what Bigelow referenced as assisting in "the discovery of beneficial resources"—space mining.

US companies have taken the lead in the field of space mining. Planetary Resources, Deep Space Industries, and Shackleton Energy have all expressed not just interest but intent to lead the way in various extraction activities. Planetary Resources is a Washington-based asteroid mining company. Its Arkyd 3 Reflight (A3R) spacecraft was launched from the ISS in July 2015 to test the technology for scouting and prospecting asteroids in anticipation of asteroid mining. The company describes the challenges on its website.

> Our spacecraft are headed into deep space. It's a challenging environment: outside Earth's protective magnetosphere where radiation is prevalent and communicating back to [E]arth is minutes away. This is where our spacecraft must thrive. That's why kilo for kilo, we build the most capable commercial space systems ever designed. To prospect the asteroids, we need miniaturized sensors that communicate effectively over long distances on an autonomous, mobile, and resilient platform.[38]

Deep Space Industries says it intends to mine the sky, beginning with prospecting.[39] Shackleton Energy is taking a different approach, focused on extracting water from the Moon, turning it into rocket fuel, and creating in-space fuel stations. They say those stations will "jump-start a multi-trillion dollar industry."[40] Clearly, these companies aim to make money. That means that all the legal bases for claiming rights to water and minerals, such as platinum, palladium, osmium, and iridium, need to be covered.

The section of the 2015 US Space Act focused on asteroid mining recognized the rights of US citizens to own the resources they obtain through the mining of asteroids.[41] Prior to the signing of that law, whether individuals had such a right was tenuous given the 1967 Outer Space Treaty provision that "outer space should be the common heritage of mankind to be used for peaceful purposes in the interests of all nations, limiting state sovereignty."[42] Commercial companies want as much certainty in regulation as possible to reassure investors. They need those rules to be relatively understood and stable through a business cycle. Referencing the 2015 US Commercial Space Launch Competitive Act, Eric Anderson, co-founder of space mining company Planetary Resources, said, "This is the single greatest recognition of property rights in history."[43]

Those supportive of the US legislation do not consider allowing the ownership of resources recovered and mined to be a declaration of sovereignty as that would be a violation of the 1967 Outer Space Treaty. The official position appears to be that US/Western property and other legal jurisprudence should pertain for the good of all, and since US companies are pursuing extraction activities first, setting good legal precedents is the best way to do that. Under that view, if China or Russia decided to pursue extraction and was able to successfully do so, that would be acceptable to the United States.

Perhaps not surprisingly though, there have been a multitude of views on the legality of space mining generally[44] and the 2015 US Space Act specifically. Canadian attorney Ram Jakhu has voiced the opinion that the Space Act potentially violates the Outer Space Treaty, while Australian attorney Ricky Lee says that it does not.[45] Gbenga Oduntan, an international lawyer at the University of Kent in Great Britain, also expressed objections to the 2015 US Space Act. "The idea that American companies can on the basis of domestic laws alone systematically exploit resources in space, despite huge environmental risks, really amounts to the audacity of greed."[46] This view represents those who see these activities as (another) form of Western exploitation. But historian Niall Ferguson made the case in his 2011 book *Civilization: The West and the Rest*[47] that it was property rights that differentiated the economic and political development of North America from that of South America. Without giving individuals a vested interest in development and private companies' incentive, development rarely ensues.

Other countries are interested in asteroid mining too, and in legislation to protect investor interests. Luxembourg's economy minister has announced that this tiny country will explore asteroid mining as a "key high-tech sector" and seek to become the hub of European commercial space efforts.[48] Whether Luxembourg is displaying tremendous foresight or pursuing a celestial pipe dream remains to be seen. Additionally, the director general of the United Arab Emirates (UAE) Space Agency announced in March 2016 that the UAE was drafting a law similar to the 2015 US Space Act, covering human space exploration and commercial activities including mining.[49] While this sort of international activity creates economic and sometimes political competition, this competition spurs development.

Projections of profits in the trillions[50] have spurred this private and public interest in asteroid mining, though those figures are only projections so far. "Platinum alone is worth around $23,000 a pound — nearly the same as gold. Mining the top few feet of a single modestly sized, half-mile-diameter asteroid could yield around 130 tons of platinum, worth roughly $6 billion."[51] The asteroid Ryugu contains tons of nickel, iron, cobalt—and water—worth an estimated $95 billion.[52]

But overly optimistic projections of commercial space opportunities have occurred before—or it could be that the projections are a harbinger of a new gold rush. Because competition is involved, though, with space competition declared part of the currently threatening space environment, there have already been headlines that "Space Mining Could Set Off a Star War."[53]

Certainly, the United States would claim foul if Russia or China claimed the Moon, or even part of the Moon, or any other celestial body. But allowing the claiming of a celestial body, in part or in its entirety, is not what the 2015 US legislation does; the legislation covers only extraction. Whether that situation will lead to another version of Star Wars, monetarily driven, or whether it is another in a long list of space activities that inherently calls for cooperative international action remains to be seen. It must be assumed, though, that the same rules hold true in space as do terrestrially in terms of environmental conditions that promote or deter development: that unless a company specifically profits from conflict, kinetic conflict does not bode well for economic development opportunities. It should also be noted that nothing being discussed for commercial development in space is as potentially valuable as the real estate in geosynchronous orbit already is and, though not without problems, users are making that work relatively well.

Stability in space is important for these private sector companies to survive and thrive. Air Force Deputy Undersecretary for Space Winston Beauchamp suggested in March 2016 that the space industry should take the lead in the development of norms for safe, predictable, and responsible space actions. "That is work best done by the industry, to develop those *de facto* norms, without the government getting involved just yet."[54] He further suggested that industry must develop ways to make small satellites, such as cubesats, visible to radar so that they can be tracked to avoid debris-creating collisions. At an April 2016 Space Business Roundtable in Washington, US regulators again admitted that they are playing catch-up with the commercial sector in terms of keeping track of and regulating "nontraditional" space actors and further urged the private sector to take the lead. George Neidle, associate administrator of commercial space transportation at the Federal Aviation Administration, reminded the audience that many of the challenges currently being faced have been known for years, with little tangible progress having been made in addressing them.[55]

The private sector has already shown more of a willingness to work together than governments in at least some areas, such as space situational awareness (SSA), through the Space Data Association (SDA). Additionally, while the SDA shares data among member satellite operators, a US commercial company, Analytic Graphics, Inc. (AGI), began offering SSA data and products in 2014, including conjunction analysis, maneuver modeling, orbit trajectory modeling, orbit determination, and rendezvous and proximity operations.[56] AGI's Commercial Space Operations Center (ComSpOC) utilizes 70 telescopes aimed primarily at geostationary Earth orbit (GEO) along with two radar sensors for low Earth orbit (LEO) to update its space observations on an hourly basis. In March 2016, AGI announced confidence that by the end of 2016, ComSpOC would be able to track the same number of objects in space as the US military's JSPOC is currently tracking.[57] Paul Welsh, vice president of business development at AGI, has stated that industry should be able to handle "80 to 90 percent of the solution"[58] to the tracking problem in 2016.

Private companies and organizations share data among members. Although Russia, China, France, and some other European countries have space-tracking capabilities of some degree, they do not routinely share that information. Only the US government routinely shares notifications of potential collisions with other countries.

In 2014, China took the unprecedented step of asking Air Force Space Command to directly share possible collision warnings. Previously, the United States had been sharing conjunction warnings with China through the State Department, though whether China paid any attention to those warnings was unknown as they were not acknowledged. The Chinese request that the data be shared directly from the Air Force, which would expedite the transfer of information, was considered a positive sign of Chinese interest in avoiding collisions and debris creation.

As private sector space development increases, the need for what has become known as "Space Traffic Management" (STM) will also increase. But it is useful to note that there are three separate aspects to usefully keeping track of what is going on in space, each likely to be done by different organizations. The first is SSA, which involves gathering data and making projections. The second is notification. Having data and delivering conjunction warnings are different. The third, management, involves "the set of technical and regulatory provisions for promoting safe access into outer space, operations in outer space and return from outer space to Earth free from physical or radio-frequency interference"[59] and requires public–public and private–public cooperation. Space Traffic Management is the terrestrial equivalent of air traffic management. Nobody wants the over 5,000 planes in the air just over the United States at any given time to be operating without rules. The International Civil Aviation Organization (ICAO) regulates international air travel, though it does not have the authority to pass or enforce internationally binding laws. Rather, it establishes standards and recommended practices for passage within each member nation. Increased space congestion suggests that the same type of standards and recommended practices will soon be needed in space as well.

While STM has been the subject of study for over a decade,[60] it will inherently limit some freedom of use in outer space. Consequently, there has been no international agreement that an STM regime is even necessary, let alone what it would look like or its parameters. At the national level, there has been discussion that the FAA should take on the same role for space as it does for aviation. That would mean a transfer of responsibility from the Pentagon. While yielding control of missions related to space data seems to contradict the military propensity for autonomy, "leaders from Air Force Space Command and US Strategic Command have said they would like to lessen the burden on military space operators [for STM] so they can concentrate on preparing for potential conflicts in space."[61]

As a positive step toward the private–public cooperation necessary in STM, agreement was reached between the SDA and the JSPOC in April 2015 to stand up a "commercial prototype cell." The idea is to allow selected space industry officials to sit inside the JSPOC to allow for better sharing of information.[62] Apparently, one of the catalysts for the prototype cell was a Schriever war game in which commercial satellite capabilities played a prominent role in decision-making; consequently, the need to include commercial operators in the JSPOC was recognized.

SpaceX, Virgin Galactic, Bigelow, and Planetary Resources are a mere sampling of the NewSpace companies that have a vested interest in stability. NewSpace Global (NSG) is the core market observer, publishing investor and market reports, market indices, and daily and monthly newsletters and bulletins. It reports that the "great innovation economy" of NewSpace is composed of nearly 1,000 companies worldwide.[63] NSG groups companies into "verticals" (including spacecraft, launch vehicle providers, human spaceflight, microgravity research, in-space services, space resources, and space-based energy) and then evaluates each company by "screens" (management, market, capital, technology). The Colorado-based Space Foundation also produces an annual report that is the benchmark for information about the more mature aerospace industries and national expenditures, but increasingly, NewSpace companies are being included in its analysis.[64]

Elliot Pulham, Space Foundation CEO, was joined by Dr. Sandra Mangus of AIAA and Eric Stallmer, president of the Commercial Spaceflight Federation, in releasing a white paper titled "Ensuring U.S. Leadership in Space" on March 4, 2016.[65] The intent was to present industry views to presidential and congressional candidates. In the paper, the challenges faced by the US space program are said to include unpredictable budgeting, foreign competition, and workforce trends. The paper offers what it considers as sensible policy recommendations to address and overcome the challenges and ensure US leadership in space:

- Commit to predictable budgets, fund robust investments, promote innovative partnerships and repeal the Budget Control Act of 2011.
- Continue global space engagement.
- Restore American access to space.
- Encourage the continued use of fully competitive, innovative partnerships.
- Maintain, strengthen, and grow the domestic industrial base.
- Commit to a robust national security space program that maintains U.S. dominance of the high ground in space.
- Maintain and expand internationally harmonized spectrum access for space.
- Define and commit to new missions to expand the frontiers of science.
- Promote STEM education and retention of U.S.-educated workers.
- Further reduce barriers to international trade whenever possible.[66]

As a consensus document, not surprisingly, it is somewhat of a "something for everybody" grab bag. It does, however, represent more than just the interests of the defense-related aerospace industries—though the "dominance of the high ground" portion certainly reflects these interests—thus, again, demonstrating the myth of "control."

Space developers remain interested in and, in some cases, need public–private partnerships and incentives. At times, this may mean asking the government to think differently about how they operate. For example, rather than investing in the acquisition of spacecraft for space data such as weather, imagery, and communications, it could buy (more) from commercial vendors. While potentially a money-saver, that approach would again require the government, especially the military and intelligence community, to turn away from the standard model of operating autonomously and trusting only its own data. A number of US states have spaceports that could be used for launches instead of those owned by federal government. In some cases, vendors are looking more directly for government funding through arrangements sometimes pejoratively referred to as "rent-seeking" agreements. For example, vendors would like to see more funded NASA Space Act agreements like those discussed in the commercial resupply and crew vehicle contracts. Another hotly debated policy and funding area is government hosted payloads (HPLs) on commercial satellites. But even among vendors, there is disagreement regarding how far and what kind of government support would be useful. Some vendors, for example, support the use of excess ICBMs as commercial launchers, while others object to that usage. Two company presidents presented their opposing views in 2016 op–eds.

Scott Lehr, President of Orbital ATK's Flight Systems Group, made the case that ending the current US ban on retired ICBMs would allow US companies to reclaim a considerable portion of the small satellite launch market. Russia's Dnepr and Rokot, Europe's Vega, and India's PSLV are all priced well below any similar US launch vehicle and so have made significant inroads into the small satellite market. Dnepr and Rokot are repurposed decommissioned ICBMs. Vega and PSLV are government subsidized.[67]

George Whitesides, CEO and President of Virgin Galactic, argued the case opposing the use of decommissioned ICBMs for small satellite launches. He pointed out that the current policy—in place with the support of the White House and Congress for over 20 years—requires that before excess ICBMs can be used for satellite launches, the Secretary of Defense must reach a determination that those ICBMs are more cost-effective than available commercial services and that they do not compete with the private sector. Basically, Whitesides argues that dumping excess ICBMs on the market would stifle NewSpace efforts to develop new launch vehicles by cutting into their potential market.[68]

Gen. Hyten has weighed into the debate in favor of using decommissioned ICBMs as launchers, but he says their use will be at a price that does not threaten commercial vendors.[69] Finding that "sweet spot" price point, however, won't be easy. The House science committee held hearings in April 2016 to hear arguments from both sides of the debate on that very issue.

NewSpace, or more broadly, commercial space, is rapidly outpacing traditional government space in innovation, operations, markets, and, most importantly, investment. In virtually every traditional area—including launch; communications; weather; positioning, navigation, and timing (PNT); remote sensing; and even SSA—industry is displacing civil and national security government development with commercial business approaches. Further, NewSpace companies are pressing the limits in areas like tourism, satellite servicing, and asteroid or Moon exploitation. As these commercial endeavors move forward, they are running into existing regulations, international treaties and agreements, and other obligations, often with little patience for the conflict avoidance legacy or the environmental debris impacts of these agreements. While the private sector is assertively moving forward with space activity, always slow and cumbersome UN multilateral governance efforts hit what many feared would be a terminal snag in 2016.

## The Multi-Pronged UN Space Efforts

The United Nations has a long history of involvement with space activity through its commitment to space being used for peaceful purposes. Early on in the space age, there was concern—justifiable concern—that "space might become yet another field for intense rivalries between the superpowers or would be left for exploitation by a limited number of countries with the necessary resources."[70] With one concern being security related and one being primarily development related, two different entities within the United Nations were tasked with responsibilities. The First Committee of the UN General Assembly is responsible for international security affairs, while the Fourth Committee handles a variety of issues under the title Special Political and Decolonization. Both are involved with space, with Fourth Committee activity dating back to 1958. The inclusiveness of the United Nations (its strength) and its need in most instances to work on a consensus basis (its weakness) have both been evident as related to its work on space issues over the years.

Ongoing multilateral work through the United Nations has largely focused on voluntary measures because legally binding measures such as a treaty have been a bridge too far, primarily for the United States. In fairness to the United States, in many cases, it has said "no" to treaties offered in these venues because they include untenable provisions included by parties for internal and global political reasons rather than as an attempt to develop a good set of space "rules." There have been efforts at prevention of an arms race in outer space (PAROS) through the UN Conference on Disarmament (CD), a forum established in 1979 to negotiate multilateral arms control and disarmament agreements. Although the Conference on Disarmament is not formally a UN organization, resolutions adopted by the UN General Assembly are often referred to the CD for consideration, and the CD in turn annually reports its activities to the General Assembly.

In 1981, for example, the General Assembly adopted two resolutions related to negotiating an international agreement on PAROS. But from its Cold War beginnings, there was disagreement on what should be the exact focus of such an agreement. One resolution, sponsored by the Western Europe and Others Group (WEOG), focused on negotiation of "an effective and verifiable agreement to prohibit anti-satellite systems," while the other resolution, sponsored by the Eastern European and other states, wanted the focus on a treaty to prohibit the stationing of any kind of weapons in outer space.[71] Given the dual-use nature of space technology, the requested focus of each group was formidable, even more so when placed in competition with each other. Further, each resolution sponsor held firm in insisting on its focus rather than negotiating a compromise, thus beginning a fairly consistent pattern of political overtones and inhibitions to PAROS efforts.

Other than intermittent periods during the Cold War when both the United States and the Soviet Union saw it in their benefit to sign and encourage a number of multilateral treaties—such as the Outer Space Treaty and the Nuclear Non-Proliferation Treaty—the United States has consistently preferred bilateralism to multilateralism. In fact, in 1990, the United States stated the view that it had identified no "practical outer space arms control measures that can be dealt with in a multilateral environment."[72] The US voting record on a PAROS Treaty resolution through the UN First Committee has consistently reflected that opposition. Though PAROS resolutions have overwhelmingly passed multiple votes over the years, the United States—occasionally with another country or two, such as Israel, Haiti, or Palau—abstains or outright votes no. US objections to multilateral negotiations stemmed largely from wanting to avoid treaty provisions that could inhibit its technical advantage and missile defense program. More recently, the United States has acquiesced to work through UN multilateral forums on some space issues.

As resolute as the United States has been in its objections to a legally binding treaty, China and Russia have been equally insistent in favor of a treaty. They first introduced the text for a Treaty on Prevention of the Placement of Weapons in Outer Space and of the Threat or Use of Force Against Outer Space Objects (PPWT), essentially banning weapons in space, to the CD in 2008 and submitted a revised version in 2014. While the PPWT bans weapons in space, it says nothing about ground-based weapons such as China used in its 2007 ASAT test. Basically, many of the flaws and ambiguities seen by critics in the 2008 version of the treaty remain in the 2014 version.[73] Much of China's and Russia's objections to an international code of conduct (ICOC) for Space stemmed from publicly stated concerns that acceptance of a code would undermine their goal of a legally binding treaty. With a treaty politically impossible and the code dead, two primary UN avenues for progress toward maintaining stability in space have remained. The first is through the Working Group on the Long-Term Sustainability of Outer Space Activities (LTS) which reports to the 83-member Committee on the Peaceful Uses of Outer Space (COPUOS). The second focuses on transparency and confidence-building measures (TCBMs) through the First Committee.

COPUOS has two subsidiary bodies: The Scientific and Technical Subcommittee (STSC) and the Legal Subcommittee, both established in 1961. The LTS is a working group of the STSC, established in 2010 to develop a set of "best practices" for space activities, focused on protecting the space environment. The best practice guidelines were intended to be technical in nature and were negotiated during inter-sessional meetings of four expert groups: (1) Sustainable space utilization supporting sustained development on Earth; (2) Space debris, space operations, and tools to support collaborative space situational awareness; (3) Space weather; and (4) Regulatory regimes and guidance for actors in the space arena. Because of the dual-use nature of space technology, while the LTS exercise was "not officially aimed at space security or military uses of space, the guidelines, if followed, would by their nature have an effect on the conduct of national security space activities."[74]

At the February 2015 meeting of the STSC in Vienna, the Russian delegation complicated what had been considered an otherwise productive exercise, successfully progressing toward the LTS goal, when they introduced a proposal to incorporate an official interpretation of "self-defense" in space.[75] They also introduced eight new, complex guidelines[76] to those already under consideration. In each case, the Russian Federation refused to accept any discussion on the guidelines—even in terms of the ponderous and often unintelligible English translation—in effect, insisting that they be accepted verbatim.

Space politics are affected by larger geopolitics; the Russian and US relationship began souring with the Russian incursion into Crimea and then especially after

Russian actions in Syria. Russian foreign policy can be as bellicose as the Russian Prime Minister Vladimir Putin is nationalistic and determined to restore Russia to superpower status. Consequently, the Russians at times appear resolute on obstruction of anything backed by the West, particularly the United States.

The intent of the COPUOS and STSC leadership was to have "guidelines" for space activity from the LTS ready to present to the COPUOS plenary in June 2016 and the Fourth Committee when it met in the fall. Toward that end, LTS Working Group Chair Peter Martinez, from South Africa, proposed what was considered a pragmatic way forward at the February 2016 LTS meeting. Guidelines were to be categorized according to how close they were to consensus approval: Category 1 for "those [11] draft guidelines for which the Working Group is very close to achieving consensus"; Category 2 for "those [10] draft guidelines for which the Working Group may reasonably expect to achieve consensus within the current work plan"; and Category 3 for "those [7] draft guidelines for which the Working Group may find it difficult to achieve consensus on all their constituent elements within the current work plan."[77] The idea, again, was to move things along—not to wait until there was consensus on every item but, rather, to move forward with those where there was consensus and hold off on the more difficult ones.

Given the assumed "accepted" nature of the 11 Category 1 guidelines, the Chair focused on moving forward on the 10 in Category 2. They included guidelines on such issues as radio frequency spectrum use, providing information on space objects and orbital events, sharing information on space debris monitoring, and development of prelaunch assessment of possible conjunctions of newly launched objects with already orbiting space objects. The Category 3 items were considered potentially more controversial as they dealt with issues such as registration of space objects. For both political and legal reasons, there has been reluctance by some countries, including the United States, China, Israel, and Saudi Arabia, to register space objects. Politically, these space objects might involve intelligence-gathering and so countries want to keep their nature and whereabouts undisclosed. Legally, countries might also be seeking to avoid liability for potential insurance claims in case of an accident or collision. While the Category 2 and Category 3 items would all have to be tackled eventually, the idea was not to hold up other consensus items in the meantime.

Most countries accepted Martinez's suggested approach. China submitted a position paper on the LTS issues, generally supportive of the process and the intended goal. "China hopes that States will promote the conclusion of a final consensus text of the LTS Working Group Report and Guidelines by following the principle of mutual understanding and seeking common ground while putting aside differences."[78] Similarly, a working paper submitted by Canada, France, Germany, Italy, Japan, Romania, Sweden, the United Kingdom, and the United States supported the work of the four expert groups that had gotten the guidelines to their current state and suggested the creation of a new expert group. The purpose of the new expert group was to:

identify and assess relevant international practices and procedures which allow for collaborative exchanges of space object and event monitoring information, to limit the probability of, and facilitate effective responses to, accidental collisions and break-ups or other accidental events in Earth orbit that might damage spacecraft, leading to loss of mission, or loss of life in the case of crewed spacecraft.[79]

Unfortunately, however, the Russians clearly came to the meeting with only one goal—obstruction—and they were successful.

The Russian Federation submitted multiple working papers. One was entitled "Russian assessment of the initiative and actions of the European Union to advance its draft code of conduct for outer space activities"; Another was "Additional considerations and proposals aimed at building up understanding of the priority aspects, comprehensive meaning and functions of the concept and practices of ensuring the long-term sustainability of outer space activities." Both of these appeared to be efforts to pull the developing countries support from the entire LTS effort, as Russia, Brazil, and China had done in the ICOC negotiations, resulting in its collapse. The gist of the Russian arguments, in both the tortured-English working papers and in bombastic floor speeches,[80] was that the process was being managed to the benefit of only a few countries—primarily the United States. Though Brazil and China both publicly supported the Chair's plan for proceeding based on category guidelines, the Russian approach was to insist on intricate, convoluted "guidelines" for reaching consensus. The Russians refused to attend any of the informal meetings where the substantive work of wordsmithing the individual draft guidelines took place in order to achieve consensual text. Then the Russian Federation made the incongruous argument that they could not accept the draft guidelines agreed to by the other states since they had not been party to the informal discussions.

Of note as well is Russia taking the opportunity to toss lots of "loaded" words at the United States in its working paper.

> It would be pertinent as well to cite as an example the national regulation of one of the States, which co-sponsor the draft code. Its basic doctrine document defines the concept of "control" in respect of outer space in terms of "freedom" (i.e. freedom of action for itself) and "denial" of access to outer space (obviously for those States, in respect of which it would be deemed reasonable to deny such access). ... It is known that some States uphold the paradigm of domination in outer space. Such a doctrine is fundamentally different from previously set targets, such as leadership and even superiority to which policies have been confined until recently. Dominance is not reduced solely to factors and considerations of technological (including military) pre-eminence; in fact, it is the equivalent to the promotion of really aggressive schemes that involve the establishment of relations of domination and dependence.[81]

The Russians also took the opportunity to specifically denounce the recent signing of the US Commercial Space Launch Competitiveness Act as an egregious breach of the 1967 Outer Space Treaty.

In the end, the Russians were successful in blocking attempts to generate an interim set of consensus guidelines for submission to the COPUOS June 2016 Plenary. They were unable to sway the developing countries to their position as they had been with the ICOC; in fact, there was perhaps an unprecedented amount of positive engagement among the States, with the exception of Russia. During the politicking that always informally occurs at these multilateral meetings, the Europeans, Japanese, Chinese, and Brazilians (on behalf of the UN Group of Latin American and Caribbean Countries [GRULAC]) made significant progress on the Category 2 guidelines as the Chair had intended. Many countries prevailed on the Russians to reconsider their position as well, but without success. Without interim guidelines going forward, many delegations expressed frustration that there was nothing to show for years of work and no clear way forward, except perhaps through the Group of Governmental Experts.

Several of the working papers submitted at the 2016 STSC in Vienna referenced the UN work previously completed by the Group of Governmental Experts (GGE) on Transparency and Confidence-Building Measures through the First Committee, initiated in 2011. The report of the GGE expressly recognized that the guidelines being developed by the LTS activity

> will have characteristics similar to those of transparency and confidence-building measures; some of them could be considered as potential transparency and confidence-building measures, while others could provide the technical basis for the implementation of certain transparency and confidence-building measures proposed by this Group of Governmental Experts.[82]

Thus the GGE provided the basis for the working papers submitted at the 2016 STSC.

The 15 members of the GGE were nominated by member states, with the permanent members of the UN Security Council guaranteed five of the spots and the rest being filling by countries selected by the United Nations based on State applications and on fair geographic representation: Brazil, Chile, Kazakhstan, Nigeria, Romania, South Africa, South Korea, Sri Lanka, and Ukraine. The Russian expert, Victor Vasiliev, effectively chaired the GGE, which began its work in 2012 and issued its first report in July 2013 prior to the souring of US–Russian relations. That report was subsequently adopted by the General Assembly during the 68th session. Theresa Hitchens, former director of the United Nations Institute for Disarmament Research (UNIDIR), explains the report's intent.

> The work of the GGE is most directly related to space security, seeking to create mutual understanding and build trust among nations in order to reduce risks of misperceptions, miscalculations, and conflict. The report lays

out basic TCBMs that could be undertaken by states, unilaterally, bilaterally, or multilaterally. The GGE report is important since it is the first UN agreement in many years to focus on improving space security.[83]

While the GGE was highly successful in development of TCBM guidelines, the difficulty lay in implementation since adherence is strictly voluntary.

After first providing an overview of global space activities and the need for TCBMs, the report then provides the general characteristics and basic principles of TCBMs and explains their nature and purpose.

> In general terms, transparency and confidence-building measures are a means by which governments can share information with an aim of creating mutual understanding and trust, reducing misperceptions and miscalculations and thereby helping both to prevent military confrontation and to foster regional and global stability.[84]

International cooperation, consultative mechanisms, outreach, and coordination are examined and encouraged as appropriate TCBMs for space, with several specific areas singled out.

- Information exchange on national space policy and goals, and exchange of information on military space expenditures;
- Information exchange on activities in outer space, including orbital parameters, possible conjunctions, natural space hazards, and planned launches;
- Notifications on risk reductions such as scheduled maneuvers, uncontrolled high-risk re-entries, emergency situations, intentional orbital breakups; and
- Voluntary visits to launch sites and command and control centers, and demonstrations of space and rocket technologies.[85]

In conclusion, the report recommended that states and international organizations review, consider, and implement the GGE's TCBMs on a voluntary basis through relevant national mechanisms, to the greatest extent practicable, and consistent with national interests. The GGE report emphasized the value of continuing dialogue between agencies, governments, organizations, and through various UN forums. The idea behind the GGE initiative was to change behavior by having those with a vested interest in space security develop guidelines to the benefit of all. The very nature of security dilemmas, though, is that politics and fear will sometimes compel countries to act not in their own best interests. However, common threats, such as from Near Earth Objects (NEOs) potentially on a collision course with Earth, can draw countries to work together.

While meeting during February 2013, the STSC Working Group on Near-Earth Objects had recommended establishment of the Space Planning Advisory

Group (SMPAG) and the International Asteroid Warning Network (IAWN), and Committee and full UN endorsement was given later in the year. "The primary purpose of the SMPAG is to prepare for an international response to a NEO threat through the exchange of information, development of options for collaborative research and mission opportunities, and to conduct NEO threat mitigation planning activities."[86] The establishment of both groups coincided with the Chelyabinsk meteor event on February 15, 2013, while the STSC was in session.

The more problematic work on space security and sustainability remained the purview of the First and Fourth Committees. A General Assembly resolution made on the basis of proposals from the 2013 GGE study report on space TCBMs mandated a joint session of those committees, which was subsequently scheduled for October 2015. Unfortunately, however, the 2014 Russian annexation of Crimea occurred in the interim between the GGE study report and the joint committee session. Consequently, when that meeting was finally held, most of what happened there simply demonstrated the intransigence of the divergent diplomatic positions to space diplomacy.

Several of the developing states were concerned about celestial bodies being expropriated through claims of sovereignty—a not particularly oblique reference to activities like asteroid mining. The vast majority expressed concern about outer space becoming an arena for an arms race with the space environment described as "congested, contested, and competitive."[87] How to avoid such an arms race, however, was the sticking point. Some countries argued in favor of addressing military and civilian activities jointly, while others insisted on distinguishing between civilian aspects of space relevant to the Fourth Committee and those matters relating to security through the First Committee. Keeping with the past, most countries supported a legally binding treaty via an inclusive and transparent process as the ultimate goal of the First Committee, though some were willing to accept non-binding consensus guidelines in the meantime.

The Russian delegation took the opportunity to again cast the United States in a negative light and to again push an initiative that it knew the United States would not support—this time, a political commitment not to be the first to deploy space weapons. Russian Federation representative Vladimir Yermakov's remarks were reported in the meeting notes.

> "Up to now, we have been able to keep outer space free of any types of weapons of inter-State military confrontation," he said. The Russian Federation supported the prevention of weapons deployment or the use of force in space, but with the development of military aspirations by some Member States, the threat of militarization was growing. Recalling the 1972 Anti-Ballistic Missile Treaty between the then Union of Soviet Socialists Republics and the United States, he expressed regret that, in 2001, the latter had unilaterally left the treaty and "freed their hands" regarding possible deployment of weapons in outer space. The Russian Federation, in order to prevent an arms race in space, had initiated the dialogue on transparency and

confidence-building measures in space, and had globalized the political commitment not to be the first to deploy such weapons. Calling on all States to "show sense" and join that international initiative, he declared, "We much not repeat the mistakes of the past." The United States was the only country that had said it wished to dominate all others in outer space, and had left the door open to the use of force.[88]

The US withdrawal from the ABM Treaty, space control and domination rhetoric, and refusal to back a PAROS Treaty or even a "no first deployment" pledge all combine to present a very primacist US space posture to much of the world, one the Russians are happy to remind them of. Russia found support for the view that the United States had ceded the moral high ground in space from other countries as well. The Indonesian representative, for example, speaking on behalf of the nonaligned movement, expressed serious concern about the abrogation of the ABM Treaty and deployment of strategic missile defense systems.[89]

The US position was reported as concern that development of anti-satellite systems by some States could trigger "dangerous misrepresentations and miscalculations" and escalate a conflict,[90] which corroborates the view that escalation concerns cannot be dismissed. The United States also rejected the Russian initiative for a pledge of "no first placement" of weapons in space as failing to satisfy the experts' criteria and the Russian/Chinese draft treaty as "fundamentally flawed." Both the draft treaty and a "no first deployment" pledge mean little if only dealing with space-based weapons and because of the dual-use nature of space hardware. Whether US objections are those of the United States acting as the adult in the room, thus allowing other countries the luxury of appearing to support a flawed treaty without fear of it being accepted, or the United States being obstructionist is a matter of perspective. Nevertheless, the optics of the United States consistently rejecting measures that most other countries appear to support do not work in its favor.

Ultimately, votes taken on several measures that largely reaffirmed the stalemate that has prevailed. The first dealt with a no first placement of weapons in outer space.

> The draft resolution ... encouraged all States, especially space-faring nations, to consider upholding as appropriate a political commitment not to be first. The draft was approved by a recorded vote of 122 in favor and 4 against (Israel, Ukraine, United States, Georgia) with 47 abstentions.[91]

The Committee also took action on a draft text calling on all States, especially those with major space capabilities, to actively contribute to the objective of the peaceful use of outer space and the prevention of an arms race there. It was approved by a "recorded vote of 173 in favor to none against, with 3 abstentions (Israel, Palau, United States)."[92]

The work at the United Nations is important as it allows for dialogue and, potentially, solutions to inherently global issues. Addressing the threat from Near

Earth Objects, for example, and even space debris are issues of concern to all States. But the United Nations is not immune to politics, especially in matters concerning national security.

Speaking at a March 2016 International Symposium on Ensuring Stable Use of Outer Space in Tokyo, Assistant Secretary of State Frank Rose, who served as the US representative to the GGE, spoke about UN efforts in positive terms.

> One promising area of TCBMs is the continued implementation of the recommendations of the UN Group of Governmental Experts, or GGE, study of TCBMs. The 2013 GGE report, which was later endorsed by consensus by the UN General Assembly, highlighted the importance of voluntary, non-legally-binding TCBMs to strengthen stability in space. We continue to encourage all states to review and implement, to the greatest extent practicable, the full range of recommendations in the 2013 consensus report. ... We hope to work constructively with all COPUOUS participants in Vienna to complete work on consensus guidelines for long-term sustainability of outer space activities in 2016.[93]

Whether the United States is prepared to change any of its positions at the United Nations or offer some kind of bargain or assurances that demonstrates its seriousness about guidelines, codes, or rules of the road for space stability, including access for all countries, remains to be seen.

While it is unlikely that the President of the United States or many at the Pentagon are familiar with the alphabet soup that deals with space issues at the United Nations—STSC, LTS, GGE, GRULAC, etc.—unless the United States is fully prepared to accept a unilateralist stance in space, the optics at the United Nations should matter. Time and again, it has been demonstrated that not caring about world opinion does not work in favor of the United States. Only through a holistic approach to addressing the complexity of dealing with space issues and the plethora of players involved in those issues, private, public, and intertwined, will a way forward be found toward achieving the dual overall US goals of space security and space development. And by virtue of its size and scope, the effects of US space policy spill over to the rest of the world.

While NewSpace rushes forward, not just in the United States but also in an increasing number of other countries that do not want to be left out of a galactic "gold rush," politics plods on at its usual pace of one step forward, two steps back. NewSpace is hard-pressing the old rules, highlighting the need for a new "code of conduct" or, even better, "rules of the road." Although hopes for multilateral guidelines for long-term space sustainability were low after the February 2016 LTS meeting, all proved not lost. Although the Russians said in February that they would not attend the June 2016 meeting, making consensus impossible, interim diplomacy proved successful and got them there, demonstrating the need for an value of persistence in diplomatic efforts. Geopolitics inherently affects space negotiations, but so does self-interest, and it seems that an increasingly number of countries are recognizing that stability in space is in their interest.

## Notes

1 Theresa Hitchens, *Forwarding Multilateral Space Governance: Next Steps for the International Community*, CISSM Working Paper, Center for International and Security Studies at Maryland, University of Maryland, College Park, MD, August 2015, p. 14.
2 Gerard K. O'Neill, *The High Frontier: Human Colonies in Space*, William Morrow and Company, New York, 1976.
3 Roger Launius, "Exploding the myth of popular support for project Apollo," Blog, August 16, 2010. https://launiusr.wordpress.com/2010/08/16/exploding-the-myth-of-popular-support-for-project-apollo/; Jeremy Hsu, "The myth of America's love affair with the Apollo Program," *Space.com*, January 12, 2011. www.space.com/10601-apollo-moon-program-public-support-myth.html
4 Roger Launius, *Historical Analogs for the Stimulation of Space Commerce*, Monographs in Aerospace History No. 54, NASA History Program Office, Washington, DC, 2014, pp. 17–18.
5 William M. Brown and Herman Kahn, *Long-Term Prospects for Developments in Space (A Scenario Approach)*, Hudson Institute, Inc., Croton-on-Hudson, NY, October 30, 1977, pp. 257–74, cited in Lanius, *Historical Analogs*, ft. 56.
6 Launius, *Historical Analogs*, 2014.
7 "Company", *SpaceX*. www.spacex.com/about
8 Cited in Elien Blue Becque, "Elon Musk wants to die on Mars," *Vanity Fair*, March 10, 2013. www.vanityfair.com/news/tech/2013/03/elon-musk-die-mars
9 Historic Landing of Falcon 9 First Stage at Landing Zone 1 [video]. https://www.youtube.com/watch?v=1B6oiLNyKKI
10 Ryan Whitwam, "SpaceX has finally nailed reusable rocket with latest Falcon 9 landing," *ExtremeTech*, April 11, 2016. www.extremetech.com/extreme/226305-spacex-has-finally-nailed-reusable-rockets-with-latest-falcon-9-landing
11 "Other Transactions Authority," *AcqNotes*. www.acqnotes.com/acqnote/careerfields/other-transaction-authority-ota
12 Jim Garmone, "Kendall describes novel way of contracting for space launch service," *U.S. Department of Defense*, January 27, 2016. www.defense.gov/News-Article-View/Article/644946/kendall-describes-novel-way-of-contracting-for-space-launch-services
13 "Commercial cargo: NASA's management of Commercial Orbital Transportation Services and ISS Commercial Resupply contracts," *NASA Office of Audits*, June 13, 2013. https://oig.nasa.gov/audits/reports/FY13/IG-13-016.pdfhttps://oig.nasa.gov/audits/reports/FY13/IG-13-016.pdf
14 NASA, *Emerging Space: The Evolving Landscape of 21st Century American Spaceflight*, NASA, Washington, DC, 2014. www.nasa.gov/sites/default/files/files/Emerging_Space_Report.pdf
15 ATK acquired Orbital Sciences in February 2015 and created Orbital ATK, retaining the Orbital Sciences CEO, Dave W. Thompson, and the ATK Chairman, Gen (Ret) Ronald Fogleman.

16 Chris Gebhardt and Chris Bergin, "NASA awards CRS2 contracts to SpaceX, Orbital ATK and Sierra Nevada," *NASAspaceflight.com,* January 14, 2016. www.nasaspaceflight. com/2016/01/nasa-awards-crs2-spacex-orbital-atk-sierra-nevada/

17 "Commercial crew program – the essentials," *NASA*. https://www.nasa.gov/content/ commercial-crew-program-the-essentials/#.Vv0qp6v1clI

18 "SpaceX completes first commercial crew transportation milestone," *NASA*. www. nasa.gov/content/spacex-completes-first-commercial-crew-transportation-milestone

19 "NASA's Journey to Mars," *NASA*. www.nasa.gov/content/nasas-journey-to-mars

20 "Human spaceflight," *Virgin Galactic*. www.virgingalactic.com/human-spaceflight/

21 Alex Davies, "Blame a catastrohic blindspot for the fatal Virgin Galactic crash," *Wired*, July 28, 2015. www.wired.com/2015/07/blame-catastrophic-blindspot-virgin-galactic-crash/

22 National Transportation Safety Board Meeting, Commercial Space Launch Accident – SpaceShipTwo, Presentation by Dr. Katherine Wilson, "Human factors and organization issues," NTSB, Washington, DC, July 28, 2014. www.ntsb.gov/news/events/ Documents/2015_spaceship2_BMG_HumanPerformancePresentation.pdf

23 "Reflections on Virgin Galactic," *Virgin*. https://www.virgin.com/richard-branson/ reflections-on-virgin-galactic

24 Mike Wall, "Stephen Hawking wants to ride Virgin Galactic's new passenger spaceship," *Space.com*, February 20, 2016. www.space.com/31993-stephen-hawking-virgin-galactic-spaceshiptwo-unity.html

25 Rachel Crane and Amanda Barnett, "Virgin Galactic unveils new spaceship," *CNN*, February 19, 2016. www.cnn.com/2016/02/19/us/virgin-galactic-new-space-plane/

26 Elizabeth Howell, "Virgin Galactic recruits female test pilot Kelly Latimer," *Space.com*, November 9, 2015. www.space.com/31072-virgin-galactic-female-test-pilot-kelly-latimer.html

27 "Lynx Spacecraft," *XCOR Aerospace*. http://aerospace.xcor.com/reusable-launch-vehicles/lynx-spacecraft/

28 "Technology," *Blue Origin*. https://www.blueorigin.com/technology

29 Caleb Henry, "Zero2infinity lays out goals for balloon-rocket launch system," *Via Satellite,*March 23, 2016. www.satellitetoday.com/launch/2016/03/23/zero2infinity-lays-out-goals-for-balloon-rocket-launch-system/

30 Jeff Foust, "Rocket Lab plans to begin launches mid-year," *SpaceNews*, March 24, 2016. http://spacenews.com/rocket-lab-plans-to-begin-launches-mid-year/

31 "Our mission," *Rocket Lab*. https://www.rocketlabusa.com/our-mission/

32 "Russian company set to usher in era of suborbital tourism," *Sputnik*, March 5, 2015. http://m.sputniknews.com/science/20160305/1035843182/russia-space-tourism.html

33 Cited in Peter B. de Selding, "Orbital ATK believes in satellite servicing, but not rocket reusability," *SpaceNews*, March 2, 2016. http://spacenews.com/orbital-atk-believes-in-satellite-servicing-but-not-in-rocket-reusability/

34 "About Bigelow Aerospace," *Bigelow Aerospace*. http://bigelowaerospace.com/about/

35 Irene Klotz, "The FAA: regulating business on the moon," *Reuters*, February 3, 2015. www.reuters.com/article/us-usa-moon-business-idUSKBN0L715F20150203

36 Doug Messier, "House Democrats slam SPACE Act as 'commercial space industry wish list,'" *ParabolicArc,*May 21, 2015. www.parabolicarc.com/2015/05/21/house-democrats-slam-space-act-commercial-space-industry-list/

37  Cited in Nick Stockton, "Congress says yes to space mining, no to rocket regulations," *Wired*, November 18, 2015. www.wired.com/2015/11/congress-says-yes-to-space-ming-no-to-rocket-regulations/

38  "Technology," *Planetary Resources*. www.planetaryresources.com/technology/#technology-overview

39  "Asteroid mining," *Deep Space Industries*. https://deepspaceindustries.com/space-resources/

40  "Overview," *Shackleton Energies*. www.shackletonenergy.com/overview#goingback tothemoon

41  "President Obama signs bill recognizing asteroid resource property rights into law," *Planetary Resources*, November 25, 2015. www.planetaryresources.com/2015/11/president-obama-signs-bill-recognizing-asteroid-resource-property-rights-into-law/

42  Cited in Joanne Wheeler, "Managing space: international space law and prospective reforms," *Harvard International Review*, March 30, 2012. http://hir.harvard.edu/a-new-empiremanaging-space/

43  Cited in "President Obama Signs Bill," *Planetary Resources*.

44  Tim Worstall, "The economic problem with Luxembourg's space mining law," *Forbes*, February 23, 2015. www.forbes.com/sites/timworstall/2016/02/03/the-economic-problem-with-luxembourgs-space-mining-law/#5a96ae4563eb

45  "US space-mining law seen leading to possible treaty violations," *CBS News*, November 27, 2015. www.cbc.ca/news/technology/space-mining-us-treaty-1.3339104

46  Cited in Brooks Hays, "New US space mining law may violate international treaty," *UPI.com*, November 25, 2015. www.upi.com/Science_News/2015/11/27/New-US-Space-Mining-Law-May-Violate-international-treaty/8751448634436; Katrina Pascual, "US space mining law is potentially dangerous and illegal: how asteroid mining act may violate international treaty," *Tech Times*, November 28, 2015. www.techtimes.com/articles/111534/20151128/u-s-space-mining-law-is-potentially-dangerous-and-illegal-how-asteroid-mining-act-may-violate-international-treaty.htm

47  Niall Ferguson, *Civilization: The West and the Rest*, Penguin, London, 2011.

48  Cited in Michael Reilly, "Luxembourg wants to lead the way in asteroid mining," *MIT Technology Review*, February 4, 2016. https://www.technologyreview.com/s/600725/luxembourg-wants-to-lead-the-way-in-asteroid-mining/

49  Lucy Barnard, "UAE to finalise space laws soon," *The National*, March 7, 2016. www.thenational.ae/business/aviation/uae-to-finalise-space-laws-soon?utm_content=buffera6520&utm_medium=social&utm_source=facebook.com&utm_campaign=buffer

50  Clive Thompson, "Space mining could set off a star war," *Wired*, January 14, 2016. www.wired.com/2016/01/clive-thompson-11/

51  Adam Mann, "Tech billionaires plan audacious mission to mine asteroids," *Wired*, April 23, 2012. www.wired.com/2012/04/planetary-resources-asteroid-mining/

52  Thompson, "Space mining could set off a star war."

53  Ibid.

54  Cited in "Senior US Air Force official urges private sector to take lead in building space norms," *Space Watch Middle East*, March 23, 2016. http://spacewatchme.com/2016/03/senior-us-air-force-official-urges-private-sector-to-take-lead-in-building-space-norms/

55 Caleb Henry, "SmallSat boom outpacing regulators in the US," *Via Satellite,* April 8, 2016.www.satellitetoday.com/regional/2016/04/08/smallsat-boom-outpacing-regulators-in-the-us/

56 "About AGI," *AGI.* www.agi.com/about-agi/

57 Caleb Henry, "ComSpOC expects to par with JSpOC's public catalog this year," *Via Satellite,* March 31, 2016. www.satellitetoday.com/technology/2016/03/31/comspoc-expects-to-par-with-jspocs-public-catalog-this-year

58 Cited in ibid.

59 The International Academy of Astronautics (IAA), "Cosmic Study on Space Traffic Management," Presentation at UN COPUOS, Vienna, June 2006. www.unoosa.org/pdf/pres/copuos2006/06.pdf

60 Kai-Uwe Schrogl, Corinne Jorgenson, Jana Robinson and Alexander Soucek, "From the 2006 to the 2016 Space Traffic Management Studies of the International Academy of Astronautics," Presentation at the 58th IISL Colloquium on the Law of Outer Space, Jerusalem,October14,2015.www.pssi.cz/download/docs/274_international-astronautical-congress-2015-ppt-presentation.pdf

61 Mike Gruss, "Washington weighs a FA role in managing space traffic," *SpaceNews,* December 3, 2015. http://spacenews.com/might-the-faa-inherit-the-space-traffic-management-role/

62 Caleb Henry, "US JSPoC to create 'commercial cell prototype' in coming months," *Via Satellite,* April 10, 2015. www.satellitetoday.com/regional/2015/04/10/us-jspoc-to-start-commercial-cell-prototype-in-coming-months/

63 Newspace Global home page. http://newspaceglobal.com/home

64 "Research and analysis," *Space Foundation.* www.spacefoundation.org/programs/research-and-analysis/space-report/

65 "Ensuring U.S. Leadership in Space," *AIAA,* March 4, 2016. www.aiaa.org/uploadedFiles/Whats_New/EnsuringUSLeadershipInSpace_FINAL.pdf

66 "Ensuring U.S. Leadership in Space," excerpts from pp. 3–5.

67 Scott Lehr, "Op–ed: ending ban on retired ICBMs would allow U.S. companies to reclaim small satellite launch market," *Space News,* April 5, 2016. http://spacenews.com/op-ed-ending-ban-on-retired-icbms-would-allow-u-s-companies-to-reclaim-small-satellite-launch-market/

68 George Whitesides, "Op–ed: dumping excess boosters on market would short-circuit commercial space renaissance," *Space News,* April 5, 2016. http://spacenews.com/op-ed-dumping-excess-boosters-on-market-would-short-circuit-commercial-space-renaissance/

69 Cited in Mike Gruss, "Hyten tries to find 'sweet spot' on surplus ICBM use," *SpaceNews,* April 16, 2016. http://spacenews.com/hyten-tries-to-find-sweet-spot-on-surplus-icbm-issue/

70 "COPUOS History," *United Nations Office for Outer Space Affairs.* www.unoosa.org/oosa/en/ourwork/copuos/history.html

71 Ambassador (ret.) Paul Meyer, "The Conference on Disarmament and the Prevention of an Arms Race in Outer Space," The CD and PAROS: A Short History, The CD Discussion Series, UNIDIR, April 2011.

72 Cited in Secure World Foundation, *Fact Sheet: Conference on Disarmament,* SWF, Superior, CO, updated July 28, 2009. See also ibid. and Theresa Hitchens, *Forwarding Multilateral Space Governance,* p. 4.

73 Michael J. Listner and Rajeswari Pillai Rajagopalan, "The 2014 PPWT: a new draft but with the same and different problems," *The Space Review*, August 11, 2014. www.thespacereview.com/article/2575/1

74 Hitchens, *Forwarding Multilateral Space Governance*, p. 4.

75 Russian Federation, "Achievement of a uniform interpretation of the right of self-defence in conformity with the UN charter as applied to outer space as a factor in maintaining outer space a safe and conflict-free environment and promoting the long-term sustainability of outer space activities," Working paper submitted to COPUOS, STSC, 52nd session, Vienna, February 2, 2015.

76 Russian Federation, "Additional considerations and proposals aimed at building up understanding of the priority aspects, comprehensive meaning, and functions of the concept and practices of ensuring the long-term sustainability of outer space activities," Working paper submitted to COPUOS, STSC, 52nd session, Vienna, February 2, 2015.

77 Chair of the Working Group on the Long-term Sustainability of Outer Space Activities, "Ideas for the way forward on the draft set of guidelines for the long-term sustainability of outer space activities," Working paper submitted to COPUOS, STSC, 53rd session Vienna, January 28, 2016, p. 2.

78 "China's position paper on the issues of long-term sustainability of outer space activities," COPUOS, STSC, 53rd session, Vienna, February 16, 2016, p. 5.

79 "Proposal by Canada, France, Germany, Italy, Japan, Romania, Sweden, the UK and the US for an expert group on space objects and events," COPUOS, STSC, 53rd session, Vienna, February 22, 2016, p. 2.

80 Recordings and documents from the Committee on the Peaceful Uses of Outer Space: Scientific and Technical Subcommittee, 53rd session, February 15–26, 2016 (provided by VIC Online Services). http://myconference.unov.org/#!/Package/VI140830A?organization=UN

81 Russian Federation, "Additional considerations and proposals aimed at building up understanding of the priority aspects, comprehensive meaning, and functions of the concept and practices of ensuring the long-term sustainability of outer space activities," Working paper submitted to COPUOUS, STSC, Vienna, February 2, 2015, p. 2.

82 "Report of the Group of Governmental Experts on Transparency and Confidence-Building Measures in Outer Space Activities," United Nations General Assembly, 68th session, July 29, 2013, para. 13. www.unidir.org/files/medias/pdfs/outer-space-2013-doc-2-a-68-189-eng-0-580.pdf

83 Hitchens, *Forwarding Multilateral Space Governance*, p. 5.

84 Office for Disarmament Affairs, *Transparency and Confidence Building Measures in Outer Space Activities*, Study Series No 34, United Nations, New York, 2013, p. 11.

85 Christopher Johnson, *The UN Group of Government Experts on Space TCBMs*, A Secure World Foundation Fact Sheet, Updated April 2014. http://swfound.org/media/109311/swf_gge_on_space_tcbms_fact_sheet_april_2014.pdf

86 "Terms of Reference for the Space Mission Planning Advisory Group," *Cosmos Portal*. www.cosmos.esa.int/web/smpag/terms-of-reference-v0

87 "As Fourth, First Committees hold joint meeting, speakers stress need for holistic handling of outer space security, sustainability," UN General Assembly Meetings Coverage, GA/DIS/3531, October 22, 2015. www.un.org/press/en/2015/gadis3531.doc.htm

88 Ibid.

89 "Divergent paths emerge in First Committee on ways to achieve outer space security, safety, sustainability, through legally or non-legally binding pacts," UN General Assembly Meetings Coverage, GA/DIS/3532, October 23, 2015. www.un.org/press/en/2015/gadis3532.doc.htm

90 Ibid.

91 "First Committee approves texts on disarmament aspects of outer space, weapons of mass destruction, in voting pattern reflecting complex security concerns," UN General Assembly Meetings Coverage, GA/DIS/3539. www.un.org/press/en/2015/gadis3539.doc.htm

92 Ibid.

93 Frank A. Rose, Remarks to International Symposium on Ensuring Stable Use of Outer Space: Enhancing Space Security and Resiliency, "Using diplomacy to advance the long-term sustainability and security of the outer space environment," Tokyo, Japan, March 3, 2016. www.state.gov/t/avc/rls/253947.htm

# 7

# SPACE AT THE TIPPING POINT

Since wars begin in the minds of men, it is in the minds of men that the defenses of peace must be constructed.

UNESCO Constitution

Sputnik announced its presence in orbit with a simple electronic beep in 1957. Only 12 years later, men walked on the Moon. Certainly, reasonable people assumed, it would just be a short matter of time before lunar colonies and planetary exploration expanded the human horizons and became routine, spurring technical advancements beyond imagination. All of that seemed inevitable. But then it was 9 years between the last Apollo flight and the first Shuttle flight, and 16 years between President Ronald Reagan's space station announcement and the first long-duration crew arriving at the ISS in 2000. Space development was not progressing as rapidly as many people had expected.

In 2016, Sputnik plus (nearly) sixty years, the outlook for space exploration and development looks different than during the Apollo years; regrettably, it is still far more aspirational than earlier anticipated. NASA is hoping to have humans reach Mars for the first time by 2035 if Congress maintains the necessary funding. The "Buck Rogers" and "Han Solo" NewSpace actors who, it was earlier assumed, would be the Henry Fords and Cornelius Vanderbilts of space are just starting to make substantial marks in the fields, their long-term viability still uncertain due to investor jitters over potential profits and the stability of the space environment. Concern about viability is warranted because, according to risk-acceptant Pentagon officials and analysts, the only thing inevitable about space is that it will be a battlefield, and they are ready to fight. There is now even discussion of plans for a limited, acceptable space war.

Space is at a tipping point. The democratization of space will play an important role in that determination. What happens over the next several years will likely make all the difference in what areas of space activity prevail: development or destruction. In Thomas Friedman's 1999 book *The Lexus and the Olive Tree*,[1] he talks about various "democratizations"—diffusions—that have occurred worldwide as the result of globalization, including the democratization of information, technology, and finance. The Internet diffuses information, good and bad. A 2012 World Bank report says 75 percent of the global population has a cell phone.[2] Microloans allow individuals in developing countries access to finance previously unavailable. These democratizations also disperse control while, simultaneously, increasing the need for understanding of the issues created by diffusion and how to manage those issues. RAND Professors Dave Baiocchi and William Welser IV similarly outline issues created by and left unattended (and in some cases, unrecognized) by "The Democratization of Space" in their so-named 2015 *Foreign Affairs* article.[3] They argue state and nonstate actors alike will be involved in what they call "the new space race" and that non-state actors may want to be involved in more than just commercial activities.

> Nongovernmental organizations may start pursuing missions that undermine governments' objectives. An activist billionaire wanting to promote transparency could deploy a constellation of satellites to monitor and then tweet the movements of troops worldwide. Criminal syndicates could use satellites to monitor the patterns of law enforcement in order to elude capture, or a junta could use them to track rivals after a coup.[4]

These possibilities, the authors point out, raise issues that governments have thought little about. But if nation-states don't overcome their often self-inflicted myopia, events may well overcome them.

Because the space weapons Rubicon remains uncrossed and because no country currently has space capabilities that actually threaten US ability to operate in space—though they are developing potentially threatening capabilities—the time is ripe for the kind of pause for reflection referenced by Allison in Chapter 3. The time is ripe to assure that there is alignment between US goals and the means being pursued to achieve them. Once that is accomplished, those means must be adequately funded and supported with the necessary manpower. What happens next is not up to the United States alone, but as the dominant global space player, especially regarding military space, US actions will influence those of others. Therefore, it is imperative that the United States "get things right" because current US emphasis on war plans, dominance, and control are only provoking potential adversaries and making a first-strike option on US space assets—assets the United States is more reliant on than their adversaries are—a compelling option to strive toward. Getting things right does not mean turning the Air Force into NASA or even the Coast Guard, foregoing the development of offensive counterspace capabilities, signing the fatally flawed Treaty on the Prevention of the Placement of Weapons in Outer Space, or withdrawing from the Outer Space Treaty. It does, however, require the United States to be strategically bold, be diplomatically proactive, proportionally embrace all aspects of layered deterrence, be rhetorically restrained, and regain the moral high ground in space. Many of those requirements are overlapping. To those individuals and organizations of a Jacksonian bent, that approach is likely as attractive as President Barack Obama's foreign policy of "don't do stupid shit"[5] given that it doesn't project a primacist posture. However, if it gets the results desired—a stable space environment within which the United States is free to operate—foregoing the myth of primacy ought not be too high a price to pay.

## A Strategically Bold Approach

In his 2015 book *Meeting China Halfway: How to Defuse the Emerging US-China Rivalry*,[6] Naval War College Professor Lyle Goldstein proposes an approach for the United States to use in dealing with China, different from those professing the inevitability of conflict, for addressing confrontation or even for rebalancing, or pivoting. It is a new way of thinking about the US–China relationship rather than merely tweaking past strategy to be more or less robust or engaging. It is an attempt to deal with China as it is, warts and all. It treats China as the United States does Saudi Arabia, Israel, Russia, Oman, Pakistan, and other countries where the US preference would be to see changes in government structure or policies but finds ways to work with them nonetheless because it furthers US national interests. Attempting to fundamentally change Chinese domestic politics through US foreign policies has been futile, and rejecting dealing with China due to Chinese domestic politics or policies has not been in US interests. The suggested new approach attempts to deal with China in ways benefiting US interests over the long term rather than with the kind of quick fixes Allison called "little more than aspirin treating cancer"[7] (see Chapter 3). Goldstein proposes trying to defuse spirals of competition—security dilemmas—and replacing them with cooperation spirals that "provide bilateral policy 'moves' for achieving substantive US progress across a range of difficult issues."[8]

While Goldstein acknowledges the difficulty in promoting cooperation, bilaterally or multilaterally, he argues that interests, reciprocity, and benefits can be powerful motivators, quoting political scientists Robert Axelrod and Robert Keohane to make his point: "A strategy based on reciprocity—such as tit for tat—can be remarkably effective in promoting cooperation … even among pure egotists."[9] Axelrod and Keohane accurately describe many space players in their assessment as egotists because of the geostrategic prestige and broad spectrum of advantages associated with space capabilities. While egotists are inherently distrustful of others, they will, nevertheless, act on measures in their own interest if properly motivated. But engagement is a prerequisite to opportunities for promoting mutual interest. Therefore, it is in the interests of all spacefaring nations, including the United States, to engage with all other spacefaring nations, including China, on a regular and consistent basis.

In his discussion of a cooperation spiral focused on the larger strategic relationship between the United States and China, Goldstein suggests, as an incremental move, that "the United States should initiate substantive space cooperation with China."[10] The rationales for doing so are several. Goldstein acknowledges the potency of space power as a geopolitical currency in coming years, the dangers of Chinese scientists working in isolation (which may have contributed to the 2007 Chinese ASAT test), and the symbolic impetus for cooperation as in the 1975 Apollo–Soyuz docking. He points out as well that cooperation "could also enable projects—for example, a Mars mission—that is simply too prohibitively expensive for one space power to undertake independently."[11] Given the Wolf amendment, supporters of US–China space cooperation have trodden carefully of late, pleased that the first meeting of the US–China Civil Space Dialogue took place in 2015,[12] but dismayed that US foreign policy is so constrained by ideology that initiating dialogue has come to be considered a bold policy move.[13]

China and the United States have recently viewed each other as rivals in space. But each has a great deal to lose if the space environment is destabilized. That is especially true if China is not looking to or willing to put its own satellites at risk through an asymmetric kinetic attack on US assets but, rather, sees space as a critical part of its own informationalized approach to defense and security. Further, it was neither the United States nor China that blocked movement of UN consensus guidelines promoting stability in 2016; it was Russia. To that point, Goldstein points out, again incorporating Axelrod and Keohane, that "[t]he most effective motive for cooperation between rivals in world politics has generally been the 'activities of a third power.'"[14] TCBMs for space are in the interests of both China and United States. Cooperation with China may open a window for the United States and China to work together toward encouraging Russia to cease its intermittent obstructionism on UN efforts other than a treaty, and get the all the major space players moving in the same direction. That would go a long way toward tamping down some of the impetus behind the United States again turning to a primacist approach to space and, instead, promoting space stability, needed for security and commercial purposes.

With the passage of the 2015 Space Act, the United States has signaled its clear intention to support commercial space development. But it is likely that China, rather than the United States, will be the next country to reach the Moon, robotically or with a crew, and similarly probable that China has or will develop the technological capability to conduct lunar mining. Given clear US intentions to pursue commercial space activity, the United States would be hard-pressed to object to Chinese commercial space development or to try to constrain it. Trying to constrain competition with Europe in the field of communication satellites ended up costing the United States a substantial portion of the commercial launch field when Europe developed the Ariane rocket for launch autonomy. Trying to constrain the sale of satellites to China after the Cox Committee fiasco cost the US satellite industry dearly. Alternatively, and in line with a new approach, it has been suggested that "China appears to be an excellent potential global partner, together with the United States and the European Union, to lead a global campaign to open the space frontier to peaceful commercial development for the benefit of all humanity."[15] Europe and China are already working together in multiple space venues, public and private, with more planned for the future. Working with China gives the United States much more of an opportunity to co-opt Chinese space efforts into peaceful purposes within sets of norms agreeable to all than does attempting to isolate China—an impossible task in a globalized world with a globalized supply chain of aerospace products.

Therefore, rather than the small, incremental steps toward US–China space cooperation that have been proposed in an effort to avoid the ire of Congress (actually a very few, but vocal and powerful Members of Congress) and given the very real potential for the commercial development of space, perhaps the time is ripe for a grand bargain whereby both sides make big concessions for potentially big gains. Maintaining the US–China relationship has long been recognized as key to maintaining globalization, which is essential to the economies of both countries.[16] Space cooperation with China in that sense becomes part of a cooperation spiral and a security initiative much like Apollo during the Cold War. But whereas Apollo was about competition between two superpowers, cooperation with China would be part of a larger, inevitable US–China power transition.

Multiple authors have considered how to address the US–China power transition to avoid Allison's Thucydides Trap. Former Australian Defense Department official Hugh White argued in his 2012 book *The China Choice*[17] that the United States and China ought to share power in Asia as the American quest to retain regional primacy is inherently incompatible with the Chinese quest to be recognized as an equal. Former Deputy Secretary of State and Deputy National Security Advisor James Steinberg and Brookings Fellow Michael O'Hanlon similarly favor "restraint" in their 2014 book *Strategic Reassurance and Resolve*.[18] In language not unlike that used in connection with multilateral space security guidelines, the authors largely focus on informal limitations that each country may unilaterally choose to adopt. Ideally, these limitations would then result in restraint upon which long-term (in this case, bilateral) cooperation may be sustainable. The authors also emphasize "reinforcement," "transparency," and "resilience" as key components of their strategy. Reinforcement means taking actions that make declared assurances more credible. Transparency allows each country to understand the other's capabilities. Resilience is necessary so that each side is less vulnerable to preemption or escalation. All are similar to the need for verification, transparency, and resilience as aspects of space stability. Most recently, George Washington University Professor Charles Glaser has proposed a grand bargain between the United States and China, intended to accommodate the rise of China in Asia while strengthening US security.

> A possibility designed to provide the benefits of accommodation while reducing its risks is a grand bargain in which the United States ends its commitment to defend Taiwan and, in turn, China peacefully resolves its maritime disputes in the South China and East China Seas and officially

accepts the United States' long-term military security role in East Asia. In broad terms, the United States has three other options—unilateral accommodation, a concert of Asian powers, and the current US rebalance to Asia. Unilateral accommodation and the rebalance have advantages that make the choice a close call, but all things considered, a grand bargain is currently the United States' best bet.[19]

A grand space bargain could be an incremental step in a larger strategic US–China grand bargain.

The idea of a grand bargain in space between the United States and China has been raised before. Theresa Hitchens and David Chen suggested such an approach in 2008.[20] There, the potential bargaining chips on offer included

> participation in the International Space Station (ISS), joint exploration missions, reform in US policies restricting sales of commercial satellite hardware, and licensing of Chinese launch services. In exchange, China might willingly restrict behaviors that could lead to strategic miscalculation in space, as well as certain forms of counter-space capabilities.[21]

Then too, perhaps the authors were reaching out to a new administration. But addressing the 2007–08 financial crisis and the continuing quagmire of the Middle East understandably held the new administration's focus. While some of the bargaining chips suggested by Hitchens and Chen have become moot, there are now more and bigger bargaining chips that could be exchanged, and both countries are now acutely aware of how much they have to both gain and lose.

The biggest chip that the United States has to offer is a partnership role for China in NASA's Journey to Mars, similar to that given to Russia on the ISS after the demise of the Soviet Union. A Mars mission potentially offers China a place in the international family of spacefaring nations that it has long coveted but was denied on the ISS. China would thereby gain domestic credibility, regional prestige, and international respect. The United States seems too frequently to forget the importance of respect in international relations, but as Friedman reminds us, "[t]he single most underappreciated force in international relations is humiliation."[22] The Chinese psyche is still affected by its century of humiliation. Chinese leaders are not oblivious to global public opinion surveys that show it having a decidedly mixed international image. "While China's economic prowess impresses much of the world, its repressive political system and mercantilist business practices tarnish its reputation."[23] The United States can use China's desire for respect to its advantage as a carrot in a grand bargain where both sides would win. International involvement in the Mars program has always been anticipated though not with China in an active role, let alone one involving leadership.

Currently, the Journey to Mars program builds on NASA's international and commercial partnerships and on multitudes of lessons learned on the ISS. NASA states that its Mars program aligns with the Global Exploration Roadmap (GER) first developed in 2011 by a contingency of space agencies from the multinational International Space Exploration Coordination Group (ISECG).[24] Although China is a member of the ISECG, the initial GER effort did not include China. The GER effort was said to reflect "a coordinated international effort to prepare for collaborative space exploration missions beginning with the International Space Station (ISS) and continuing to the Moon, near-Earth asteroids and Mars."[25] With China consistently banned from ISS participation and NASA prohibited from bilateral cooperation— even communication—with China regarding space, initial Chinese exclusion from the group is not surprising from a political perspective. Realistically, however, Chinese exclusion from the group made no sense given its ambitious space plans. Ma Xingrui, head of the Chinese National Space Agency, said in 2013 that China would gladly join the effort if invited.[26] China has since been included;[27] this is allowable under the Wolf amendment since the GER is a multinational, rather than bilateral, effort. This multilateral structure could be built upon.

Ironically, however, a potential issue to be considered regarding a space "grand bargain" between the United States and China might be Beijing's hesitancy to commit itself and Chinese resources to Journey to Mars as it feels the program is subject to Congress' fickle budgeting and political whims. There are precedents of the United States not being seen as a particularly good "space partner" on multinational programs dating back to the 1980s; specifically, this relates to the International Solar Polar Mission (ISPM) and the ISS,[28] which the Chinese are certainly aware of. Consequently, a strong show of commitment—both financial and symbolic—to a joint Mars venture would be required by the United States.

Those dismissive of diplomacy and symbolic declarations often assert that words mean little to bad actors; they do bad things and don't care. But who is a bad actor, even in terms of trustworthiness, is a matter of perspective. After the United States canceled its ISPM spacecraft, Europeans were leery of committing to the ISS for fear the United States would again pull out and leave Europe with no legal recourse since no international agreement, treaty, or executive agreement can commit the resources of the United States. Only Congress can commit resources. So, instead, the Europeans insisted that the intergovernmental agreement being negotiated be "visually enhanced" by such mechanisms as the status of the signatory, surrounding publicity, and congressional resolutions of support. The idea was that if the United States (again) tried to back out of its commitment, the Europeans wanted the ability to try to embarrass the United States into upholding it. It is likely the United States would again have to offer such visual enhancements to bilateral agreements to work cooperatively on the Journey to Mars.

Additionally, part of the US commitment would have to include a budget commensurate with supporting a security-related program as opposed to a nice-to-have but expendable science and exploration program. A budget increase—new money not simply money reprogrammed from within NASA—would be needed to accommodate the inherent structural and organizational costs of cooperation and to assure a stable timeline. This increased funding would flow to the big aerospace contractors, though different divisions of their corporate structure than those that support weapons programs, and NewsSpace companies.

The returns on investment from space, both in terms of dollars back from dollars spent and technology development, make space exploration and development a good investment of American tax dollars. That then begs the question of why the public is not more supportive. The simple reason is a lack of knowledge. A 2007 poll showed that, at that time, Americans thought NASA received a whopping 25 percent of the US budget when, in fact, it received just 0.58 percent.[29] In 2013, a poll conducted by the nonprofit group Explore Mars and aerospace contractor Boeing asked the public whether they would support 1 percent of the federal budget being spent for a Mars mission—which would basically double NASA's budget; a resounding 76 percent agreed.[30]

Because most polls focus on whether the public thinks "more" or "less" should be spent on space, with the public having little actual knowledge of what is spent, it is not surprising that the answer is often "less." Therefore, rather than playing on the public's fear with doomsday pronouncements and television segments alluding to the imminent dangers of a Space Pearl Harbor—or, at least, "in addition to" this—public education on how much is actually spent on civilian space programs and the tangible benefits of space development would serve long-term US interests well. Neil deGrasse Tyson has been among the prominent voices trying to convey that message;[31] though, without the video-game-like attraction of space warfare, it has been more difficult for the message to resonate with the public.

## Diplomatically Proactive

The *quid pro quo* in return for the invitation to China to join the Journey to Mars would be China's commitment to actively support full implementation of LTS guidelines. The LTS guidelines are a strong beginning toward not just a code of conduct but "rules of the road" that will maintain the stability in space that the United States seeks. Working together, the United States and China could be diplomatically persuasive with other countries, including Russia.

NASA's Journey to Mars could assume a management system similar to that of the ISS, including countries interested and capable but with the United States and China taking the lead—perhaps eventually joined by Russia if conditions were right and agreeable to all. Such an arrangement would also be able to benefit from the many "lessons learned" available from the ISS experience.[32] Just as on the ISS, technology transfer issues can be addressed through compartmentalization of contributions. The entanglement advantages of such an arrangement whereby both the United States and China have vested interests in continued operation and success have already been demonstrated by the ISS experience in the midst of tense relations between the United States and Russia. Chinese scientists would no longer be working in isolation and would instead have a vested interest in maintaining good relations with the United States, thus acting as a stakeholder for those relations within China—something they have had no reason to do in the past. All in all, such a grand bargain in space between the United States and China can significantly add to US layered deterrence.

## Layered Deterrence

At its most elemental levels, layered deterrence requires a benefit to the party or parties sought to be deterred, appropriate signals about both the benefits and the risks of not being deterred, and that the deterring party have credibility regarding its capability to carry through on both benefits and threats. While the United States has been clear in the past about recognizing the benefits of a layered defense and has been vocal about its capability to carry through on threats, there is still considerable room for proportional effort in the other areas. Focusing on the threat of retaliation alone isn't enough. As RAND analyst Karl Mueller has pointed out, "if the enemy has nothing to lose, even a very risky action may be preferable" to maintaining the status quo.[33] In this case, the external perception of the status quo is the United States advancing toward having a virtually unbreachable space technology gap with other countries, allowing it to dictate how others can use space. As part of a grand bargain or not, proactive diplomacy to build toward reciprocal constraints—deterrence through international norms—and deterrence by entanglement can play important roles.

Proactive policymaking takes commitment, manpower, and money. A quick look at the money and manpower devoted to diplomacy in the US State and Defense departments compared to the resources available for the hardware-producing military–industrial complex efforts described in Chapter 5 is enlightening. The Assistant Secretary of State for Arms Control, Verification, and Compliance (AVC) leads space-related diplomacy in the State Department. The AVC Bureau is responsible for "all matters related to the implementation of certain international arms control, nonproliferation, and disarmament agreements and commitments; this includes staffing and managing treaty implementation commissions."[34] The AVC arms control portfolio includes nuclear, biological, and chemical weapons and all related issues. The AVC section charged with space issues is the Office of Emerging Security Challenges; this office also handles missile defense issues and the promotion of transparency, cooperation, and building confidence regarding cybersecurity. As of financial year 2013, AVC had a budget of $31.2 million and 141 employees[35] to be active participants and leaders in all of these issues.

By way of comparison, the Space Security and Defense Program, a joint program of the DoD and the Office of the Director of National Intelligence (ODNI) was programmed for a similar budget amount in financial year 2015: $32.3 million. That program is described as a "center of excellence for options and strategies (materiel, non-materiel, cross-Title, cross-domain) leading to a more resilient and enduring National Security Space (NSS) Enterprise."[36] A majority of SSDP funding is allocated to the development of offensive space control strategies. So basically, the same budget is allocated for all US global space diplomacy efforts as for an in-house Pentagon think tank to devise counterspace strategies.

Within the Pentagon, the Deputy Assistant Secretary of Defense for Space Policy is charged with all issues related to space policy, including diplomacy. The responsibilities of the Space Policy office are to:

- Develop policy and strategy for a domain that is increasingly congested, competitive, and contested
- Implement across DoD — plans, programs, doctrine, operations — and with the IC and other agencies
- Engage with allies and other space-faring countries in establishing norms and augmenting our capabilities.[37]

The breadth of those responsibilities, which includes reviewing space acquisitions, means that there may be only a handful of individuals actually engaged in multilateral diplomatic efforts, acting, for example, as advisors to diplomatic discussions such as those through the United Nations. Additionally, the expanse of the Pentagon results in a chain of command that makes organizational competition for attention to subject matter challenging at best. The Deputy Assistant Secretary of Defense for Space Policy reports to the Assistant Secretary of Defense for Homeland Defense, who then reports to the Principle Deputy Secretary of Defense for Homeland Defense and Global Security, who then reports to the Under Secretary of Defense for Defense Policy. There are also a multitude of space players in other governmental organizations to coordinate and contend with, particularly within the Air Force and intelligence communities. Personnel are spread thin.

US government-wide space diplomacy needs a mandate, manpower, and a supporting budget. Diplomacy, especially multilateral diplomacy, can be time-consuming, manpower-intensive, and frustrating; and patience is not a strong American virtue. The recent experience in the UN LTS Working Group is emblematic of everything that causes the United States to shun multilateralism. Under the auspices of this group, countries had worked in good faith over the past five years to develop technical guidelines as reciprocal constraints, as insisted upon by the developing countries when they rejected the ICOC. Yet group success appeared thwarted at the February 2016 meeting of the LTS Working Group by one country, Russia.

But although Moscow vowed subsequently to boycott a follow-up COPUOS meeting in June 2016, they did not follow through on this. In fact, tangible progress was made during the session, including adoption of 12 guidelines considered by the LTS Working Group.[38] Those guidelines will be included in a compendium of LTS guidelines that is to be finalized in 2018 as per a new two-year work plan adopted at the June meeting.

Consequently, the time for the United States to step up and take a proactive leadership role. In continuing the effort to move the LTS guidelines forward, the United States demonstrates its commitment to using all its tools of national power: DIME rather than just the "M" component.

Theresa Hitchens offered several "next step" options that countries might take toward multilateral space governance after the completion of the GGE recommendations.[39] She suggested that they be adopted "on a voluntary unilateral, bilateral, regional, or multilateral basis opens the path for leadership by the major space-faring states, especially the United States, but also Russia and China."[40] Russia, another country with a serious humiliation hangover, likes nothing better than to claim credit for foreign policy successes where both the United States and Russia are involved.[41] Even though it was Russia that nearly derailed the LTS guidelines in 2016, Russian willingness and eagerness to claim credit for advancements should not be underestimated; witness the Russian role in the Syrian chemical weapons debacle in 2013 and again in 2016 with the ceasefire. The United States—and other countries eager to pass and implement all of the LTS guidelines—can and should take advantage of this characteristic of modern Russian diplomacy. Furthermore, efforts toward bilateral or trilateral moves forward with Russia and China are worth the effort, if only for the diplomatic visuals.

Regardless of a willingness to cooperate by partners and competitors, there are a number of unilateral actions and initiatives based on the GGE recommendations that the United States could take or, even better, lead on. For example, the identification of focal points and creating contacts for data exchange is needed as these are particularly important in crisis situations, including potential collisions. Being able to quickly contact a key counterpart in another country is a simple but essential aspect of crisis control. Unfortunately, however, these contacts do not exist for space incidents in many cases. This lack of a basic "space phonebook" heightens the opportunities for mishaps, misperceptions, and miscalculations to occur and escalate. Similarly, the GGE recommendations call for universal adherence to the 1976 Convention on the Registration of Objects Launched into Outer Space, which is currently lacking. The United States is among those countries whose compliance is less than complete. Although, in the past, there have been accusations that the United States was deliberately misleading or "muddying the waters" about its space assets,[42] more recently, noncompliance has been considered a problem largely of poor oversight and accountability rather than policy. Taking the initiative to address and, wherever possible, correct registration issues and encourage other countries to do so as well would enhance space situational awareness, transparency, and the quality of data available to all spacefaring nations.

Hitchens pointed out that there is a wealth of data being collected by various private and public organizations and networks, formal and informal, including amateur organizations. While the data is valuable, utility is not maximized because each system uses different collection, reporting, and analysis methodologies. The data is not usefully available from a single source. While likely a job better suited to being run by an independent organization than a government agency, the United States could initiate and support the effort.

An initiative that would bring all of this data together and provide a "master" catalog in the process would provide a public service and arguably enhance ongoing government efforts. A crowd-sourced database, run by an independent organization, could serve as a kind of "halfway house" between what is publically available today and the higher quality data kept by the United States and other states for national security purposes. In particular, an independently operated space object catalog could provide much needed transparency to those states and space operators that have little or no SSA capability.[43]

While none of these efforts will directly lead to mutual restraints, a code of conduct, rules of the road, or full adoption and implementation of the LTS guidelines, they would demonstrate US diplomatic involvement and leadership, contribute to better SSA, and be part of retaking the moral high ground. Sharing data can also be a component of deterrence by entanglement. While the United States has been known to be somewhat "stingy" with data sharing, even with allies,[44] there are welcome indications that this situation could improve.

In March 2015, Lt. Gen. John W. Raymond, commander of the Joint Functional Component Command for Space, reported to the House Armed Services Strategic Forces Subcommittee that STRATCOM is developing a new "tiered SSA Sharing Strategy." He noted the existence of 46 SSA sharing agreements already in place with 46 commercial firms, 8 nations and 2 intergovernmental organizations, and another 10 in development. Perhaps the most important element in Raymond's remarks was the reference to a "tiered" system. Development of such a system requires the DoD to determine what data to share, with whom, and at what level of specificity and accuracy—all of which have been difficult questions with inconsistent answers in the past. It is because of the past problems associated with these questions that the European Union, for example, decided to launch its own independent SSA efforts in 2009.[45]

Additionally, the United States might advocate for a follow-on GGE with representatives from countries different than the first round to discuss implementation efforts. This would have the benefit of expanding the number of countries with a vested interest in success, allow for more in-depth study toward guidelines in areas like active debris removal, and keep at least some momentum alive for implementing the GGE guidelines. It would also be another area where the United States could demonstrate interest in space diplomacy rather than just warfare.

As part of diplomacy, there is also a role for international law to play in maintaining stability in space. The development of a Manual on International Law Applicable to Military Uses of Outer Space (MILAMOS) has been suggested. The idea would be to provide clarity on international laws that are in place which are applicable to military and security activities in outer space.[46] Clearly, development of such a manual would require broad representation of legal views, but it could be a useful reference in differentiating agreed upon legal views from minority opinions.

Significant overlap exists between deterrence by international norms and deterrence by entanglement due to the unprecedented levels of economic interdependence evidenced in this latest iteration of globalization. Information technology has made the expanse of this iteration much broader and the speed of change much faster than in past, including in the colonial era and in the Cold War. While the 2008–09 global economic crisis curbed the lure of unrestrained capitalism, globalization did not go into a full retreat. The world is still intertwined through an expansive system for exchange of goods, a global financial system, and two global utilities, the Internet and GPS.

A particular example of the necessity of space-enabled global utilities is the connective tissue provided by GPS. GPS signals have been incorporated into global electric and transportation grids, financial systems, international commerce, and public services, creating technological entanglements that, were GPS to be no longer available, would result in far-reaching, devastating loss—economic and otherwise. An argument can be made that the more space actors there are, the more entanglement works to benefit all countries but especially those like the United States that are heavily dependent on space assets. Harrison, Jackson, and Shackelford described the basic premise of entanglement thus:

> The example of GPS demonstrates entanglement when civilian applications of a system originally built for a military purpose proliferate globally. In such cases, the effects of any attempts to deny the original military function would not be confined to one country in a crisis, but would unavoidably draw in other states who have become reliant upon space over time. The reverse situation also obtains. Communications systems originally built for civilian, commercial purposes now carry a variety of necessary military traffic, including data from unmanned air systems.[47]

Entanglement can be achieved in numerous ways.

Government hosted payloads, where government payloads are matched to commercial space assets, have been considered a potential avenue for cost-effective access to space by government and for entanglement. But there have been difficulties due to the complexity involved in making government contracts conform to commercial practices, as considered in Chapter 6. Air Force programs have been particularly problematic. In 2013, the Air Force's Space and Missile Center in Los Angeles stated it would

> award multiple indefinite-delivery, indefinite-quantity contracts to a stable of prequalified companies. These selected companies, expected to be a mix of satellite operators and space hardware manufacturers, would be in position to support the inclusion of dedicated government payloads and capabilities aboard commercial satellites.[48]

Nevertheless, hosted payloads remain an underutilized avenue for both cost savings and entanglement.

According to industry analyst Kay Sears, and in line with the distinction drawn in Chapter 6 between "commercial" space vendors and NewSpace vendors, "the perceived hurdles to implementing hosted payloads are primarily cultural in nature, not technical."[49] Five reasons, or excuses, have been suggested as holding up the adoption of more hosted payloads.[50] First, they are not part of any Air Force architecture for its primary programs. Therefore, the easy approach for the Air Force is to simply operate as it has always done and buy more of what it has always bought. Second, the military claims that, procedurally, there is a lack of integration into existing concepts of operations (CONOPs), though that is true with any new space program. Third, military requirements for launch flexibility are potentially in conflict with commercial launch timelines and planning. Fourth, there can be timing issues because the commercial world operates on the premise that time is money, whereas government planning, programming, and budgeting wheels turn at a much slower bureaucratic pace. And finally, use of hosted payloads can be viewed as threatening to a major program of record. Organizational culture changes are often the most difficult to address and are rarely accomplished solely through new or altered processes that the military favors as change levers. But given that hosted payloads offer cost-effectiveness and can play an important part in deterrence by entanglement, addressing those issues must be part of a genuine effort at layered deterrence.

Beyond entanglement, resilience and disaggregation can also play key roles in a layered defense by denying any advantage an adversary would gain from an attack. The advantages and premises underlying deterrence by denial in space have been discussed for many years.[51] Gen. Shelton began seriously talking about it to the Senate Armed Services Committee in 2013.

> Our satellites provide a strategic advantage for the US, and as such, we must consider the vulnerabilities and resilience of our constellations. My staff at Headquarters Air Force Space Command, alongside the team at the Space and Missile System Center, is leading efforts at balancing resilience with affordability. They are examining disaggregated concepts and evaluating options associated with separating tactical and strategic capability in the missile warning and protected communications mission areas. We are also evaluating constructs to utilize hosted payloads and commercial services, as well as methods to on-ramp essential technology improvements to our existing architectures. Beyond the necessity of finding efficiencies and cost savings, we may very well find that disaggregated or dispersed constellations of satellites will yield greater survivability, robustness and resilience in light of environmental and adversarial threats.[52]

Rather than relying on large, "exquisite-class" satellites that are potentially vulnerable, the underlying idea of disaggregation is to diffuse capabilities and so make any specific single system less vulnerable, thereby denying potential adversaries the intended benefit of an attack. Disaggregation also links to increased hosting of government payloads on commercial satellites; these targets are more fraught with the potential for damage that would impact a large customer base and, thus, elicit condemnation of the attacking country.

Similarly, satellites developed and deployed as part of international partnerships also increase the risk to an attacking country and are, therefore, considered part of disaggregation. For example, the Wideband Global Satcom (WGS) constellation of satellites represents a partnership between originally the United States and Australia, joined later by Canada, Denmark, Luxembourg, The Netherlands, and New Zealand. More partnerships are another way to reduce satellites' vulnerability to attack.

At a 2014 briefing, Undersecretary of the Air Force Eric Fanning stated, "The Air Force is committed to disaggregation."[53] Resilience and disaggregation were intended to play a key role in future Air Force satellite architectures beginning in 2015. However, consequent to the Space Portfolio Review, the Air Force cooled considerably on the idea of disaggregation. Deterrence by denial—a key part of layered deterrence—appears abandoned or downplayed in favor of deterrence by punishment as part of the still amorphous "space protection" strategy. This effectively compromises layered deterrence, thus negating potential levers against adversaries.

Resiliency is also part deterrence by denial, and it is included in the 2011 NSSS as a priority for space operations. The DoD provided a definition of resilience in 2011.

> Resilience is the ability of an architecture to support the functions necessary for mission success in spite of hostile action or adverse conditions. An architecture is "more resilient" if it can provide these functions with higher probability, shorter periods of reduced capability, and across a wider range of scenarios, conditions, and threats. Resilience may leverage cross-domain or alternative government, commercial or international capabilities.[54]

As a classic approach to deterrence by denial, resilience includes elements of avoidance, robustness, reconstitution, and recovery, each of which the DoD has defined as follows:

- *Avoidance*: countermeasures against potential adversaries, proactive and reactive defensive measures taken to diminish the likelihood and consequence of hostile acts or adverse conditions
- *Robustness*: architectural properties and system of systems design features to enhance survivability and resist functional degradation
- *Reconstitution*: plans and operations to replenish lost or diminished functions to an acceptable level for a particular mission, operation, or contingency
- *Recovery*: program execution and space support operations to re-establish full operational capability and capacity for the full range of missions, operations, or contingencies.[55]

How each of these is handled and whether there is any proportionality—balance—among efforts is unclear, though each appears at least minimally considered.

Current avoidance efforts appear focused on increased countermeasures, linking deterrence by denial with deterrence by punishment. Cyber-hardening of satellites can be considered part of robustness, as would efforts such as increased security for ground stations. The Office of the Secretary of Defense also specifically created an Operationally Responsive Space (ORS) program office toward development of rapid reconstitution capabilities, which stood up at Kirkland Air Force Base in 2007. However, Air Force interest in ORS has waxed and waned and it has tried to shut down the office more than once. The Air Force argument for closure has been that ORS could be handled at the Space and Missile Systems Center in Los Angeles. But that office manages GPS, missile warning, communications satellites—the large, "exquisite" satellites that Congress was urging the Air Force to move away from. Congress blocked closure fearing Air Force organizational culture at the Space and Missile Systems Center would overcome congressional intent. More recently, in 2015, the Air Force stated it was considering ORS management of Space-Based Surveillance and Defense Weather System follow-on programs.[56] Recovery efforts appear to focus on training operators to work under degraded conditions, which involves development of a Space Mission Force. How much attention, backed by support for funding, the Space Portfolio Review conclusions and recommendations have or will place on each aspect of resiliency remains unclear.

Whether through disaggregation, comprehensive resilience, or some other still-unspecified manner, deterrence by denial cannot be overlooked. The United States has very publically—in multiple venues from *60 Minutes* to the annual Space Symposium in Colorado Springs—made it clear that it has the capabilities, the wherewithal, the resolve, and the right to punish adversaries who attack US space systems. That is the stated rationale for development of counterspace systems and space control programs—capabilities that have been explicitly and tacitly demonstrated over the years through Operation Burnt Frost, the XSS-11 program, various high-energy laser programs, and others. The punishment layer of the deterrence strategy appears well covered and should be maintained as such as a hedge, but *in conjunction with* other layers so as not to exacerbate a space arms race. That can be done through hedging, first demonstrated as a space strategy during the Carter Administration. Carter wanted to initiate negotiations on ASATs with the Soviet Union while also developing advanced ASAT technologies. The idea was both to hedge against potential Soviet activities and to provide the Soviets with a compelling incentive to avoid a space arms race. Today, the Defense Advanced Research Projects Agency (DARPA), founded in response to Sputnik and responsible for milestone inventions including the Internet, GPS, and stealth aircraft, is the cornerstone of providing the technology that is an integral part of hedging efforts. Further, US goals would be better served without chest-thumping rhetoric about US capabilities and primacist intentions

## Strategic Communication

The United States would do well to heed the cautionary words of the 2010 RAND study cited in Chapter 1 regarding the need to resist openly declaring US intentions to dominate space. Primacist rhetoric does nothing to deter others from attacking US space assets and, in fact, can be counterproductive in terms of driving other countries to consider first-strike options. It is another prong of the current, internally inconsistent US policy, professedly aimed at protecting the space environment and the ability of the United States to use that environment. The United States must be the dominant space player with a full arsenal of deterrent options, but it will never dominate space in the sense of effective space control. It cannot deny other countries or private entities access to space or control use of their space assets on any broad or sustained basis. That is both an empty promise and self-damaging rhetoric.

Changing the US rhetoric about space security is also an integral part of regaining the moral high ground, currently challenged by language riddled with "do as we say, not as we do" platitudes, jingoistic three-word catchphrases, and conveniently ambiguous space terminology. For example, when the Secretary of the Air Force stated on *60 Minutes* that the United States does not have any weapons in space at this time, that was (likely) a true statement due to the dual-use nature of space technology. But it is also true that Congress is vigorously boosting funding for potential preventive offensive counterspace operations, including a first-strike attack capability on an adversary's space assets. The *de facto* mixed and inconsistent messages are unsettling to allies and competitors alike. Not being able to decipher US actions and intentions without a NewSpeak dictionary or having to read between the lines increases the perception that the United States is attempting to hide something, is acting nefariously, or is acting the hegemon—a role which has not served it well.

Words matter. US language rollbacks on what "rights" in space accrue to all nations, especially access, versus what rights accrue to the United States and its allies is provocative at best. More possibly, it potentially puts the United States at odds with the Outer Space Treaty, one of the few widely adopted space arms control measures. And while the United States now says it is not against space arms control, adding the condition of verifiability adds a host of other conditions and can appear a canard for rejecting arms control without openly stating such.

Clarity of the message matters as well. For example, reference was made in Chapter 1 to the 2016 CNAS report stating that "senior responsible US officials have telegraphed that the United States would indeed not necessarily respond massively to attacks against its space assets."[57] The messages telegraphed in the CNAS references, however, seem muddled and fairly opaque compared to others.

Reference is made in the report, for example, to remarks by then Assistant Secretary of Defense for Global Strategic Affairs Madelyn Creedon at the Stimson Center in 2013,[58] especially comments offered as assurance during the question and answer period. That fairly obscure reference does not seem to telegraph a message equal to those regarding "inevitable space warfare" from Washington.

Speeches by USSTRATCOM Commander Admiral Cecil Haney and Deputy Secretary of Defense Robert Work are also referenced. Speaking at a 2015 Deterrence Symposium in Omaha that focused largely on nuclear issues, Haney said, "our nation is prepared to manage escalation"; he further asked, but did not answer, how the United States might "develop the appropriate off-ramps to deter further violent, egregious activity by influencing the adversaries' decision-making so that we de-escalate in our favor?"[59] Work's comments were that the United States "must be able to respond in an integrated, coordinated fashion."[60] US ability and readiness to respond to and perhaps even preventively address threats are clear; telegraphed assurances of limited or proportional responses to attacks are less so.

There is a time for tough talk, such as after China's 2007 ASAT test that irresponsibly polluted the space environment with debris or in relation to North Korea's continued reckless nuclear and missile testing. Both events engendered global condemnation. But a constant drum beat of pugilistic language from the United States that centers on "domination" and "control"—likely intended to show strength and resolve—smacks of the kind of hubris that the public opinion polls cited in Chapter 5 have shown work against the United States rather than in its favor. Well-measured wordss and actions, both discrete and bold, serve US interests better than the perpetuation of a primacist self-image. The United States has been grappling with how to execute its global leadership position in one way or the other since the end of the Cold War. Knowing it must be a leader, and determining how to effectively do so in an increasingly complex world has presented the US with a conundrum. While often clumsy with its power, and unabashedly self-interested, it nevertheless wishes no harm on any country that works within international norms and does not seek to harm the US. Part of its current challenge is conveying that message in manner that other countries will believe. Doing so involves (re)taking the moral high ground.

## Retaking the Moral High Ground

A number of ways have been suggested to help the United States incrementally retake the moral high ground in space. Banning specific behaviors has been suggested as a potentially productive way to begin a set of rules for space, perhaps focusing first on those behaviors that create space debris. In other words, rather than trying to eat the whole elephant all at once, do it one bite at a time. The United States rejected a "no first deployment" pledge at the United Nations. While a "no testing" pledge would be a welcome incremental step toward banning a specific action, it still carries with it a considerable amount of ambiguity.

Unfortunately as well, the incline of the required ascent for the United States to retake the moral high ground in space is such that bold action is necessary to demonstrate seriousness about wanting to maintain the stability and sustainability of space. A "no first use" pledge by the United States, accompanied by a promise that an attack on any US space asset will bring a reciprocal response from the United States at a time, place, and manner of its choosing, is such a bold action as well as being clear and unambiguous. It would go a long way toward re-establishing the United States as holding the moral high ground and, thus, leadership in space diplomacy. It would also benefit the United States in diplomatic efforts toward pressuring other countries to make a similar pledge.

Scott Sagan argued in favor of a "no first use" pledge for nuclear weapons in a 2009 article in *Survival* and then invited experts to critique his perspective.[61] The arguments made by Sagan and others about nuclear weapons are pertinent to space weapons as well. Sagan explains his position as follows:

> Previous analyses of the appropriate role and missions for US nuclear forces, including earlier official nuclear posture reviews, have been too narrow, focusing exclusively on the contribution of nuclear weapons to deterrence and not examining the effects of the American nuclear posture and declaratory policy on the wider set of US and allied objectives regarding non-proliferation and nuclear terrorism. Because of this focus, previous government and academic analyses have both exaggerated the potential military and diplomatic costs of a no-first-use doctrine and have seriously underestimated its potential benefits.[62]

Much the same might be said about space weapons.

Morton Halperin's cogent summary of the argument made by opponents of a "no first use" position states that the United States "should not make any 'promise' to a potential adversary that might make it easier for an opponent to plan an effective military action."[63] Both he and Sagan counter the "don't make it easier for the opponent" argument by saying that "the threat to use nuclear weapons in these situations is not credible and the implication that nuclear weapons are necessary reduces the credibility of the conventional deterrent."[64] The more difficult argument to counter, per Halperin, is the domestic political firestorm that a president declaring a "no first use" nuclear policy would encounter. But there is a significant difference between nuclear weapons and space weapons that could be effectively used to counter similar angst in response to a "no first use" space weapons pledge. The genie is out of the bottle regarding nuclear weapons—let loose by the United States. But the Rubicon of space weapons remains to be crossed, if only by convenient ambiguity created by dual-use technology. A "no first use" pledge would put the United States in a leadership position toward avoiding the creation of a space version of the multi-headed Hydra of nuclear proliferation.

Admittedly, soft power on its own is ineffective, but US foreign policy excursions into Iraq and Afghanistan have shown that so too is hard power. A bold new strategic approach to China, assuming a proactive leadership role in space diplomacy, being rhetorically restrained, and retaking the moral high ground are all means that would serve the United States well toward achieving its space goals. Further, an effective layered deterrence posture in space can be said to be premised on quotes from two US presidents, one Republican and one Democrat. From Ronald Reagan, the following statement: "The defense policy of the United States is based on a simple premise: The United States does not start fights. We will never be an aggressor."[65] From Theodore Roosevelt, the phrase "Speak softly and carry a big stick." The United States must be ready to fight, but it must also actively try to avoid that fight. It must take the offensive on diplomacy as well as on the development and deployment of counterspace capabilities.

## Conclusion

A new US administration will have the opportunity to make new decisions about how space will evolve. While the United States must be ready to fight and win a war in space, it must be equally committed to preventing conflict. There will undoubtedly be pressure on a new administration from the Pentagon and intelligence communities to act quickly and move forward with the direction and programs realigned after the Space Portfolio Review. But prudence requires that a more thorough and broader assessment of all aspects of US space policy be conducted: a review and reaffirmation of space goals; the validity and implications of space being congested, competitive, and contested; how each of the deter, defend, and defeat military missions are being pursued; an assessment of both the capabilities and the range of possible intentions of non-US national space actors; the potential effects of NewSpace development on national security space; and how to best utilize bilateral and multilateral diplomatic avenues for the establishment of useful space norms. This sort of comprehensive review would require reaching out beyond those who would benefit from a "more of the same" approach to include nontraditional views.

There have been "the sky is falling" alarms ringing since 1998 regarding national security space, though the United States continues to be the dominant global military player by a considerable margin. Therefore, there is time to reassess and formulate a proactive, balanced approach to national security space that moves toward achieving its stated goals. Policy would thereby be guided by rational decision-making as opposed to allowing governmental politics to prevail. Space assets are too important to leave to the pulling and hauling of politics as usual.

## Notes

1 Thomas Friedman, *The Lexus and the Olive Tree*, Farrar, Straus and Giroux, New York, 1999.
2 "Mobil phone access reaches three quarters of planet's population," World Bank Press Release, July 17, 2012. www.worldbank.org/en/news/press-release/2012/07/17/mobile-phone-access-reaches-three-quarters-planets-population
3 Dave Baiocchi and William Welser IV, "The democratization of space," *Foreign Affairs*, May/June 2015. www.foreignaffairs.com/articles/space/2015-04-20/democratization-space

4   Ibid., p. 100.

5   David Rothkopf, "Obama's 'don't do stupid shit' foreign policy," *Foreign Policy,* June 4, 2014. http://foreignpolicy.com/2014/06/04/obamas-dont-do-stupid-shit-foreign-policy/

6   Lyle J. Goldstein, *Meeting China Halfway: How to Defuse the Emerging US-China Rivalry,* Georgetown University Press, Washington, DC, 2015.

7   Graham Allison, "The Thucydides Trap: are the US and China headed for war?" *The Atlantic,* September 24, 2015. www.theatlantic.com/international/archive/2015/09/united-states-china-war-thucydides-trap/406756/

8   Ibid., p. 12.

9   Goldstein, *Meeting China Halfway,* p. 13, quoting Robert Axelrod and Robert Keohane, "Achieving cooperation under anarchy: strategies and institutions," in *Neorealism and Neoliberalism: The Contemporary Debate,* ed. David A. Baldwin, Columbia University Press, New York, 1993, pp. 85–9: 101, 103.

10  Goldstein, *Meeting China Halfway,* p. 349.

11  Goldstein, *Meeting China Halfway,* p. 350.

12  Office of the Spokesperson, "The first meeting of the US-China dialogue," US Department of State, September 28, 2015. www.state.gov/r/pa/prs/ps/2015/09/247394.htm

13  Joan Johnson-Freese, "Found in space: cooperation," *China-US Focus,* October 9, 2015. www.chinausfocus.com/foreign-policy/u-s-china-space-cooperation-a-welcome-dialogue-begins/

14  Goldstein, *Meeting China* Halfway, p. 13.

15  Vid Beldavs, "Prospects for US-China space Cooperation," *The Space Review,* December 7, 2015. www.thespacereview.com/article/287c/1

16  Thomas P. M. Barnett, "Mr. President, here's how to make sense of your second term, secure your legacy, and oh yeah, create a future worth living," *Esquire,* August 18, 2010. http://thomaspmbarnett.com/globlogization/2010/8/18/blast-from-my-past-mr-president-heres-how-to-make-sense-of-y.html

17  Hugh White, *The China Choice,* Black, Inc., Collingwood, VIC, Australia, 2012.

18  James Steinberg and Michael O'Hanlon, *Strategic Reassurance and Resolve,* Princeton University Press, Princeton, NJ, 2014.

19  Charles Glaser, "A US-China Grand Bargain?" *International Security,* 29(4), Spring 2015, 49–90. https://www.wilsoncenter.org/article/us-china-grand-bargain

20  Theresa Hitchens and David Chen "Forging a Sino-US 'grand bargain' in space," *Space Policy,* 24(3): 128–31.

21  Ibid., 130.

22  Thomas L. Friedman, "The humiliation factor," *The New York Times,* November 9, 2003. www.nytimes.com/2003/11/09/opinion/the-humiliation-factor.html

23  David Shambaugh, "China's soft-power push: the search for respect," *Foreign Affairs,* July/August 2015, p. 99. www.foreignaffairs.com/articles/china/2015-06-16/china-s-soft-power-push

24  "Frequently asked questions," *International Space Exploration Coordination Group.* www.globalspaceexploration.org/wordpress/?page_id=257

25  International Space Exploration Coordination Group, *The Global Exploration Roadmap,* NASA, Washington, DC, August 2013. https://www.nasa.gov/sites/default/files/files/GER-2013_Small.pdf

26 Cited in Peter B. de Selding, "CNSA chief says China would gladly join space roadmapping group if asked," *SpaceNews*, September 23, 2013. http://spacenews. com/37360cnsa-chief-says-china-would-gladly-join-global-space-roadmapping-group-if/

27 Kathleen C. Laurini, Bernard Hufenbach, Juergen Hill, and Alain Ouellet, "The Global Exploration Roadmap and expanding human/robotic exploration mission collaboration opportunities," 66th International Astronautical Congress, Jerusalem, 2015. www. globalspaceexploration.org/wordpress/wp-content/uploads/2015/10/GER-HR-Jerusalem-paper-vfinal.pdf

28 Joan Johnson-Freese, "The International Solar Polar Mission," *Space Policy*, 3(1), February 1987, 24–37; Wulf von Kries, "Flunking on Space Station Cooperation?" *Space Policy*, 3(1), February 1987, 10–12.

29 Phil Plait, "NASA's budget … as far as Americans think," *Discover*, November 21, 2007. http://blogs.discovermagazine.com/badastronomy/2007/11/21/nasas-budget-as-far-as-americans-think/#.Vv6bi6v1eII; the NASA portion of the federal budget reached 4 percent during the Apollo program.

30 Curtiss Thompson, "Poll: Americans overwhelmingly support doubling NASA's budget, Mission to Mars," *Penny4NASA*. www.penny4nasa.org/2013/05/15/poll-americans-overwhelmingly-support-doubling-nasas-budget-mission-to-mars/

31 Chris Barth, "Neil deGrasse Tyson: invest in NASA, invest in US economy," *Forbes*, March 13, 2012. www.forbes.com/sites/chrisbarth/2012/03/13/neil-degrasse-tyson-invest-in-nasa-invest-in-u-s-economy/#41e8576925dc

32 Kathleen C. Laurini, Georgy Karabadzhak, Naoki Satoh, and Bernard Hufenbach, "International Space Station (ISS) lessons learned and their influence on preparations for human exploration for human exploration beyond low Earth orbit," 62nd International Astronautical Congress, Cape Town, South Africa, 2011. www.globalspaceexploration. org/wordpress/wp-content/uploads/IAC62/IAC-11.B3.2.1%20ISECG%20ISS%20 Lessons%20Learned.pdf

33 Karl Mueller, "The absolute weapon and the ultimate high ground: why nuclear deterrence and space deterrence are strikingly similar, and profoundly different," in *Anti-Satellite Weapons, Deterrence and Sino-American Space Relations*, ed. Michael Krepon and Julia Thomas, The Henry L. Stimson Center, Washington, DC, September 2013, pp. 41–60: p. 43.

34 "Bureau of Arms Control, Verification and Compliance (AVC)," *U.S. Department of State*. www.state.gov/t/avc/

35 United States Department of State and the Broadcasting Board of Governors, *Inspection of the Bureau of Arms Control, Verification, and Compliance*, Office of the Inspector General of the Department of State, Arlington, VA, June 2014. https://oig.state.gov/system/ files/228996.pdf

36 Budget item justification for the Space Security and Defense Program, March 2014. www.globalsecurity.org/military/library/budget/fy2015/usaf-peds/0603830f_4_ pb_2015.pdf

37 "Deputy Assistant Secretary of Defense for Space Policy: Mission," *Under Secretary of Defense for Policy*. http://policy.defense.gov/OUSDPOffices/ASDforHomelandDefense GlobalSecurity/SpacePolicy.aspx

38 Annex to Draft Report, agreed by the Working Group on the Long-term Sustainability of Outer Space Activities, submitted to Committee on the Peaceful Uses of Outer

Space, 59th session, Vienna, June 15, 2016. www.unoosa.org/res/oosadoc/data/documents/2016/aac_105l/aac_105l_306add_6_0_html/AC105_L306Add06E.pdf

39 Theresa Hitchens, *Forwarding Multilateral Space Governance: Next Steps for the International Community*, CISSM Working Paper, Center for International and Security Studies at Maryland, University of Maryland, College Park, MD, August 2015. http://cissm.umd.edu/publications/forwarding-multilateral-space-governance-next-steps-international-community

40 Ibid., p. 14.

41 Elena Holodny, "Putin likes the Iran deal," *Business Insider*, July 14, 2015. www.businessinsider.com/putin-likes-the-iran-deal-2015-7; Neil MacFarquhar and Anne Barnard, "Vladimir Putin calls Syria operation a success, says it'll lead to peace," *The New York Times*, March 17, 2016. www.nytimes.com/2016/03/18/world/europe/vladimir-putin-syria-russia.html?_r=0

42 "Jonathan McDowell's Statement on United States Non-Compliance with UNR1721B," *Planet4589*, August 16, 2001. http://planet4589.org/space/un/untxt.html

43 Hitchens, *Forwarding Multilateral Space Governance*, p. 23.

44 E. L. Zorn, "Israel's quest for satellite intelligence," *Central Intelligence Agency*. https://www.cia.gov/library/center-for-the-study-of-intelligence/kent-csi/vol44no5/html/v44i5a04p.htm; Joseph Fitchett, "Spying from space: US to sharpen the focus," *International Herald Tribune*, April 10, 2001. http://fas.org/irp/news/2001/04/iht041001.html

45 "SSA programme overview," *European Space Agency*. www.esa.int/Our_Activities/Operations/Space_Situational_Awareness/SSA_Programme_overview

46 Ram S. Jakhu, Cassandra Steer, and Juan-Wei (David) Chen, "Conflicts in Space and the Rule of Law," McGill University Institute for Air and Space Law, December 2015.

47 R. G. Harrison, D. R. Jackson, and C. G. Shackelford, "Space deterrence: the delicate balance of risk," *Space and Defense*, 3(1), 1–30, 2009: p. 21.

48 Cited in Mike Gruss, "Air Force hosted payload contracting vehicle seen as 'game changer,'" *SpaceNews*, July 29, 2013. http://spacenews.com/36508military-space-quarterly-air-force-hosted-payload-contracting-vehicle/

49 Kay Sears, "What's holding back the adoption of hosted payloads?" *SatCom Frontier*, March 8, 2016. www.intelsatgeneral.com/blog/whats-holding-back-the-adoption-of-hosted-payloads/

50 Ibid.

51 Brian Weeden, "Protecting space assets through denial deterrence," *Space Security and Defense Conference*, Las Vegas, NV, December 8–9, 2008. http://swfound.org/media/17810/weeden%20-%20deterring%20attacks%20on%20us%20space%20assets.pdf

52 Air Force Space Command, *Resiliency and Disaggregated Space Architectures*, White Paper. www.afspc.af.mil/shared/media/document/AFD-130821-034.pdf

53 Cited in Mike Gruss, "Disaggregation gets traction in 2015 Pentagon budget request," *SpaceNews*, March 7, 2014. http://spacenews.com/39773disaggregation-gets-traction-in-2015-pentagon-budget-request/

54 US Department of Defense, *Fact Sheet: Resilience of Space Capabilities*, 2011. http://archive.defense.gov/home/features/2011/0111_nsss/docs/DoD%20Fact%20Sheet%20-%20Resilience.pdf

55 Ibid.

56 Amy Butler, "USAF operationally responsive space office could oversee next SSA, Weather Sats," *Aviation Week*, February 12, 2015. http://aviationweek.com/space/usaf-operationally-responsive-space-office-could-oversee-next-ssa-weather-sats

57 Elbridge Colby, *From Sanctuary to Battlefield: A Framework for a U.S. Defense and Deterrence Strategy for Space*, Center for a New American Security, Washington, DC, January 2016, p. 18.

58 Madelyn Creedon, Remarks on Deterrence, Stimson Center, Washington, DC, September 17, 2013. www.stimson.org/images/uploads/Creedon_Stimson_Speech.pdf

59 Admiral Cecil D. Haney, Opening Remarks, Deterrence Symposium, Omaha, NE, July 29, 2015. https://www.stratcom.mil/speeches/2015/136/Deterrence_Symposium_Opening_Remarks/

60 Cited in Colin Clark, "DepSecDef work invokes 'space control;' analysts fear space war escalation," *Breaking Defense*, April 15, 2015. http://breakingdefense.com/2015/04/depsecdef-work-invokes-space-control-analysts-fear-space-war-escalation/

61 Scott D. Sagan, "A case for no first use," *Survival*, 51(3), June–July 2009, 163–82.

62 Ibid., p. 164.

63 Morton H. Halperin, Bruno Tertrais, Keith B. Payne, K. Subrahmanyam, and Scott D. Sagan, "The case for no first use: an exchange," *Survival*, 51(5) October–November 2009, 17–46. www.iiss.org/en/publications/survival/sections/2009-5f8e/survival--global-politics-and-strategy-october-november-2009-ce61/51-5-04-forum-02b1

64 Ibid.

65 Ronald Reagan, Speech on Defense and National Security (Star Wars), March 23, 1983. www.ff.org/library/reagan-legacy/speech-reagan-1983-03-23/

# INDEX